# Bézier and Splines in Image Processing and Machine Vision

Sambhunath Biswas • Brian C. Lovell

# Bézier and Splines in Image Processing and Machine Vision

🐴 Springer

Sambhunath Biswas
Indian Statistical Institute
Kolkata, India

Brian C. Lovell
The University of Queensland
Brisbane, Australia

British Library Cataloguing in Publication Data
A catalogue record for this book is available from the British Library

Library of Congress Control Number: 2007939448

ISBN: 978-1-84628-956-9          e-ISBN: 978-1-84628-957-6

© Springer-Verlag London Limited 2008

Printed on acid-free paper

9 8 7 6 5 4 3 2 1

springer.com

To my late parents, **Kali Kinkar Biswas and Niharbala Biswas**, who were always inspiring

Sambhunath Biswas

To my wonderful and supportive wife, **Vicki**, and my beautiful daughters, **Adeleine, Quetta, and Tess**, who were very understanding during the many hours spent writing this manuscript, both at home and abroad

Brian C. Lovell

# Preface

The rapid development of spline theory in the last five decades—and its widespread applications in many diverse areas—has not only made the subject rich and diverse, but also made it immensely popular within different research communities. It is well established that splines are a powerful tool and have tremendous problem-solving capability. Of the large number of splines discovered so far, a few have established permanent homes in computer graphics, image processing, and machine vision. In computer graphics, their significant role is well documented. Unfortunately, this is not really the case in machine vision, even though a great deal of spline-based research has already been done in this area. The situation is somewhat better for image processing. One, therefore, feels the need for something in the form of a report or book that clearly spells out the importance of spline functions while teaching a course on machine vision. It is unfortunate that despite considerable searching, not even a single book in this area was found in the market. This singular fact provides the motivation for writing this book on splines, with special attention to applications in image processing and machine vision.

The philosophy behind writing this book lies in the fact that splines are effective, efficient, easy to implement, and have a strong and elegant mathematical background as well. Its problem-solving capability is, therefore, unquestionable. The remarkable spline era in computer science started when P. E. Bézier first published his work on UNISURF. The subject immediately caught the attention of many researchers. The same situation was repeated with the discovery of Ingrid Daubechi's wavelets. Different wavelet splines are now well known and extensively found in the literature. As splines are rich in properties, they provide advantages in designing new algorithms and hence they have wide-scale applications in many important areas. Bézier and wavelet splines, can, therefore, be regarded as two different landmarks in spline theory with wide application in image processing and machine vision, and this justifies the title of the book.

In writing this book, therefore, we introduce the Bernstein polynomial at the very beginning, since its importance and dominance in Bézier spline models for curve and surface design and drawing are difficult to ignore. We omitted the design problems of curves and surfaces because they are dealt with in almost all books on computer graphics. Some applications in different image processing areas, based on the Bézier-Bernstein model, are discussed in depth in Chapters 1, 2, 3, and 4, so that researchers and students can get a fairly good idea about them and can apply them independently. Chapter 1 provides a background for Bézier-Bernstein (B-B) polynomial and how binary images can be viewed, approximated, and regenerated through Bézier-Bernstein arcs. Chapter 2 explains the underlying concept of graylevel image segmentation and provides some implementation details, which can be successfully used for image compression. In Chapter 3 of this book, we will show how one can use one dimensional B-B function to segment as well as compress image data points. Chapter 4 depicts image compression in a different way, using two dimensional B-B function.

B-splines, discussed in Chapter 5, are useful to researchers and students of many different streams including computer science and information technology, physics, and mathematics. We tried to provide a reasonably comprehensive coverage. Attention has been devoted to writing this chapter so that students can independently design algorithms that are sometimes needed for their class work, projects, and research. We have also included applications of B-splines in machine vision because we believe it also has strong potential in research. The beta splines discussed in Chapter 6 are relatively new and much work remains to be done in this area. However, we tried to discuss them as much as possible and indicated possible directions of further work.

In Chapter 7, discrete splines are discussed, along with the feasibility of their use in machine vision. The application is appropriate and informative. It shows how the problem of recovering surface orientations can be solved through a system of nonlinear equations. Splines in vision is an open area and much attention needs to be paid for further research work. Wavelet splines are relatively new, so we took special care to write the theory in a clear, straightforward way in Chapter 8. To aid in understanding, we used examples whenever necessary.

Snakes and active contours are explained in Chapter 9, and we discuss their intimate relationship with mathematical splines. Minimizing snake energy using both the original calculus of variations method and the dynamic programming approach are discussed. This chapter also includes problems and pitfalls drawn from several applications to provide a better understanding of the subject. Chapter 10, on the other hand, discusses powerful globally optimal energy minimization techniques, keeping in mind the need of students and researchers in this new and promising area of image processing and machine vision.

Finally, we believe that this book would help readers from many diverse areas, as it provides a reasonably good coverage of the subject. We believe this book can be used in many different areas of image processing and machine vision. It is our hope that this book differs from many other books, as we made a considerable effort to make these techniques as easy to understand and implement as possible. We do hope the reader will agree with us.

*Sambhunath Biswas*
Indian Statistical Institute
Kolkata, India
March 2007

*Brian C. Lovell*
The University of Queensland
Brisbane, Australia
March 2007

# Acknowledgments

We have freely consulted different books, articles from reputed journals and conference proceedings, and Ph.D theses. All of them are listed in the bibliography. We gratefully acknowledge all the authors whose contributions we have used in some minor forms. Among them, we express our sincere acknowledgement to Roberto Cipolla and Andrew Blake for the application of B-spline in machine vision; Brian Andrew Barsky for beta splines; Cohen, Lyche and Risenfeld, David Lee and B.K.P. Horn for some of the properties of discrete splines and application, respectively. We believe these works are befitting and informative. We extend our acknowledgments to Charles K. Chui and S. Mallat for inclusion of a few articles on wavelet splines. Chapter 10 outlines a number of research themes currently being pursued within the Intelligent Real-Time Imaging and Sensing Group and National ICT Australia. We would like to acknowledge the contributions of Terry Caelli, Hugues Talbot, Peter Kootsookos, and Brian's current and former students Pascal Bamford, Ben Appleton, Carlos Leung, David McKinnon, Christian Walder, Stephen Franklin, and Daniel Walford. We would also like to acknowledge the ANU Centre for Mental Health for providing the labeled brain images.

# Contents

## Part II Intermediate Steps

## Part III Advanced Methodologies

# Part I

## Early Background

# 1

# Bernstein Polynomial and Bézier-Bernstein Spline

## 1.1 Introduction

Bernstein polynomial, its significance, different properties, and detection of its order for approximation of a data set, are very important and useful as a first course material to study splines. In fact, Bernstein polynomial can be thought of as the gateway to splines, namely the Bézier spline. Its strong relation with the Bézier spline can, in no way, be forgotten. Bézier polynomial can be made to act in either of these ways: as a spline or as a non-spline. When it acts as a spline, it does piecewise approximation of a data set with some smoothness conditions satisfying at the break points, but when it acts as a non-spline to approximate, it does not take into consideration the smoothness conditions to satisfy at the break points. Readers interested in details of Bernstein polynomial may consult any standard text book on mathematics. Bézier curves, on the other hand, show how their geometry is influenced by Bernstein polynomials. As Bézier curves and surfaces are driven by Bernstein basis, they can also be thought of, respectively, the Bernstein polynomial pieces of curves and surfaces. P. E. Bézier, a French designer in the automobile industry for Rénault, suggested a revolutionary concept for the interactive design of curves and surfaces. He suggested that these curves behave exactly the same way as humans do until satisfaction reaches a maximum. For this, he artfully incorporated [22] the Bernstein basis and some control points in his design. This concept of control points and their positioning play the most significant and vital role in his interactive design mechanism.

## 1.2 Significance of Bernstein Polynomial in Splines

Bernstein polynomial is well known in the mathematical theory of function approximation. It can be used to approximate known, as well as unknown, functions with any desired degree of accuracy. Besides, this polynomial possesses a number of significant properties that have made it attractive to many researchers for its use in diverse areas. The success behind the efficient applications of this polynomial in many fields has also made it widely popular. The basic philosophy behind the Bernstein polynomial approximation is that this polynomial is very convenient to free-form drawing. In fact, some of the properties of this polynomial are so attractive that no sooner than the technique was published by Bézier, it became widely popular in many industries. In order to design the body of an automobile, Bézier developed a spline model that became the first widely accepted spline model in computer graphics and computer-aided design, due to its flexibility and ease over the then-used drawing and design techniques. Since Bézier used the Bernstein polynomial basis as the basis function in his spline model, the justification of the name "Bézier-Bernstein" spline immediately applies and hence, the Bernstein basis dominates the performance of the Bézier spline. This model, therefore, helps to design and draw smooth curves and surfaces of different shapes and sizes, corresponding to different arbitrary objects, based on a set of control points.

Bézier spline model, though is extensively used for free-form drawing, can also be used to approximate data points originated from different functions. The problem of function approximation is essentially the problem of estimation of control points from a data set. Drawing and function approximation are essentially different in nature, though approximation is done in both cases. In the curve and surface design, approximation error is not of prime concern. Visual effect or the aesthetics of the shape of the object is the sole objective. So, one should observe how accurately a drawn object depicts the shape of its corresponding target object. Notice that Bézier spline-based drawing technique starts from the zeroth order Bernstein approximation (which is exactly the line drawing between control points) of the data points and goes to some higher order (quadratic or cubic) approximation, until it mimics the shape of the object. Step by step through interactions, a designer can make necessary corrections to achieve perfection in shape of the object. On the other hand, in a data approximation problem, we justify the approximation by the error in approximation. This is a purely mathematical problem where we are in no way concerned with the graphics involved behind the approximation. Furthermore, if the data set corresponds to a graylevel image, the error in approximation becomes subjective. We accept small or large error depending on the nature of applications. Such an approximation of image data points is useful in compression and feature extraction.

The concept of control points in Bézier-Bernstein spline is implicit in the definition of the Bernstein polynomial and it was Bézier who made it explicit. Later on, the concept of control points was generalized to knots in B-spline to keep the interaction locally confined, so that the global shape of curves and surfaces is least affected. The generalization, therefore, introduces more drawing flexibility in the B-spline model.

## 1.3 Bernstein Polynomial

Bernstein polynomial approximation of degree p to an arbitrary real valued function $f(t)$ is

$$B_p[f(t)] - \sum_{i=0}^{p} f(\frac{i}{p})\phi_{ip}(t) \qquad\qquad 0 \le t < 1, \qquad (1.1)$$

where the function $\phi$ is the Bernstein basis function. The ith basis function is precisely given by

$$\phi_{ip}(t) = \binom{p}{i} t^i (1-t)^{p-i}, \qquad\qquad i \in [0, p]. \qquad (1.2)$$

Some of the elementary properties of $\phi_{ip}(t)$ are:

(1) $\forall i \in [0, p]: \phi_{ip} \ge 0; \forall t \in [0,1]: \sum_{i=0}^{p} \phi_{ip}(t) = 1.$

(2) $\forall i \in [1, p-1]: \phi_{0p}(0) = 1; \; \phi_{ip}^{(i)}(0) = \frac{p!}{(p-i)!}.$
$\forall r \in [0, i-1]: \phi_{ip}^{(r)}(0) = 0; \forall s \in [0, p-i-1]: \phi_{ip}^{(s)}(1) = 0.$

(3) $\forall r \in [0, p-1]: \phi_{pp}^{(r)} = 0; \; \phi_{pp}(1) = 1.$

(4) $\phi_{ip}^{(p-i)}(1) = (-1)^{p-i}\frac{p!}{(p-i)!}.$

(5) $\phi_{ip}(\frac{i}{p}) = \binom{p}{i} i^i (p-i)^{(p-i)} > \phi_{ip}(t) \quad$ if $t \ne \frac{i}{p}.$

Properties (2) and (3) imply that the end point values, $f(0)$ and $f(1)$, are the only values that are interpolated by the Bernstein polynomial. From the condition for $\phi_{ip}(t)$ listed above, the end-point derivatives of $B_p$ can be obtained as follows:

$$\frac{d^r}{dt^r}B_{ip}[f(t)]|_{t=0} = \frac{p!}{(p-r)!}\sum_{i=0}^{r}(-1)^{r-i}\binom{r}{i}f(\frac{i}{p}) \qquad (1.3)$$

and,

$$\frac{d^r}{dt^r}B_{ip}[f(x)]|_{t=1}\frac{p!}{(p-r)!}\sum_{i=0}^{r}(-1)^{i}\binom{r}{i}f(\frac{p-i}{p}). \qquad (1.4)$$

Hence, the rth derivative at the end points, $t = 0$ and $t = 1$, is determined by the values of $f(t)$ at the respective end point and at the r points nearest to that end point. Specifically, the first derivatives are equal to the slope of the straight line joining the end point and the adjacent interior point.

Bernstein polynomials satisfy the Weierstrass approximation theorem, i.e., they converge uniformly, with increasing p, to the function they approximate. Also, $B_p(f(t))$ is smoother than $f$ itself if smoothness is measured in terms of the number of oscillations about a given straight line. Despite all these interesting features, Bernstein polynomials are never widely used to approximate the minimal norm. This is because they converge very slowly to the uniform norm.

### 1.3.1 Determination of the Order of the Polynomial

To judiciously fit a Bernstein curve over a set of data points, we need to know the order of the polynomial. Once the order is known, one can fit a curve over the data points using any standard method. We shall present here a classical approach to determine the order of the polynomial to approximate a one dimensional function. Extension to two or higher dimensions is not very difficult. We shall later consider a relatively simple approach to determine the order of a Bézier-Bernstein polynomial for approximating image intensity (pixels) values.

Let $f(t)$ be defined and finite on the closed interval $[0, 1]$. The Bernstein polynomial [113] of degree p for the function $f(t)$ is

$$B_{kp}(t) = \sum_{k=0}^{p} \binom{p}{k} f(k/p) t^k (1-t)^{p-k}. \qquad (1.5)$$

Since $f(t)$ is continuous on $[0, 1]$, it is uniformly continuous, i.e., for every $\epsilon > 0$ there will exist a $\delta > 0$ such that $|f(t_1) - f(t_2)| < \epsilon$ whenever $|t_1 - t_2| < \delta$. Let us select an arbitrary t on $[0, 1]$. Then

$$f(t) = \sum_{k=0}^{p} f(t) \binom{p}{k} t^k (1-t)^{p-k}$$

since

$$\sum_{k=0}^{p} \binom{p}{k} t^k (1-t)^{p-k} = 1.$$

Hence,

$$\begin{aligned} | B_{kp}(t) - f(t) | &= | \sum_{k=0}^{p} (f(k/p) - f(t)) \binom{p}{k} t^k (1-t)^{p-k} | \\ &\leq \sum_{k=0}^{p} | f(k/p) - f(t) | \binom{p}{k} t^k (1-t)^{p-k}. \end{aligned} \qquad (1.6)$$

Now we divide the set of integers $0, 1, 2, \cdots$ into two sets $A$ and $B$ according to the following rule: an integer $k \in A$ if $| k/p - t | < \delta$, k is in $B$ otherwise. Therefore, the sum on the right of the equation (1.6) can be broken into two different sums, one for each of the two sets $A$ and $B$.

If k is in $A$, we have according to the definition of $\delta$

$$| f(k/p) - f(t) | < \epsilon.$$

Therefore,

$$\sum_{k\in A} |\ f(k/p) - f(t)\ | \binom{p}{k} t^k (1-t)^{p-k} \ < \ \epsilon \sum_{k\in A} \binom{p}{k} t^k (1-t)^{p-k}$$

$$< \ \epsilon \sum_{k=0}^{p} \binom{p}{k} t^k (1-t)^{p-k} \quad (1.7)$$

$$< \ \epsilon,$$

since the extended sum is unity.

Let us now estimate the second sum where k is in set $B$. Since $f$ is continuous and $[0,1]$ is compact, there is an $M_t$ such that $|f(t)| \leq M_t$. $M_t = |f(t)|_{max}$, $0 \leq t \leq 1$. So, we get $|\ f(k/p) - f(t)\ | \leq 2M_t$ considering the worst case (when $f(k/p) = -f(t)$ or when $f(k/p)$ and $f(t)$ are of opposite sign). Therefore,

$$\sum_{k\in B} |\ f(k/p) - f(t)\ | \binom{p}{k} t^k (1-t)^{p-k} \leq 2M_t \sum_{k\in B} \binom{p}{k} t^k (1-t)^{p-k}.$$

If k is in $B$, then $(k/p - t)^2 \geq \delta^2$ or $\frac{(k-pt)^2}{p^2\delta^2} \geq 1$. Now one can prove the identity

$$\sum_{k=0}^{p} (k-pt)^2 \binom{p}{k} t^k (1-t)^{p-k} \leq \frac{p}{4}. \quad (1.8)$$

Using equation (1.8), we can show that

$$\sum_{k\in B} \binom{p}{k} t^k (1-t)^{p-k} \leq \sum_{k=0}^{p} \frac{(k-px)^2}{p^2\delta^2} \binom{p}{k} t^k (1-t)^{p-k}.$$

The second sum is, therefore,

$$\sum_{k\in B} |f(k/p) - f(t)| \binom{p}{k} t^k (1-t)^{p-k}$$

$$\leq \frac{2M_t}{p^2\delta^2} \sum_{k\in B} (k-pt)^2 \binom{p}{k} t^k (1-t)^{p-k}$$

$$\leq \frac{2M_t}{p^2\delta^2} \sum_{k=0}^{p} (k-pt)^2 \binom{p}{k} t^k (1-t)^{p-k} \quad (1.9)$$

$$\leq \frac{2M_t}{p^2\delta^2} \frac{p}{4}$$

$$= \frac{M_t}{2p\delta^2}.$$

Considering equations (1.6), (1.7), and (1.9) $\forall t \in [0,1]$ we can write,

$$|\ B_{kp}(t) - f(t)\ | \leq \epsilon + \frac{M_t}{2p\delta^2}.$$

Therefore, $|\ B_{kp}(t) - f(t)\ | < 2\epsilon$ whenever $\frac{M_t}{2p\delta^2} < \epsilon$. Thus, we get,

$$p > \frac{M_t}{2\epsilon\delta^2}. \tag{1.10}$$

From equation (1.10) it is clear that $2\epsilon$ is the error for a given approximation. So, once we choose the error for an approximation, $\epsilon$ then corresponding to this $\epsilon$, we can search the data set and determine $\delta$ and hence the order of the polynomial. For two dimensions, the extension is straightforward.

**Example**

Approximate $f(t) = \frac{1}{1+t}$ with a Bernstein polynomial for which $|B_p(t) - f(t)| < 0.9$.
We have,

$| B_{kp}(t) - f(t) | < 2\epsilon$ whenever $\frac{M_t}{2p\delta^2} < \epsilon$. Thus, we can write,

$|\frac{1}{1+\bar{t}} - \frac{1}{1+t}| < 0.45$ whenever $|\bar{t} - t| < \frac{2}{3}$. So we consider $\delta = \frac{2}{3}$. Also, from equation (1.10),

$$\frac{M_t}{2\epsilon\delta^2} < \frac{1}{2(0.45)(2/3)^2} = 2.5.$$

Since, $p > \frac{M_t}{2\epsilon\delta^2}$ we can choose, $p = 3$ (considering the nearest integer). Hence,

$$B_3(t) = \sum_{i=0}^{3} \binom{3}{i} f(\frac{i}{3}) \, t^i(1-t)^{3-i}$$
$$= (1-t)^3 + 9/4 \, t(1-t)^2 + 9/5 \, t^2(1-t),$$

is the required polynomial. Here, $f(0) = 1$, $f(1/3) = 3/4$, $f(2/3) = 3/5$ and $f(1) = 1/2$).

### 1.3.2 Bézier-Bernstein Polynomial

The elementary properties of the Bernstein polynomial show that during approximation of a data set, having some ordered representative points $f(\frac{i}{p})$, the approximating polynomial always remains confined within the convex hull of the representative points of the data set. The polynomial interpolates the end points of the ordered representative set of points. All other points are approximated by the polynomial.

Bézier-Bernstein polynomial (BBP) of degree p is mathematically defined as

$$P(t) = \sum_{i=0}^{p} \phi_{ip}(t)V_i \qquad 0 \leq t \leq 1.$$

The polynomial is based on the Bernstein basis or the blending function, given by

$$\phi_{ip}(t) = \binom{p}{i} t^i(1-t)^{p-i}, \qquad i \in [0, p].$$

$\phi_{ip}$ is the ith basis function of order p. $V_i$, for $i = 0, 1, \cdots p$ defines a polygon known as the Bézier control polygon. Bézier based his approximation method on the classical *Bernstein polynomial approximation*. The Bernstein polynomial approximation of degree p to an arbitrary real valued function $f(t)$ is

$$B_{ip}[f(t)] = \sum_{i=0}^{p} f(\frac{i}{p})\phi_{ip}(t) \qquad\qquad 0 \le t \le 1.$$

Bézier's approach, therefore, specifies a well-ordered set of points, say p+1 in number to do the approximation. These points $\{V_i, i = 0, 1, \cdots p\}$ define a p-sided polygon that is well suited to the problem of interactive design of smooth free-form curves. Changing the values of $V_i$ changes the polygon and hence, changes the shape of the curve. Thus, the shape of the curve is controlled through the shape of the polygon. In two dimensions, B-B polynomial represents a surface patch or a piece of a surface. The free-form drawing of curves and surfaces is very useful in computer graphics. The ordered representative points $f(i/p)$ in equation (1.1) in the approximation mode are, therefore, the guiding or control points in the design mode for curves.

**Some Properties**

One dimensional Bézier-Bernstein polynomial represents a curve that can be generated from a set of ordered representative points, called the control points or the guiding points. The line joining these control points is called the control line of the polynomial. It reflects the shape of the curve that one wants to draw or generate. Such curves have the following attractive properties:

- They always interpolate the end control points, and the line joining two consecutive points at either end is a tangent to the curve at that end point.
- They remain always enclosed within the convex hull defined by the control points.
- They have the variation diminishing property, i.e., they do not exhibit any oscillating behavior about any line more often than a sequence of lines joining the control points.
- They have the axis independence property, i.e., the drawing of the curve does not depend on any axis.
- They are affine invariant.
- Determination of the polynomial order in drawing a curve is easy and straightforward. It is always one less than the number of vertices of the control polygon.

# 1.4 Use in Computer Graphics and Image Data Approximation

Due to the attractive properties of the Bézier-Bernstein polynomial, one can successfully use them in both computer graphics and image data approximation. Their use in computer graphics is well known, while the use in image data approximation for image compression or feature extraction is challenging. We shall discuss the efficiency of the polynomial in each area. Before doing that, we shall elaborate on Bézier curves.

### 1.4.1 Bézier-Bernstein Curves

This class of curves was first proposed by Bézier [22, 17]. The parametric form of the curves is

$$X = P_x(t) \tag{1.11}$$

$$Y = P_y(t). \tag{1.12}$$

Let $(x_0,\ y_0)$, $(x_1,\ y_1) \cdots (x_p,\ y_p)$ be $(p+1)$ ordered points in a plane. The Bézier curve associated with the polygon through the aforementioned points is the vector valued Bernstein polynomial and is given by

$$P_x(t) = \sum_{i=0}^{p} \phi_{ip}(t)\ x_i \tag{1.13}$$

$$P_y(t) = \sum_{i=0}^{p} \phi_{ip}(t)\ y_i \tag{1.14}$$

where $\phi_{ip}(t)s$'s are the binomial probability density function of (1.2). In the vector form, equation (1.13) and equation (1.14) can be written as

$$P(t) = \sum_{i=0}^{p} \phi_{ip}(t)\ V_i. \tag{1.15}$$

The points $V_0,\ V_1, \cdots, V_p$ are known as the guiding points or the control points for the curve P(t). From equation (1.15) it is seen that

$$P(0) = V_0 \quad and \quad P(1) = V_p.$$

Thus, the average of t significantly extends from 0 to 1. The derivative of $P(t)$ is

$$P'(t) = -p(1-t)^{p-1}v_0 + \sum_{i=1}^{p-1} \binom{p}{i} \{it^{i-1}(1-t)^{p-i}$$
$$-(p-i)t^i(1-t)^{p-i-1}\}V_i + pt^{p-1}v_p.$$

Now $P'(0) = p(V_1 - V_0)$ and $P'(1) = p(V_p - V_{p-1})$. Thus the Taylor series expansion near zero is

$$P(t) = P(0) + tP'(0) + \ higher\ order\ terms\ of\ t$$
$$= V_0(1 - pt) + \cdots$$

and an expansion near one is

$$P(t) = P(1) - (1-t)P'(1) + \text{ higher order terms of } t$$
$$= V_p\{1 - p(1-t)\} + p(1-t)V_{p-1}.$$

We observe that as $t \to 0$, the Bézier polynomial lies on the line joining $V_0$ and $V_1$, and for $t \to 1$ on the line joining $V_{p-1}$ and $V_p$. This concludes that these lines are tangents to the curve P(t) at $V_0$ and $V_p$. one can choose, therefore, the end control points in such a way that that they lie on a straight line. Hence, two pieces of curves can be easily drawn to maintain continuity at their joining point, and as a result, this provides effectively a single spline curve. For the B-B basis function in the model, the spline curve so obtained is known as B-B spline curve and the underlying spline function is known as the B-B spline or simply the Bézier spline.

Since $\sum\limits_{i=0}^{p} \phi_{ip}(t) = 1$, the Bézier curve lies inside the convex hull defined by the control points. For cubic Bézier curve, $p = 3$. The control polygon corresponding to $p = 3$ consists of four control vertices, namely, $V_0$, $V_1$, $V_2$, $V_3$, and the Bézier curve is

$$P(t) = (1-t)^3 V_0 + 3t(1-t)^2 V_1 + 3t^2(1-t)V_2 + t^3 V_3. \tag{1.16}$$

The Bernstein basis functions in this case are as follows:
$$\phi_{03}(t) = 1 - t^3 = 1 - 3t^2 + 3t - t^3$$
$$\phi_{13}(t) = 3t(1-t)^2 = 3t - 6t^2 + 3t^3$$
$$\phi_{23}(t) = 3t^2(1-t) = 3t^2 - 3t^3$$
$$\phi_{33}(t) = t^3.$$

Though the cubic Bézier curve is widely used in computer graphics [133], one can use, as well, its quadratic version to speed up the procedure, without degrading the quality of drawing. For a quadratic Bézier curve, $p = 2$ and the control polygon consists of three points. The Bernstein basis in this case are
$$\phi_{02}(t) = (1-t)^2 = 1 - 2t + t^2$$
$$\phi_{12}(t) = 2(1-t)t = 2t - 2t^2$$
$$\phi_{22}(t) = t^2.$$

In the polynomial form, the Bézier curve is

$$P(t) = t^2(V_0 + V_2 - 2V_1) + t(2V_1 - 2V_0) + V_0. \tag{1.17}$$

This is a second degree polynomial and can be computed much faster than in Horner's process [133].

One should note that for a cubic Bézier curve, the basis function $\phi_{13}$ attains its maximum at $t = \frac{1}{3}$ and the maximum value is

$$\phi_{13}\left(\frac{1}{3}\right) = \frac{4}{9}, \tag{1.18}$$

while $\phi_{23}$ has the maximum at $t = \frac{2}{3}$ with

$$\phi_{23}\left(\frac{2}{3}\right) = \frac{4}{9}. \tag{1.19}$$

Figure 1.1 shows the behavior of the basis functions for different values of the parameter $t \in [0,1]$, for cubic Bézier-Bernstein polynomial.

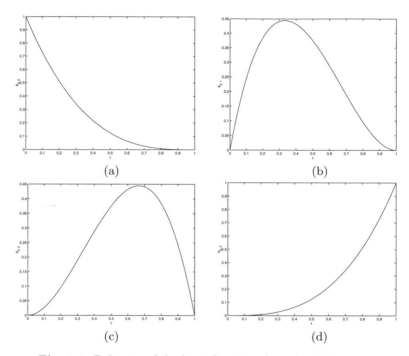

**Fig. 1.1.** Behavior of the basis functions for cubic B-B curve.

Consider the equation of a Bézier curve in a matrix form for compact representation. For a cubic curve, we have

$$P(t) = \left( (1-t)^3 \; 3t(1-t)^2 \; 3t^2(1-t) \; t^3 \right) \begin{pmatrix} V_0 \\ V_1 \\ V_2 \\ V_3 \end{pmatrix}. \tag{1.20}$$

This can be written as

$$P(t) = \left( t^3 \; t^2 \; t \; 1 \right) \begin{pmatrix} -1 & 3 & -3 & 1 \\ 3 & -6 & 3 & 0 \\ -3 & 3 & 0 & 0 \\ 1 & 0 & 0 & 0 \end{pmatrix} \begin{pmatrix} V_0 \\ V_1 \\ V_2 \\ V_3 \end{pmatrix} \tag{1.21}$$

$$= (T)(C)(V).$$

Cohen and Risenfeld [42] have generalized this representation to

$$P(t) = (T)(C)(V)$$

where $( T ) = ( t^p, \ t^{p-1}, \ \cdots 1 )$,

$$
( C ) =
\begin{pmatrix}
\binom{p}{0}\binom{p}{p}(-1)^p & \binom{p}{1}\binom{p-1}{p-1}(-1)^{p-1} & \cdots & \binom{p}{p}\binom{p-p}{p-p}(-1)^0 \\
\binom{p}{0}\binom{p}{p-1}(-1)^{p-1} & \binom{p}{1}\binom{p-1}{p-2}(-1)^{p-2} \cdots & & 0 \\
\vdots & \vdots & \vdots & \vdots \\
\binom{p}{0}\binom{p}{1}(-1)^1 & \binom{p-1}{0}(-1)^0 & \cdots & 0 \\
\binom{p}{0}\binom{p}{0}(-1)^0 & 0 & \cdots & 0
\end{pmatrix}
\tag{1.22}
$$

and $( V )^T$ is $(V_0, \ V_1 \ , V_2, \cdots V_p)$.

## 1.4.2 Bézier-Bernstein Surfaces

A Bézier-Bernstein surface is a tensor product surface and is represented by a two-dimensional Bézier-Bernstein (B-B) polynomial. If we designate the surface patch by $S(u, v)$, then

$$
S(u,v) = \sum_{i=0}^{p} \sum_{j=0}^{q} \phi_{ip}(u)\phi_{jq}(v)V_{ij},
\tag{1.23}
$$

where $0 \leq u \leq 1$ and $0 \leq v \leq 1$. $V_{ij}$ is the (i,j)th control point. $\phi_{ip}$ is the $i$th basis Bernstein basis function of order p and $\phi_{jq}$ is the Bernstein basis of order q. When $p \neq q$, the Bézier-Bernstein surface is defined on a rectangular support. This support becomes a square for $p = q$. Thus, for $p = 3$ and $q = 3$, we get a bicubic surface on a square support.

All the properties mentioned for 1-d B-B curves also hold for 2-d B-B surfaces. Once again, for selection of control points for two pieces of a surface, it is possible to draw a single piece of a spline surface.

## 1.4.3 Curve and Surface Design

One dimensional Bézier-Bernstein splines are used to design curves. To draw a curve with a definite shape, a designer inputs a set of ordered control points, which when joined in succession, produces the polygonal shape corresponding to the shape of the object that the designer wants to draw. The designer refines the shape, changing a few control points, through adequate interaction. Figure 1.2 shows two important cubic curves.

A 2-d Bézier spline is used to design a surface. The control points in this case define a control polygonal surface, which upon interactive refinement produces a desired surface. However, a quadratic spline provides some advantage from the computational point of view. For actual drawing, interested readers can consult books on computer graphics.

We now discuss the problem of data approximation in relation to binary image approximation and reconstruction.

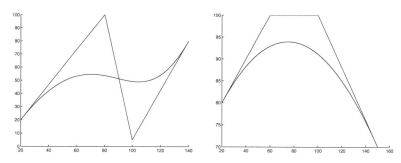

**Fig. 1.2.** Cubic Bézier-Bernstein curves.

### 1.4.4 Approximation of Binary Images

Data approximation, for binary images, based on Bézier-Bernstein spline model is the inverse of drawing mechanism used in computer graphics. So, instead of supplying the control points from outside, they are extracted from within images. The extraction, in general, uses the local geometry. As the control points are viewed as key pixels [26], i.e., knots on the discrete boundary of objects in the discrete image plane, they are extracted using local discrete geometry.

Image boundaries, in general, have many discontinuities and we need to preserve them during an approximation so that the approximated version of an image boundary does not appreciably change from its original one. It is, therefore, wise to carry out the polynomial approximation instead of polynomial spline approximation. The main reason is that we do not want to incorporate smoothness at points where two pieces of boundary segments join in. Smoothness can appreciably change the shape of a boundary and as a result, the underlying image may change noticeably. For successful approximation, one can search for a set of key pixels on contours and, based on them, decompose the contour into a set of arcs and line segments. Regeneration of an arc may use vertices of the corresponding Bézier characteristic triangle. It is possible to eliminate one of the vertices and use an intercept instead. Regeneration for straight line segments may use Bresenham's algorithm [29] and Bézier method for generation of arc segments. For regeneration, key pixels are considered to be the guiding or control pixels, and their locations are, therefore, in no way disturbed. This maintains the basic definition or shape of image boundaries (binary image). To preserve them and to maintain the connectivity property, sometimes we may need some intermediate operations (e.g., deletion and shifting of undesirable pixels, generated by Bézier approximation, and insertion of new pixels).

Difference in area as well as the compactness between the input and output versions of an image may serve as a measure for regeneration error.

**Bresenham's Algorithm**

Given two end points, restricted to an octant, Bresenham's algorithm [29] for generating points for a straight line segment between them checks the proximity of the actual line to the desired grid location. Let $(x_1, y_1)$ and $(x_2, y_2)$ be the two points through which a discrete straight line segment is needed. Intercept of the line segment with the line at $x = x_1 + 1$, $x_1 + 2, \cdots, x_2$ is first considered. If the intercept with the line at $x = x_1 + 1$ is closer to the line at $y = y_1 + 1$, then the point $(x_1 + 1, y_1 + 1)$ better approximates the line segment in question than the point $(x_1 + 1, y)$. This means if the intercept is greater than or equal to half the distance between $(x_1 + 1, y)$ and $(x_1 + 1, y_1 + 1)$, then the point $(x_1 + 1, y_1 + 1)$ is selected for approximation; otherwise, the point $(x_1 + 1, y)$ is selected. Next, intercept of the line segment with the line at $x = x_1 + 2$ is considered, and the same logic is applied for the selection of points.

Now instead of finding the intercept, an error term $e$ is used for the selection purpose. Initially, $e = -\frac{1}{2}$, and the initial point $(x_1, y_1)$ is selected. The slope of the line, $\frac{\triangle y}{\triangle x}$, is added to $e$, and the sign of the current value of $e = e + \frac{\triangle y}{\triangle x}$ is tested. If it is negative, then the point is selected along the horizontal line, i.e., $x$ is incremented by one and $y$ remains the same. The error term is then updated by adding the slope to it. However, if the error term is positive (or two) then the point is selected along the vertical line, i.e., both $x$ and $y$ are incremented by one. The error term is then updated by decreasing it by one. For integer calculation, $e$ is initialized to $\bar{e} = 2\triangle y - \triangle x$ because $2\triangle y - \triangle x = 2e\triangle x = \bar{e}$(say). The flow chart as shown in Figure 1.3 provides details of the algorithm for the first octant.

## 1.5 Key Pixels and Contour Approximation

### 1.5.1 Key Pixels

In the analytic plane, contours of an object may exhibit sharp maxima and minima, and we can detect these points almost accurately without much difficulty. However, when a contour is digitized in a two dimensional array space of $M \times N$ points or pels or pixels, the sharpness in the curvature of the contour is destroyed due to the information loss inherent in the process of digitization. The error is known as the digitization error. Consequently, it becomes rather difficult and complicated to estimate the points of maxima and minima. We can always seek an approximate solution to this problem. We define a set of pixels and call them key pixels, which are close to the points of maxima and minima.

Consider, for example, a function $f(x)$ in the discrete plane. When $f(x)$ is constant in an interval $[k_1, k_2]$, the corresponding function $f_a(x)$ may exhibit

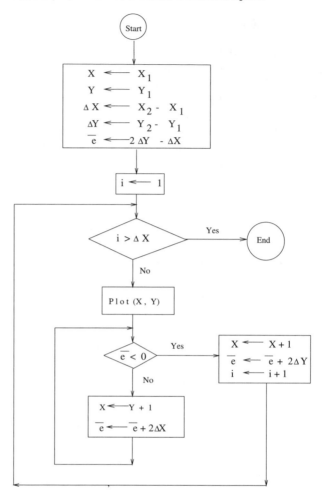

**Fig. 1.3.** Flow chart for Bresenham's algorithm in the first octant.

local maxima and minima (or a global maximum or minimum) anywhere within the interval as shown in Figures 1.4(a) and 1.4(b).

If we get pixels either directly connected or outward-corner connected to the end pixels of the interval $[k_1, k_2]$ such that both the values $f(x)$ at these pixels are larger or smaller than its value in the interval, then we assume a maximum or minimum to exist at the midpoint of the interval, i.e., at $x = (k_1 + k_2)/2$ if $(k_1 + k_2)$, is even and at $x = (k_1 + k_2 + 1)/2$ if $(k_1 + k_2)$, is odd. Consider this point or pixel in the discrete plane to be a key pixel. Another example for the existence of a key pixel is depicted in Figure 1.5 for which $f(x)$ is not constant over an interval.

**Definition**

A function $f(x)$, constant in $[k_1, k_2]$, in the discrete plane is said to have a key pixel $P$ at $x = c$ (where $c = (k_1+k_2)/2$ or $(k_1+k_2+1)/2$ corresponding to even and odd values of $(k_1 + k_2)$) provided $\delta_1, \delta_2 \in \{0, 1\}$ exist such that in both the intervals $[(k_1 - \delta_1), k_1]$ and $[k_2, (k_2 + \delta_2)]$ either $f(c) > f(x)$ or $f(c) < f(x)$ when $k_1 = k_2 = c$; the definition is applicable for Figure 1.5 where $\delta_1 = \delta_2 = 1$. Note that the foregoing definition corresponds to Figures 1.4 and 1.5, where key pixels lie on a horizontal sequence of pixels for the interval $[k_1, k_2]$ of $x$. Similarly, key pixels can also be defined for a vertical sequence of pixels for the interval $[k_1, k_2]$ of $y$.

**Contour Approximation**

Let $k_1, k_2, \cdots, k_p$ be $P$ key pixels on a contour. The segment (geometrical entity, GE) between two key pixels can be classified as either an arc or a straight line. If the distance of each pixel from the line joining the two key pixels is less than a pre-specified value, say $\delta$, then the segment is considered to be a straight line (Figure 1.6(c)); otherwise, it is an arc. The arc may again be of two types, with all the pixels either lying on both sides (Figure 1.6(a)) or lying on the same side (Figure 1.6(b)) of the line joining the key pixels. We denote the GE in Figure 1.6(c) by $L$ (line) and that in Figure 1.6(b) by $CC$ (curve). GE in Figure 1.6(a), therefore, is nothing but a combination of two $CCs$ meeting at a point $Q$ (point of inflection). Key pixels on the contour of a two-tone picture can hence be used to decompose the contour into two types of GEs, namely, arcs and lines.

Consider Figure 1.7, where the curve $CC$ in Figure 1.6(b) is enclosed within a right triangle $ABC$. $AC$, the line joining $k_j$ and $k_{j+1}$, is the hypotenuse, whereas $AB$ and $BC$ are the two other sides.

Proposition 1 justifies that the arc $CC$ will always be confined within a right triangle $ABC$. A line $DF$ is drawn parallel to the hypotenuse $AC$ and passing through the pixel $E$ of maximum displacement with respect to $AC$. The sub-triangles, $ADE$ and $CFE$, so constructed may be taken as the characteristic triangles to approximate the curve $CC$ by the quadratic Bézier approximation technique. Information preservation of Bézier characteristic triangles with the key pixels forms the basis of the underlying concept of the generation scheme.

**Proposition 1**

In the discrete plane, all pixels on the arc between two key pixels remain always on or inside a right triangle, with the line joining the key pixels as the hypotenuse. The other two sides of the right triangle are the horizontal and vertical lines through the key pixels.

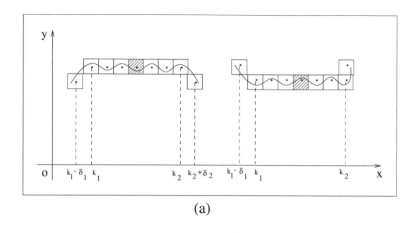

(a)

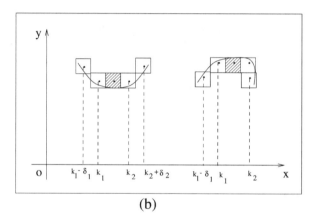

(b)

**Fig. 1.4.** Possible behavior of $f_a(x)$ when $f(x)$ is constant. (a) Considering local maxima/minima of $f_a(x)$; (b) considering global maximum/minimum of $f_a(x)$, • denotes the position of key pixel.

*Proof*: When the key pixels are on the horizontal line at $x = c$, it follows from the definition of key pixel that
*either* $f(c) > f(x)$
or      $f(c) < f(x)$
in both the intervals $[(k_1 - \delta_1), K_1]$ and $[K_2, (k_2 + \delta_2)]$, where $f(x)$ is constant in $[K_1, K_2]$ and $\delta_1, \delta_2 \in \{0, 1\}$. Thus,

(1) the pixels at $K_1$ and $K_2$ are either corner connected or direct connected or its combination to the neighboring pixels outside the interval $[K_1, K_2]$; or

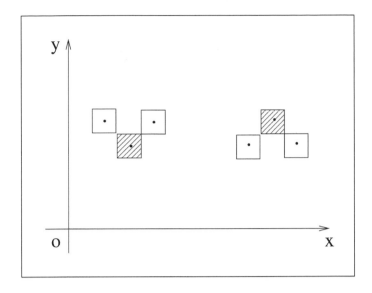

**Fig. 1.5.** Position of key pixel when $K_1 = K_2 = C$.

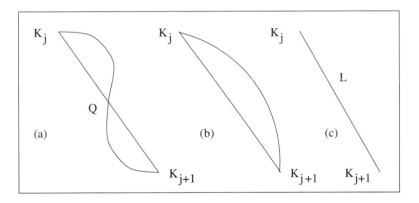

**Fig. 1.6.** Types of GE: (a) Arc with inflection point; (b) arc; (c) straight line.

(2) when $K_1 = K_2 = C$, the key pixels will have at least one corner connection to its neighboring pixels. Similar arguments hold when the key pixel lies on a vertical line.

Let $ANB$ be the arc, with $A$ and $B$ being two successive key pixels as shown in Figure 1.8. A pixel on the arc can go outside the line $AC$ or $BC$ if and only if a sequence of collinear pixels exists such that its end pixels are either corner connected or direct connected or a combination thereof, or a pixel exists that has at least one corner connection with its neighboring pixel.

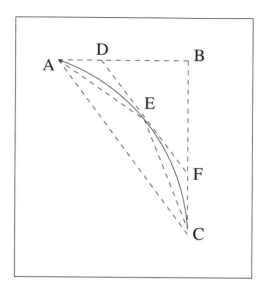

**Fig. 1.7.** Bézier characteristic triangles for an arc $AEC$.

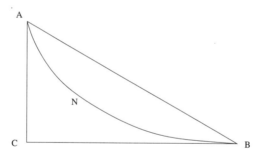

**Fig. 1.8.** Arc with its associated right triangle.

Both of these conditions lead to the existence of another key pixel outside the line $AC$ or $BC$.

This is a contradiction.

### Algorithm for Key Pixel Extraction

The following algorithm can be used for extraction of key pixels.

*Algorithm for extraction of key pixels.*

We assume:

$\{P_i\}_{i=1}^{n}$ are the contour points in the binary image and $\{(x_i, y_i)\}_{i=1}^{n}$ are their position coordinates.

Since for a closed contour there is a possibility of missing the first key pixel, we need to examine a few more points after the starting point is reached to enable us to get the same back.

Step 1: Set $i \leftarrow 1$, *count* $\leftarrow 1$. Find the initial direction code between $P_i$ and $P_{i+1}$ according to Freeman's chain code system. Let it be $d_1$.

Step 2: Increment $i \leftarrow i+1$; if i $=$ n, go to step 7; otherwise, find the directional code between $P_i$ and $p_{i\,|\,1}$; let it be $d_2$.

Step 3: If $d_1 = d_2$, go to step 2; otherwise, if $d_1$ *div* $2 = 0$ and $d_2$ *div* $2 = 0$ or if $\mid d_1 - d_2 \mid = 3$ *or* 5, then return $(x_i, y_i)$.

Step 4: Set $i \leftarrow i+1$; if i $=$ n, go to step 7; otherwise, find the direction code between $P_i$ and $P_{i+1}$; let it be $d_3$.

Step 5: If $d_3 = d_2$, then count$\leftarrow$ count+1 and go to step 4; otherwise, if $\mid d_1 - d_3 \mid = 0$ *or* 1, then set count$\leftarrow$ 1, $d_1 \leftarrow d_3$, and go to step 2 else do step 6.

Step 6: If count *div* 2 $=0$, then return $(x_{i-\ count/2},\ y_{i-\ count/2})$; otherwise return $(x_{i-\ count\ div\ 2},\ y_{i-\ count\ div\ 2})$.

Step 7: Stop.

### 1.5.2 Detection of Inflection Points

It is rather difficult to detect the points of inflection in a digital or discrete contour (a string of pixels). Due to discretization of an analog curve or contour, many inflection points (in the analytical sense) may be present, although all of them may not be properly justified from the standpoint of discrete geometry in relation to discrete straight line [143, 32, 176]. It is possible to find inflection points between two key pixels in a way somewhat similar to that in the analytical plane. Detection of inflection points also helps in maintaining the curvature of the contour during reconstruction and, as a result, the reconstruction quality is improved.

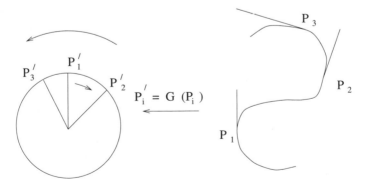

**Fig. 1.9.** Gaussian circle and its image detecting points of inflection.

**Gaussian Circle**

Consider a unit circle in the plane of a curve and draw radii in the direction of tangents at points $P_1$, $P_2$, and $P_3$, thus providing points $P_1'$, $P_2'$, and $P_3'$ as shown in Figure 1.9. The process, which assigns $P_i$ to $P_i'$, is known as the Gaussian map and the points on the circle are the Gaussian image of the curve. Therefore, if $G$ is the Gaussian map, then

$$G(P_i) \longrightarrow P_i'.$$

$G$ maps every single point $P_i$ on the curve to a unique point $P_i'$ on the circle, though $G^{-1}(P_i')$ may stand for two or more points on the curve depending on the directions of tangents at these points. Two points $P_i$ and $P_j$ appear to be the same under $G$ if tangents at these points have the same directions. In other words, it is quite likely that $G^{-1}(P_i')$ equals $P_i$ and $P_j$ both.

Note that as we move on, from $P_i$ to $P_{i+1}$ and from $P_{i+1}$ to $P_{i+2}$, it is not necessary that the same sequential order is maintained by their $G$-images. With this effect, we can make the following classification.

- The sequential order of the Gaussian image points $P_i'$ is the same as that of the points $P_i$ of the curve—we get regular points.
- The sequential order of $P_i's$ reverses, whereas that of $P_i s$ remains the same—we get point of inflection.
- The order of $P_i s$ reverses, i.e., the direction of the tangents at these points reverses, whereas that of motion of $P_i's$ remains the same—we get cusp of the first kind.
- The order of $P_i s$ as well as that of $P_i's$ gets reversed—we get cusp of the second kind.

Figure 1.10 shows all these four classifications. In the discrete domain, tangent to a discrete curve at a point is not defined in the existing literature. Therefore, it is very difficult to get the Gaussian image of a discrete curve. To detect between two key pixels on a discrete contour segment, an approximate position of a pixel as the position of a point of inflection, we first approximate the contour segment by straight line segments and these line segments are used to obtain the Gaussian image. If a reversal of order in the Gaussian image is detected for any line segment, then a point of inflection is marked at the midpoint of the previous line segment.

The process is repeated for all the pixels between other key pixels. Thus, all the key pixels and points of inflection can be extracted from the entire contour. Between any two key pixels or between a key pixel and a point of inflection or vice versa, the set of pixels can be viewed either as a line or a convex/concave arc segment.

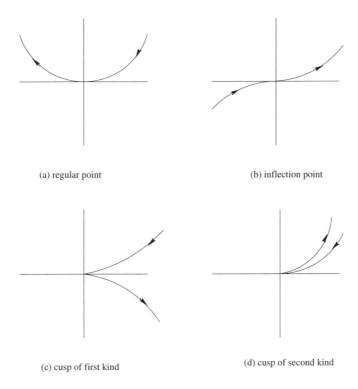

(a) regular point          (b) inflection point

(c) cusp of first kind          (d) cusp of second kind

**Fig. 1.10.** Classification of different G-images:(a) regular point; (b) inflection point; (c) cusp of first kind; (d) cusp of second kind.

## 1.6 Regeneration Technique

Below we depict two different methods of regeneration of a contour from its approximate information. These regenerations of arcs and line segments are simple and straightforward, and are helpful in data reduction.

### 1.6.1 Method 1

Method 1 considers only two points, namely $E$ and $C$ (Figure 1.7) of the characteristic triangle for the regeneration of an arc when the starting point $A$ is known beforehand. $D$ is the point of intersection of the horizontal line through $A$, and the line through $E$ and parallel to $AC$. So, one can easily get the Bézier characteristic triangle and regenerate the arc. If the GE between two key pixels is found to be a straight line, then it is generated by the Bresenham algorithm as already mentioned.

### 1.6.2 Method 2

Method 2 generates an arc in a slightly different way. It uses the information of the intercept along the horizontal or vertical line to extract the vertices of the Bézier characteristic triangles. Coordinates of the end point of the intercept may be computed using the following simple approach.

Consider $(x_1, y_1)$ and $(x_2, y_2)$ to be the initial and final points of an arc as shown in Figure 1.11. Let us now imagine a set of mutually perpendicular reference axes placed at the point $(x_1, y_1)$. Also, let $h$ be the value of the intercept and $(X', Y')$ be the coordinate of the end point of the intercept.

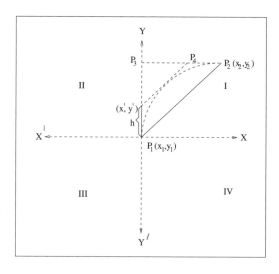

**Fig. 1.11.** Detection of Bézier characteristic triangles for Method 2.

Since an arc may lie either in the left (clockwise) or in the right (counterclockwise) side of the line joining $(x_1, y_1)$ and $(x_2, y_2)$, $X'$ and $Y'$ may have the values

$$X' = x_1 \qquad\qquad Y' = y_1 + h \ \ or,$$

$$X' = x_1 + h \qquad\qquad Y' = y_1$$

corresponding to the two possible senses of the arc in quadrant I where $x_2 > x_1$ and $y_2 > y_1$.

Similarly, for the other quadrants, where $x_2 < x_1$ and $y_2 > y_1$ (quadrant II), $x_2 < x_1$ and $y_2 < y_1$ (quadrant III), and $x_2 > x_1$ and $y_2 < y_1$ (quadrant IV), we have

$$X' = x_1 - h \qquad\qquad Y' = y_1 \ \ or,$$

$$X' = x_1 \qquad\qquad Y' = y_1 + h,$$

for quadrant II.

$$X' = x_1 \qquad\qquad Y' = y_1 - h \;\; or,$$

$$X' = x_1 - h \qquad\qquad Y' = y_1,$$

for quadrant III and,

$$X' = x_1 + h \qquad\qquad Y' = y_1 \;\; or,$$

$$X' = x_1 \qquad\qquad Y' = y_1 - h,$$

for quadrant IV, corresponding to the two possible senses.

Having determined the point $(X', Y')$, the next task is to construct the line passing through $(X', Y')$ and parallel to $P_1P_2$ so that it meets the line $P_2P_3$ at some point $P_4$. The midpoint of this line, together with the pairs of points $(X', Y')$, $(X_1, Y_1)$, and $((X_2, Y_2), P_4)$ then constitutes the Bézier characteristic triangles for the arc.

### 1.6.3 Recursive Computation Algorithm

The recursive algorithm for computation of values for the second-order Bézier approximation curve uses the forward difference scheme. Let

$$y = at^2 + bt + c$$

be a polynomial representation of (1.17), where the constant parameters $a$, $b$, $c$ are determined by the vertices of the Bézier characteristic triangle. Suppose a number of points (values of y) on the arc are to be evaluated for equispaced value of the independent variable $t$. The usual Newton's method of evaluating the polynomial results in multiplications and does not make use of the previously computed values to compute new values.

Assume that the parameter $t$ ranges from 0 *to* 1. Let the incremental value be $q$. Then the corresponding y values will be $c$, $aq^2 + bq + c$, $4aq^2 + 2bq + c$, $9aq^2 + 3bq + c, \cdots$. The difference Table 1.1 for recursive computation of points for Bézier curve then takes the following form. Observe that

**Table 1.1.** Difference table for recursive computation of points.

| t | y | $\Delta y$ (1st difference) | $\Delta^2 y$ (2nd difference) |
|---|---|---|---|
| 0 | $c$ | $aq^2 + bq$ | $2aq^2$ |
| q | $aq^2 + bq + c$ | $3aq^2 + bq$ | $2aq^2$ |
| 2q | $4aq^2 + 2bq + c$ | $5aq^2 + bq$ | $2aq^2$ |
| 3q | $9aq^2 + 3bq + c$ | $7aq^2 + bq$ | |
| 4q | $16aq^2 + 4bq + c$ | | |

$$\triangle^2 y_j = 2aq^2$$

and

$$y_{j+2} + 2y_{j+1} + y_j = 2aq^2, \quad for\ all\ j \geq 0.$$

This leads to the recurrence formula $y_2 = 2y_1 - y_0 + 2aq^2$ which involves just three additions to get the next value from two preceding values at hand. Therefore, we see that one does not need to store all the points on the curve.

### 1.6.4 Implementation Strategies

After approximating a contour of single pixel width, we get a set of key pixels with some labels. The labels indicate the geometrical entity between any two key pixels. We can use this set of key pixels in many applications. When we pay attention to regeneration of the contour, we immediately see that it results in its approximated version (output). During regeneration of a closed contour, only the outer contour is traced using Freeman's chain code (clockwise sense), assuring the positions of the key pixels on it. In other words, key pixels are considered to be the guiding pixels (important for preserving the input shape) during regeneration.

Note that due to the approximation scheme, sometimes the following undesirable situations may arise:

- The regenerated contour may not have single-pixel width.
- The key pixel may become an interior pixel of the contour.

To overcome these situations, the contours can be traced from the ordered regenerated data set, keeping the following operations in mind.

### Deletion of Pixels

While tracing a contour with the enclosed region lying on the right, if a pixel on the contour finds more than one neighbor in its eight-neighborhood domain, that neighbor is selected as the contour pixel for which the other neighboring pixels become interior pixels, and they are then deleted. But, if there is a key pixel falling in such a neighborhood, then the key pixel is retained as the contour pixel and the rest are deleted. This enables us to keep the key pixel always on the contour, and thus, improves approximation of the input. Figures 1.12(a) and (b) depict the situation. Considering "c" to be current pixel and "p" the previous pixel, the contour (clockwise) is "a" for the situation as shown in Figure 1.12(a), but if the situation is as in Figure 1.12(b), the next pixel on the contour is then k (the key pixel).

$$
\begin{array}{ccc}
 & & a \\
p & c & b \\
 & e & d
\end{array}
\qquad\longrightarrow\qquad
\begin{array}{ccc}
 & & a \\
p & c & b \\
 & e & \\
 & & k
\end{array}
$$

(a)                                        (b)

**Fig. 1.12.** Deletion of pixels: (a) In absence of key pixel; (b) in presence of key pixel.

## Shifting of Pixels

Suppose a GE is generated, and a key pixel is reached. Now during the generation of a following GE, its first data point may put the preceding key pixel on the interior contour. For example, consider the Figure 1.13(a). Here $abk$ is a part of the GE already generated. Now generating the next GE $kcd\cdots$, the first move from $k$ to $c$ makes the key pixel ($k$) lie on the interior of the contour (assuming the enclosed region is on the right).

In such cases, the data point $c$ is shifted as shown in Figure 1.13(b). This preserves connectedness of the pixel $c$ with both the GEs and also ensures single-pixel width of the contour.

(a)                                        (b)

**Fig. 1.13.** Shifting of pixels: (a) Contour before shifting; (b) contour after shifting.

## Undesirable Loop

Sometimes in the vicinity of key pixels an undesirable loop (contour with a single pixel hole) may appear due to the generation procedure. For example, consider Figure 1.14. Here GEs $ak_1k_2k_3$ are already generated. The next move from $k_3$ to $b$ creates an undesirable loop having a single-pixel hole.

To overcome this situation, the pixel $b$ is shifted along with an insertion of a new pixel $e$ (as shown in Figure 1.14(b)). Since the shifting of $b$ alone loses the connectivity property between $k_3$ and the subsequent pixels, it necessitates insertion of a new pixel whose location is governed by the concept of a minimum connected path.

(a)                                    (b)

**Fig. 1.14.** Undesirable loop: (a) Before cleaning; (b) After cleaning.

## 1.7 Approximation Capability and Effectiveness

So far, we have dealt with different approximation techniques based on Bézier-Berntein spline polynomial. Here we show their approximation capability. Consider the Figures 1.15 and 1.17(a) of two different digital contours, namely a butterfly and a chromosome. Key pixels and the points of inflection detected on them are marked by "3" and "**I**" respectively. Images regenerated by Meth-

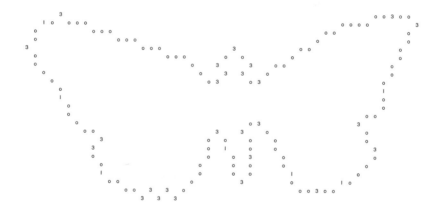

**Fig. 1.15.** Butterfly input.

ods 1 and 2 corresponding to the butterfly and chromosome images are shown in Figures 1.16(a), (b), and (c), and 1.17(b) and (c), respectively. Positions of key pixels in both the input and output remain unaltered.

As a typical illustration, section 1.6.4 shows the effectiveness of the cleaning operations on the generated points for the butterfly image. Figure 1.16(b) shows such an intermediate state for Method 1 before its final reconstructed output. Here, $d$ denotes a pixel to be deleted and $X$ corresponds to the position where a pixel is to be inserted to keep connectivity.

**Fig. 1.16.** (a) Method 1 after cleaning; (b) Method 1 before cleaning; (c) Method 2 after cleaning.

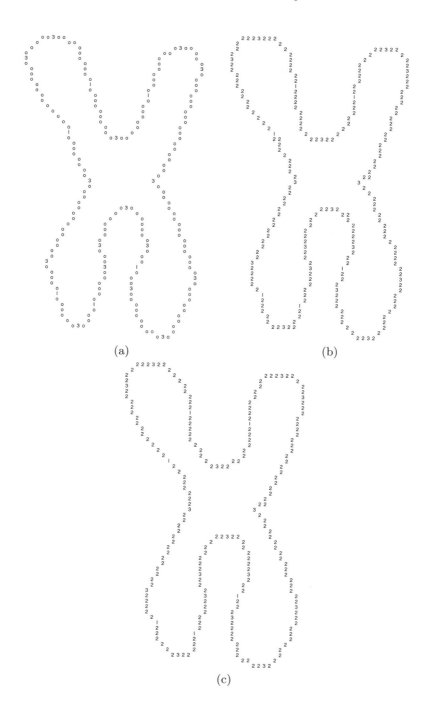

**Fig. 1.17.** (a) Chromosome input; (b) Method 1; (c) Method 2.

A reconstructed image normally deviates from its original version if the reconstruction is not perfect. Therefore, to observe the deviation of the image quality, one can compute different objective measures. One such is to provide the error in area and shape compactness between the original and reconstructed images. Kulpa [96] provided a good way to compute the area and perimeter. Since the key pixels are always on the contour and the reconstructed arcs between them are restricted by the respective Bézier characteristic triangles, the maximum error for an arc is the area of its pair of Bézier characteristic triangles. Also, for this constraint, shape compactness is a good measure for distortion in reconstructed images.

**Table 1.2.** Error in regeneration.

| Figure | % error in area Mtd 1 | Mtd 2 | Compactness of original Figure | Compactness generated figure by Mtd 1 | Mtd 2 |
|---|---|---|---|---|---|
| Butterfly | 8.63 | 10.07 | 0.024635 | 0.025393 | 0.025551 |
| Chromosome | 6.8 | 6.28 | 0.016061 | 0.016672 | 0.016359 |

Table 1.2 shows both the percentage error and the compactness of images associated with the two different methods. The reconstructed image in each case is a faithful reproduction of its input version. The butterfly contour, having the larger number of GEs, incurs the higher percent of error in their regeneration. Furthermore, since the regeneration/reconstruction procedure uses the quadratic Bézier approximation, the reconstruction is very fast.

## 1.8 Concluding Remarks

Bernstein polynomial together with its properties and approximation capabilities provides a major step in the formulation of Bézier spline model. Some of the properties of this polynomial are very powerful, and they serve the basic background for the development of a new branch in mathematics as well as in computer graphics. The widespread use and importance of B-spline mathematics is basically a generalization of Bézier-Bernstein spline. Similarly, the formulation of computer graphics algorithms for curve and surface design, based on this spline model, plays a major role in various engineering design and painting of computer drawn pictures.

The illustrative example provided in the text, to find the order of the Bernstein polynomial, is helpful to readers to approximate a function in the continuous domain by the Bernstein polynomial. The techniques and strategies discussed in this chapter for approximating a set of data points in the discrete domain are clear and explicit, and provide insight to handle various image data. We have not included any curve and surface design examples in this chapter because readers can find them almost in all graphics textbooks. However, one can use the recursive computation algorithm for curve and surface design to achieve some speed in algorithms.

# 2

# Image Segmentation

## 2.1 Introduction

We pay attention to segmentation, as it plays a significant role not only in image processing but also in pattern recognition. Segmentation of an image is its subdivision or partition, such that each partition is homogeneous in some sense. Partitions may be neither geometrically nor physically meaningful, i.e., an input image that shows, say, different industrial parts, may not be divided into regions, each describing one complete physical object (i.e., an industrial part of its input) or a single geometrically defined object (which means a completely circular, cylindrical or of any other definition from the input). Such a segmentation is very difficult and needs semantic knowledge at different levels of subdivisions, so that division and integration, or the split and merge of image regions, can successfully exploit this knowledge. Unfortunately, most of the time we do not have this knowledge. Consequently, segmentation becomes a difficult task. In the simplest case, one can use the graylevel threshold values to segment images. Obviously, different segmentations for an input image are possible, depending on different applications. As an example, segmented homogeneous regions, along with their contours, may be useful for designing image compression algorithms, whereas segmentation into known geometric entities may be useful for industrial inspection and medical diagnosis. A lot of research work has already been done in the area of segmentation, though we believe that segmentation still needs attention for semantic partition. An ideal segmentation or the ultimate objective of segmentation is to separate a physical object out from a scene.

## 2.2 Two Different Concepts of Segmentation

Segmentation can be broadly classified into two different groups: contour-based and region-based segmentation. The idea of segmentation into different image parts can be viewed as a pixel classification process, where we view the problem as a clustering problem. Given an image, we therefore try to form several clusters by assigning each pixel into a cluster. The assignment of a pixel into a cluster may depend on the image properties. One should keep in mind, while forming a cluster, that the distance between any two points of a cluster is smaller compared to the distance between any two points of different clusters. A cluster can be thought of as an image region.

### 2.2.1 Contour-based Segmentation

Contours or edges are the line segments (curved or straight) that separate one region from the other. Therefore, an edge detection technique can be used for segmentation. One of the major drawbacks of this segmentation technique is that it does not provide any guarantee for connected edges. However, we can use an edge linking algorithm to connect fragmented edges. Since edge is a feature of an image, edge-based or contour-based segmentation can also be thought of as a feature-based segmentation. Different techniques for edge detection are already in use.

### Gradient Operator

The simplest edge detection procedure is the gradient operator. The magnitude of the gradient $\sqrt{\frac{\partial f}{\partial x} + \frac{\partial f}{\partial y}}$ can be used to locate the edge pixels. On the edges, values of the gradient magnitude are high, while in object and background regions, it is low.

### The Laplacian Operator

The Laplacian operator over an image $f(x, y)$ is given by $\frac{\partial^2 f}{\partial^2 x} + \frac{\partial^2 f}{\partial^2 y}$. Edges are located at pixels where the Laplacian changes its sign.

### Laplacian of Gaussian Operator

Marr and Hildreth [119] suggested the Laplacian of the Gaussian operator for edge detection. The Gaussian, G(x,y) is given by

$$G(x, y) = \frac{1}{2\pi\sigma^2} e^{-\frac{x^2+y^2}{2\sigma^2}}.$$

Laplacian of Gaussian is, therefore

$$\nabla^2 G = -\frac{1}{2\pi\sigma^4} \left(2 - \frac{x^2 + y^2}{2\pi\sigma^2}\right) e^{-\frac{x^2+y^2}{2\sigma^2}}. \tag{2.1}$$

They developed a refined approach considering difference of Gaussian operator, given by

$$DOG(\sigma_1, \sigma_2) = \frac{1}{\sqrt{2\pi\sigma_1^2}} e^{-\frac{x^2}{2\sigma_1^2}} + \frac{1}{\sqrt{2\pi\sigma_2^2}} e^{-\frac{y^2}{2\sigma_2^2}}. \tag{2.2}$$

## 2.2.2 Region-based Segmentation

Region-based segmentation mainly depends on either thresholding or region growing, merge, and splitting. Selection of thresholds has an important role in threshold-based segmentation, e.g., single level thresholding produces a partition in the way that

$$f(x,y) = \begin{cases} f(x,y) & when \ f(x,y) \geq T, \\ 0 & otherwise, \end{cases} \qquad (2.3)$$

where $f(x,y)$ is the gray value in the image and T is a threshold. There are many ways by which one can calculate T. The simplest way is to use the histogram of the image. Equation (2.3) provides binary segmentation or object/background segmentation when $f(x,y)$ is taken as 1 for $f(x,y) \geq T$ and zero otherwise.

For multilevel thresholding, we choose

$$f(x,y) = \begin{cases} f(x,y) & when \ T_i \leq f(x,y) \leq T_{i+1} \quad i = 1,2,\cdots k, \\ 0 & otherwise. \end{cases} \qquad (2.4)$$

By multilevel thresholding we can separate out different segments of an image corresponding to different ranges of gray values. This corresponds to different objects or different portions of an object in an image.

Recursive thresholding can also be used for good segmentation. For this, segment an image corresponding to a threshold and if that segmentation does not fulfill certain objectives, then re-segment the segmented image through an iterative computation of a new threshold. So, segmentation and re-segmentation go on continuously until the criterion is satisfied for a definite task.

### Region Growing, Merge, and Split

Region growing normally starts from a small region, and merges small nearby regions to grow in size. If the merge is successful, neighborhood regions are further merged depending on a condition for successful merge. The process can keep on running if the merge passes the test, otherwise, the merge is declared unsuccessful, and split of the previous merge is carried out.

## 2.3 Segmentation for Compression

We now discuss how we can obtain a good segmentation of an image for image data compression. Choose the region-based segmentation of an image rather than the contour-based segmentation. Region-based segmentation is more useful and effective in image data compression because region contours are not disconnected like edges. Keep in mind that a contour-based segmentation may always produce disconnected edges. For background reading in this area, readers can consult [33, 97, 98, 152], whereas a broad over-view of segmentation can be found in [68, 133, 144].

To get compact homogeneous regions (or patches), we describe a segmentation method that recursively uses an object/background thresholding algorithm [130]. Unlike the region growing [133] or adaptive region growing [97] technique, it provides a number of compact regions of similar graylevels for a given threshold. We call this collection of regions for a given threshold a *subimage*. This segmentation method produces a number of subimages depending on the number of computed thresholds. Then it merges small regions depending on a criterion, and uses some quantitative indices for objective evaluation of the segmented regions.

## 2.4 Extraction of Compact Homogeneous Regions

Segmentation is objective oriented. Assume for illustration purposes, that we are using segmentation for image compression. We can think of a compression scheme that is based on modeling compact homogeneous regions or patches using Bézier-Bernstein polynomial function. Given an image, we therefore first try to extract from it the homogeneous subimages. There are many approaches [173, 65, 74] to achieve this goal. For example, it can be based on pixel level decision making such as iterative pixel modification, region growing, or adaptive region growing, or it can be based on multilevel thresholding. Each of these categories of algorithms, except multilevel thresholding, produces one region of similar graylevels at a time and, therefore, it forces local approximation for a region. Such methods may be called local thresholding schemes as a decision is made at the pixel level. It does not provide any information about other regions of similar gray values. Hence, from the standpoint of compression, segmentation algorithms based on local region growing are not very attractive. On the other hand, global thresholding based segmentation algorithms, (where the entire image is partitioned by one or a few thresholds), such as multilevel thresholding algorithms [174, 58, 35], depend on the number of local minima in the one or two dimensional histogram of gray values in the image. The extraction of these minima from the histogram information sometimes may not be very reliable, because all desirable thresholds may not be reflected as deep valleys in the histogram. Also, the detection of thresholds is influenced by all pixels in the image.

Several authors [1, 87, 131, 132, 135, 136] have used entropy as the criterion for object/background classification. All methods described in [87, 135, 136] use only the entropy of the histogram, while the methods in [1, 131, 132] use the spatial distribution of gray levels, i.e., the higher order entropy of the image. For the set of images reported in [130], authors found that conditional entropy of the objects and background based on Poisson distribution produced better results compared to the methods in [135, 136, 87, 91]. All these methods produce only an object/background (two level) partitioning of the image. Here in a segmentation problem, such a bi-level thresholding is not adequate. But, one can consider an algorithm for hierarchical extraction of homogeneous patches using the conditional entropy thresholding method. The conditional entropy we can define in terms of the second order co-occurence matrix.

a. *Co-occurrence Matrix*

Let $F = [f(x, y)]$ be an image of size $M \times N$, where $f(x, y)$ is the gray value at $(x, y)$, $f(x, y) \in G_L = \{0, 1, 2, \cdots, L-1\}$, the set of graylevels. The co-occurrence matrix of the image $F$ is an $L \times L$ dimensional matrix that gives us an idea of the transition of intensity between adjacent pixels. In other words, the $(i, j)th$ entry of the matrix gives the number of times the graylevel "j" follows the graylevel "i" in a specific way.

Let "a" denote the $(i, j)$th pixel in $F$ and let "b" be one of eight neighboring pixels of "a", i.e.,

$$b \in a_8 = \{(i, j-1), (i, j+1), (i+1, j), (i-1, j), (i-1, j-1),$$
$$(i-1, j+1), (i+1, j-1), (i+1, j+1)\} .$$

Define $t_{ik} = \sum_{a \in F, \, b \in a_8} \delta,$

where $\delta = 1$ if the graylevel of "a" is "i" and that of 'b' is 'k', $\delta = 0$ otherwise.

Obviously, $t_{ik}$ gives the number of times the gray level 'k' follows graylevel 'i' in any one of the eight directions. The matrix $T = [t_{ik}]_{L \times L}$ is, therefore, the co-occurrence matrix of the image $F$. One may get different definitions of the co-occurrence matrix by considering different subsets of $a_8$, i.e., considering $b \in a_8'$, where $a_8' \subseteq a_8$.

The co-occurrence matrix may again be either asymmetric or symmetric. One of the asymmetrical forms can be defined considering

$$t_{ik} = \sum_{i=1}^{M} \sum_{j=1}^{N} \delta$$

with $\delta = 1$ if $f(i, j) = i$ and $f(i, j+1) = k$,
$\qquad\qquad f(i, j) = i$ and $f(i+1, j) = k$,
$\quad \delta = 0$ otherwise.

Here only the horizontally right and vertically lower transitions are considered. The following definition of $t_{ik}$ gives a symmetrical co-occurence matrix.

$$t_{ik} = \sum_{i=1}^{M} \sum_{j=1}^{N} \delta,$$

where $\delta = 1$ if $f(i, j) = i$ and $f(i, j+1) = k$,
$\quad$ or $f(i, j) = i$ and $f(i, j-1) = k$,
$\quad$ or $f(i, j) = i$ and $f(i+1, j) = k$,

$$\text{or } f(i,\ j)\ =\ i \text{ and } f(i-1,\ j)\ =\ k,$$
$$\delta\ =\ 0, \text{ otherwise.}$$

b. *Conditional Entropy of a Partitioned Image*

The entropy of an n-state system as defined by Shannon [151] is

$$H = -\sum_{i=1}^{n} p_i \ln p_i \ , \tag{2.5}$$

where $\sum_{i=1}^{n} p_i\ =\ 1$ and $0 \le p_i \le 1$, $p_i$ is the probability of the $i$-th state of the system. Such a measure is claimed to give information about the actual probability structure of the system. Some drawbacks of (2.5) were pointed out by Pal and Pal [131] and the following expression for entropy was suggested:

$$H\ =\ \sum_{i=1}^{n} p_i e^{1-p_i}, \tag{2.6}$$

where $\sum_{i=1}^{n} p_i\ =\ 1$ and $0 \le p_i \le 1$. The term $-\ln p_i$, i.e., $\ln(1/p_i)$ in (2.5) or $e^{1-p_i}$ in (2.6) is called gain in information from the occurrence of the $i$-th event. Thus, one can write,

$$H\ =\ \sum_{i=1}^{n} p_i \triangle I(p_i), \tag{2.7}$$

where $\triangle I(p_i)\ =\ \ln(1/p_i)$ or, $e^{1-p_i}$ depending on the definition used.

Considering two experiments $A(a_1,\ a_2,\ \cdots,\ a_m)$ and $B(b_1,\ b_2,\ \cdots,\ b_n)$ with respectively $m$ and $n$ possible outcomes, the conditional entropy of $A$ given $b_l$ has occurred in $B$ is

$$H(A \mid b_l)\ =\ \sum_{k=1}^{m} p(a_k \mid b_l) \triangle I(p(a_k \mid b_l)), \tag{2.8}$$

where $p(a_k \mid b_l)$ is the conditional probability of occurrence of $a_k$ given that $b_l$ has occurred. We can write the entropy of $A$ conditioned by $B$ as

$$\begin{aligned}
H(A \mid B) &= \sum_{l=1}^{n} p(b_l)\ H(A \mid b_l), \\
&= \sum_{l=1}^{n} \sum_{k=1}^{m} p(b_l)\ p(a_k \mid b_l) \triangle I(p(a_k \mid b_l)), \\
&= \sum_{l=1}^{n} \sum_{k=1}^{m} p(a_k,\ b_l) \triangle I(p(a_k \mid b_l)),
\end{aligned} \tag{2.9}$$

where $p(a_k, b_l)$ is the joint probability of occurrence of $(a_k, b_l)$.

Let $p(i \mid j)$ be the probability that a gray value i belongs to the object, given that the adjacent pixel with gray value j belongs to the background, $\sum_i p(i \mid j) = 1$. Thus, for a given threshold s, the conditional entropy of the object given the background, as defined by Pal and Bhandari [130] (using (2.9)) is

$$
\begin{aligned}
H_s(O \mid B) &= \sum_{i \,\in\, object} \sum_{j \,\in\, background} p_o(i, j) \triangle I \left( p_o(i \mid j) \right), \\
&= \sum_{i=0}^{s} \sum_{j=s+1}^{L-1} p_o(i, j) \triangle I \left( p_o(i \mid j) \right),
\end{aligned}
\tag{2.10}
$$

where

$$
p_o(i, j) = \frac{t_{ij}}{\displaystyle\sum_{i=0}^{s} \sum_{j=s+1}^{L-1} t_{ij}}
\tag{2.11}
$$

and

$$
p_o(i \mid j) = \frac{t_{ij}}{\displaystyle\sum_{i=0}^{s} t_{ij}}
\tag{2.12}
$$

for $0 \le i \le s$ and $s + 1 \le j \le L - 1$. Here $t_{ij}$ is the frequency of occurrence of the pair $(i, j)$. The conditional entropy of the background given the object can similarly (using(2.9)) can defined as

$$
H_s(B \mid O) = \sum_{i \,\in\, background} \sum_{j \,\in\, object} p_b(i,j) \triangle I \left( p_b(i \mid j) \right)
\tag{2.13}
$$

where

$$
p_b(i, j) = \frac{t_{ij}}{\displaystyle\sum_{i=s+1}^{L-1} \sum_{j=0}^{s} t_{ij}}
\tag{2.14}
$$

and

$$
p_b(i \mid j) = \frac{t_{ij}}{\displaystyle\sum_{i=s+1}^{L-1} t_{ij}}
\tag{2.15}
$$

for $s + 1 \le i \le L - 1$ and $0 \le j \le s$. Then the total conditional entropy of the partitioned image is

$$
H_T{}^C = H_s(O \mid B) + H_s(B \mid O).
\tag{2.16}
$$

For an image, the conditional entropy of the object, given the background, provides a measure of information about the object when we know about the existence of the background. Entropy is a measure of expected gain in information or expected loss of ignorance with an associated probability distribution. Thus, $H(O \mid B)$ can also be viewed as average loss of ignorance about the object when we are told about the background. Similar interpretation is also applicable to $H(B \mid O)$. Hence, maximization of $H_T{}^C$ is expected to result in a good threshold. $H_T{}^C$ can also be viewed as a measure of contrast.

Let $th$ be the correct threshold for an object/background segmentation. Now if $th$ is used to partition the co-occurrence matrix, entries in quadrants two and four in Figure 2.1 will have low frequencies, but expected to be more or less uniformly distributed. Similarly, for the first and third quadrants, frequencies also will be uniformly distributed but with high values, because within a region, frequencies of transition from one level to another will be high. However, as far as the two dimensional probability distribution is concerned, all cells will have more or less uniform probability mass function. Now suppose the assumed threshold $s$ is less than $th$. The second quadrant will have some high frequencies that are actually transitions within the object. In addition to this, it will also have actual low frequency transitions from object to background (i.e., across the boundary). Thus, the second quadrant will have a highly skewed probability distribution resulting in a drastic lowering of $H_T{}^C$.

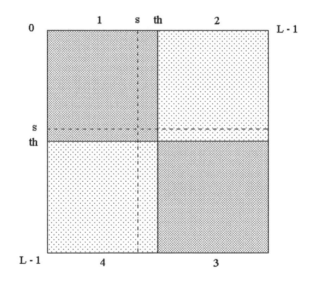

**Fig. 2.1.** Partitioning of the co-occurrence matrix for thresholding.

The uniformity of quadrant one will be maintained, but that of quadrants three and four will be affected causing a lowering of entropy of quadrants three and four. Similarly, if the assumed threshold is more than $th$, $H_T{}^C$ will be reduced. Hence, its maximization with respect to $s$ is expected to provide a good object/background segmentation.

Next, we provide a schematic description of the algorithm.

c. **Algorithm** *Cond_threshold*$(X,\ th)$
**begin**

    Compute Co-occurrence matrix, $t = [t_{ij}]_{L \times L}$.

    $s = 0$ ; max $= 0$ ;

    th $= 0$ ;  th is the threshold for segmentation

    while $(s < L - 1)$ do

        compute $H_T{}^C$ by (2.16)

        if ( $H_T{}^C(s)$ > max ) then **begin**

$$\text{th} = s\ ;$$
$$\text{max} = H_T{}^C(s)$$

           **end**

        s $=$ s+1 ;

    **endwhile;**

**end**;

    Here, we use $\triangle I(p_i) = e^{1-p_i}$ in equation (2.16).

### 2.4.1 Partition/Decomposition Principle for Gray Images

Explore the possibility of using the object/ background thresholding algorithm (*Cond_threshold*) for the extraction of homogeneous patches from a graylevel image. To partition the image into several subimages, one should keep in mind the following points:

- Each subimage consisting of different regions should be approximated well by some low order function.
- Number of subimages should be as low as possible.
- Homogeneity within a region and contrast between regions should be reasonably good.

In order to achieve this goal, one can use either a multilevel thresholding algorithm [174, 58, 35] or an object/background thresholding algorithm. The multilevel thresholding algorithm depends on the number of local minima in the histogram of the image. The extraction of these minima from the histogram information sometimes may not be very reliable, because some of them may not be strong enough to be detected by the objective function being used. The object/background algorithm, on the other hand, relies on a single threshold to extract the object from the background. Consider a scheme that repeatedly uses an object/background segmentation algorithm for extraction of homogeneous patches.

Consider an L-level image $F_0(x,\ y)$. The input gray image $F_0(x,\ y)$ initially provides a threshold, $s$ on application of the object/background thresholding algorithm. The threshold, $s$ partitions the image $F_0(x,\ y)$ into two subimages $F_{01}(x,\ y)$ and $F_{02}(x,\ y)$. The graylevels in $F_{01}(x,\ y)$ lie in the interval

$[0, s]$ and in $F_{02}(x, y)$, it is limited to $(s, L - 1]$. From the standpoint of object/background thresholding, $F_{01}(x, y)$ can be viewed as the object while $F_{02}(x, y)$ is the background, without loss of generality.

To check the feasibility of global approximation of the subimages so obtained, we approximate, first of all, $F_{01}(x, y)$ by a polynomial of order $p \leq q$ ($q$ is a predefined upper limit on the order of polynomials) satisfying a criterion C. It should be noted that $F_{01}(x, y)$ may consist of a number of isolated regions or patches, say, $\Omega_1, \Omega_2, \cdots \Omega_r$. If the approximation satisfies the criterion C, we accept the subimage $F_{01}(x, y)$. Otherwise, even when a polynomial surface of order $q$ cannot approximate the subimage subject to C, we compute the variance in each of the regions. Next, we fit a global surface of order $q$ over the entire subimage and a local surface of order less than $q$ over the residual errors (defined with respect to surface of order $q$) of the most dispersed region. This may give rise to one of the following four different situations:

(1) The criterion C is satisfied for the most dispersed region (with respect to global and local surface fitting) and also for rest of the regions (with respect to global fitting).

(2) C is satisfied for the most dispersed region but not for rest of the regions.

(3) C is not satisfied for the most dispersed region but satisfied for rest of the regions.

(4) C is not satisfied for both the most dispersed region and rest of the regions.

In situation in (1), both local and global fits are satisfied. Hence, it implies that all segmented regions or surface patches are homogeneous and we accept the subimage.

In situation (2), additionally fit a local surface of order less than $q$ over the residual errors (defined with respect to surface of order $q$) of the second most dispersed region. The process may continue for all regions in the subimage, only in case of failure for the global surface approximation. But if the local surface fit fails to satisfy the criterion C at any stage (cases 3 and 4), it indicates the need for further decomposition and hence, we seek a new threshold for the subimage $F_{01}(x, y)$. We accept the partition, $F_{01}$ when both local and global fits satisfy the criterion C.

A new threshold $s_1$ divides the image $F_{01}$ into $F_{011}(x, y)$ and $F_{012}(x, y)$. The graylevels in $F_{011}(x, y)$ extend from zero to $s_1$ while in $F_{012}(x, y)$, they extend from $s_1 + 1$ to $s$. In other words, the graylevel bands are $[0, s_1]$ and $(s_1, s]$ respectively for $F_{011}(x, y)$ and $F_{012}(x, y)$. The image $F_{02}(x, y)$ may likewise be examined and segmented if needed. The segmentation, therefore, follows a binary tree structure as shown in Figure 2.2.

The criterion C plays a crucial role in the determination of polynomial orders. If the segmented regions are more or less uniform, then low order polynomials will fit the data reasonably well. However, if the approximation criterion C is very strict and if the spatial distribution of gray values over a region deviates from uniformity, higher order polynomial will be required to justify the fit. This will result in better reconstruction of the image at the cost of compression ratio. Hence, the choice of C should be made based on a compromise between the quality of reconstructed image and the compression ratio. Sections 2.4.2–2.4.4, provide details of approximation, along with a new approach for the determination of polynomial order. In most of the cases, order is seen to be 2 but it can go up to 3 or 4 depending on variations in the segmented regions and the criterion, C.

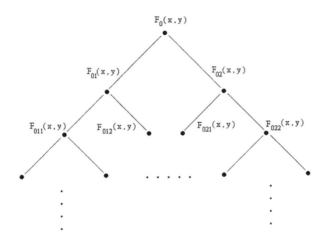

**Fig. 2.2.** Binary tree structure for hierarchical segmentation.

## 2.4.2 Approximation Problem

For approximation, one can first formulate the problem using Bézier-Bernstein polynomial and then can consider the issue of the polynomial order determination. Choose the Bézier-Bernstein polynomial because the segmentation algorithm we are considering is for image compression, for which Bézier-Bernstein polynomial provides a number of merits during reconstruction. However, one can use also other functions. The Bézier-Bernstein surface is a tensor product surface and is given by

$$
\begin{aligned}
s_{pq}(u,v) &= \sum_{r=0}^{p}\sum_{z=0}^{q}\phi_{rp}(u)\phi'_{zq}(v)\,V_{rz}, \\
&= \sum_{r=0}^{p}\sum_{z=0}^{q}B_{rp}D_{zq}\,u^{r}\,(1-u)^{p-r}\,v^{z}\,(1-v)^{q-z}\,V_{rz},
\end{aligned}
\tag{2.17}
$$

where $u,\,v \in [0,1]$ and $B_{rp} = \frac{p!}{(p-r)!r!}$, $D_{zq} = \frac{q!}{(q-z)z!}$. $p$ and $q$ define the order of the Bézier-Bernstein surface.

To approximate an arbitrary image surface $f(x, y)$ of size $M \times M$, $f(x, y)$ should be defined in terms of a parametric surface (here $s_{pq}$) with the parameters $u$, $v$ in $[0, 1]$. Therefore, the function $f(x, y)$ can be thought in terms of $g(u, v)$ where $u = \frac{(i-1)}{(M-1)}$; $i = 1, 2 \cdots, M$ and $v = \frac{(j-1)}{(M-1)}$; $j = 1, 2 \cdots, M$.

Now choose the weighted least square technique for estimation of parameters $V_{rz}$ for reconstruction of the decoded surface. Although the total squared error for the conventional unweighted least square approximation may be less than that for the weighted least square, the approximation produced by the latter may be visually more appealing than that by the former, provided weights are chosen judiciously. For an image, edge points are more informative than the homogeneous regions. Edges are the distinct features of an image. Thus, edges should be given more emphasis while approximating an image patch and this can be done through weighted least square.

The weighted squared error we can write as

$$
\begin{aligned}
E^2 &= \sum_u \sum_v [W(u, v)(g(u, v) - s_{pq}(u, v))]^2, \\
&= \sum_u \sum_v [W(u, v)(g(u, v) - \sum_{r=0}^{p} \sum_{z=0}^{q} \phi_{rp}(u)\phi'_{zq}(v) V_{rz})]^2,
\end{aligned}
\tag{2.18}
$$

where $W(u, v)$ is the weight associated with the pixel corresponding to (u, v). For p = q, the surface $s_{pq}(u, v)$ is defined on a square support. Since $W(u, v)$ is the weight associated with each pixel, it is considered constant for that pixel. Therefore, one needs to find out the weight matrix before solving equations for the weighted least square. Once $W(u, v)$ is known, these equations reduce to a system of linear equations and can be solved by any conventional technique.

We emphasize for order determination the unweighted approximation scheme.

### 2.4.3 Polynomial Order Determination

The order of the polynomial can be determined using either the classical approach as discussed in Chapter 1 or the image quality index IQI [25]. Since IQI reflects the average contrast (with respect to background) per pixel in the image, we can say if the original and approximated image have nearly the same IQI, the approximated image is expected to preserve the boundary contrast in the average sense. Therefore, very small $\triangle IQI$ between the input and approximated subimages is an indicator of the adequacy of the polynomial order. In order to determine optimal polynomial, one can increase the order of the polynomial unless the following condition is satisfied

$$
| (IQI)_{input} - (IQI)_{approximated} | \leq \epsilon_a,
\tag{2.19}
$$

where $\epsilon_a$ is a small positive number.

To calculate IQI we find, first of all, the total contrast K of the image. For an $M \times N$ image, K is be defined as

$$K = \sum_{i=1}^{M} \sum_{j=1}^{N} c_{ij}. \tag{2.20}$$

The contrast $c_{ij}$, at the pixel position $(i,\ j)$ is written using the concept of psycho-visual perception as [73]

$$\begin{aligned} c_{ij} &= \frac{|\ B\ \ B_{ij}\ |}{B}, \\ &= \frac{|\ \Delta B\ |}{B}, \end{aligned} \tag{2.21}$$

where $B$ is the immediate surrounding luminance of the $(i,\ j)$th pixel with intensity $B_{ij}$. Equations (2.20) and (2.21) reveal that the contrast of pixels in a perfectly homogeneous region is zero everywhere except near the boundary points. The contribution to K of the image, therefore, comes mainly from its noisy pixels and contrast regions (edge points). Thus the image quality index or the average contrast per pixel is defined as

$$IQI = \frac{K}{n_k}, \tag{2.22}$$

where $n_k = MN - n_h$, $n_k$ = total number of significant contrast points, $n_h$ = total number of significant homogeneous points, and $MN$ = number of pixels in the image. Note that the average is taken over only those pixels that mainly contribute to the contrast measure, K; the pixels of homogeneous regions, being least contributory, have been discarded.

To find out $n_h$ we define the homogeneity, $h_{ij}$ of the $(i,j)$th pixel as

$$h_{ij} = \frac{\sum_{r=1}^{8} exp - |B_{ij} - B_r|}{8}, \tag{2.23}$$

where $B_r$ indicates the intensity of a background pixel in the $3 \times 3$ neighborhood, $N_3(i,j)$, of $(i,\ j)$. From equation (2.23), it is seen that when each background pixel is equal to the central pixel, the tiny region around the central pixel is perfectly homogeneous, and the homogeneity measure at the central pixel is equal to unity. For other cases, homogeneity value of a pixel exponentially drops with its difference from the background intensity.

Therefore, if we compute total homogeneity of an image as

$$H = \sum_{i=1}^{M} \sum_{j=1}^{N} h_{ij}, \tag{2.24}$$

then the major contribution to H comes only from the pixels that lie in perfectly homogeneous regions. Thus, H will be a good *approximation* to $n_h$. Therefore,

$$IQI = \frac{\sum_{i=1}^{M}\sum_{j=1}^{N} \mid \triangle B_{ij} \mid /B}{MN - \sum\sum h_{ij}}. \tag{2.25}$$

The condition in equation (2.19) follows a psycho-visual criterion. A low value of $\epsilon_a$ psycho-visually produces a good quality of image. Note that for an ordinary least square approximation using polynomial surface, the error over the boundary points normally is higher than that over the interior points. Therefore, any polynomial with order determined relative to an error function measured over the boundary points is expected to provide a good approximation for the interior points.

### 2.4.4 Algorithms

#### Method 1: Variable order global approximation

Here we determine the order of the global approximation over data points in each subimage obtained under different thresholds. A schematic description of the global approximation scheme is given below. We assume that there are k number of thresholds for an image and $N_1, N_2, \cdots N_k$ are the number of regions in these k subimages.

    **Algorithm** *global_approx(input_image, th, $\epsilon_a$, p)*
**begin**

        step 1: compute the weights as the gradients of the image;
        step 2: find an acceptable subimage corresponding to a threshold *th*
            obtained during segmentation by **Algorithm** *Cond_threshold*
            (assuming W(i,j)=1 $\forall$ i,j);
        step 3: find the value of IQI of the subimage using equation (2.25);
        step 4: set the order of the polynomial, p = 1;
        step 5: approximate the subimage with weights as computed in
            step 1.
        step 6: find IQI of the approximated image.
        step 7: if $\mid (IQI)_{subimage} - (IQI)_{approximated} \mid \leq \epsilon_a$ then return p
            and goto step 8 else set p = p+1 and goto step 5;
        step 8: stop;
**end**;

#### Method 2: Variable/fixed-order local approximation

If the variable order global approximation over subimages does not provide good approximation for some regions in a subimage, then we do local correction. The global approximation is performed over each of the k subimages using a variable order polynomial function. The residual error surface patches are computed using the globally approximated surface $s_{pp}(u, v)$ and the original input surface (here, the input subimage). Let us denote *l*-th error surface patch of the *i*-th subimage by $e^i{}_l(u, v)$. Considering $N_i$ error surface patches that need local correction in the *i*-th subimage, we see that

$$e^i{}_l(u, v) = g(u, v) - s_{pp}(u, v), \qquad i = 1, 2, \cdots k \quad and \; l = 1, 2, \cdots, N_i.$$

Each of these error surface patches is approximated locally using a fixed or variable order polynomial. A schematic description of variable order local surface approximation is given below.

**Algorithm** *local_approx* (*input_image*, *th*, $\epsilon_a$, *q*, *p*)
**begin**
        step 1: find the most dispersed region, $\Omega_k$ in the input_image; find
              the residual error surface for it with respect to order $q$;
        step 2: find p using the **Algorithm** *global_approx* ($\Omega_k$, *th*, $\epsilon_a$, *p*);
        step 3: if $p \geq q$, a pre-assigned positive integer then goto step 4 else
              assign an index for the region and return p;
        step 4: stop;
**end**;

To summarize, this scheme is a two stage process. In stage 1, first determine a threshold. This threshold partitions an image into two subimages, $F_{01}$ and $F_{02}$. Determine the order of a polynomial minimizing *unweighted* least square error for approximating a subimage $F_{01}$. If the order of the polynomial is less than a predefined order, say, $q$ then accept the partition $F_{01}$, else do a local correction for one or more regions. Local correction is always with respect to the global surface of order q. If the global approximation together with local correction(s) is all right, then accept the subimage, $F_{01}$, else compute a new threshold to subdivide $F_{01}$ into $F_{011}$ and $F_{012}$. The process goes on subdividing the subimages hierarchically until all of them are approximated by *global_approx* and *local_approx*. The same is also true for $F_{02}$. The segmentation algorithm may produce some small isolated patches. After the partition of the entire image, all single pixel and small regions or patches are merged to the neighboring regions depending on some criteria, which are described in section 2.4.5. Note that all approximations in stage 1 are unweighted, i.e., $W(i, j) = 1 \; \forall i, j$ in approximation algorithms. In stage 2, for encoding one can approximate the subimages minimizing a *weighted* least square error with a polynomial of the same order as determined in stage 1. The same order can be used because the order (global and also local) of a subimage or the nature of approximation is not expected to change due to merging of small regions. However, one can once again find the order of approximation before encoding.

## 2.4.5 Merging of Small Regions

Merge is always used for better segmentation. Obviously, small noninformative regions are merged to nearby regions. Two issues are raised: which regions are to be merged and where are they to be merged. In order to detect regions of small size for possible merge to one of its neighboring regions, a merge index is often very helpful. Consider a merge index, MI, as the ratio of a measure of within region interactions to that of between regions interactions. Assume that for a nontrivial region, the within region interaction should be more than that across the boundary, i.e., $MI > 1$. A very simple measure of within region interaction is the number of transitions within the region. Similarly, the between region interaction can be defined as the number of transitions across the border of the region. Thus, MI can be computed as

$$MI = \frac{Number\ of\ transitions\ within\ a\ region}{Number\ of\ transitions\ across\ the\ border\ of\ the\ region}. \qquad (2.26)$$

Note that MI cannot be computed directly from the co-occurence matrix discussed earlier because more than one isolated regions may contribute to the computation of $t_{ij}$ for a particular $(i, j)$. In the present context we need to consider only the transitions with respect to one region. This is a very simple, yet effective, measure of interaction.

Small regions detected by MI are the potential candidates for merge and they are merged if the magnitude of the average gradient computed over their region boundaries is less than a preassigned positive value. This criterion will avoid merging small but informative regions. High contrast small regions are usually informative, e.g., the white spot in the eye ball in a face image. The average gradient over a region, say $\Omega_1$, may be computed as

$$\bar{G} = \sum_{(i,\ j)\ \in\ \partial\Omega_1} \frac{G(i,\ j)}{p}, \qquad (2.27)$$

where p is the perimeter of the region $\Omega_1$ and $G(i, j)$ is the gradient at the position $(i, j)$. The average gradient over other regions can likewise be computed. We have used the following gradient functions. Let $g_{i,j}$ and $g_{k,l}$ be two adjacent pixels belonging to two different regions, say, $\Omega_i$ and $\Omega_k$, then

$$G(i,\ j) = max \mid g_{i,j}\ -\ g_{k,l} \mid \qquad (2.28)$$

$$k \in \mathcal{N}_3(i,\ j),$$

where $\mathcal{N}_3(i,\ j)$ is the $3 \times 3$ neighborhood of $(i,\ j)$. Note that rechecking of the segmentation criteria may be avoided because of merging small regions with low gradients across the boundary positions. It is expected that the condition will be satisfied and our computational experience indeed supports this fact. However, to ensure the validity of the condition, one can once more check the thresholding after merging.

*Single Pixel Merge*: Sometimes, single pixel region can occur in a thresholded image. This should be merged to the neighboring region having the closest gray value in the $3 \times 3$ neighborhood of the single pixel region.

## 2.5 Evaluation of Segmentation

Evaluation of segmentation is very important, though adequate attention is not always paid. For evaluation of segmentation, one can consider region homogeneity and contrast along the boundary points. A good segmentation technique should create homogeneous regions or patches with high contrast at the inter-region boundaries. Merging should have very little effect on the over-all contrast of the image. The following objective measures for quantitative evaluation of segmentation are helpful.

a. *Correlation*

Correlation has already been used as a criterion for graylevel threshold-ing and evaluation [31]. In the present context, it can be used to examine the graylevel similarity between the segmented region/patches and the origi-nal image. Consider the segmented image where all patches under respective thresholds are replaced by their average value. The correlation between the segmented and input images provides an idea about how a segmented patch is nearer to the corresponding region in the original input image. For a good segmentation, the correlation coefficient between the two images should be very high. However, if the segmented patches are not homogeneous, i.e., if they have edges in them, the variance of the corresponding regions would be high and as a result, the correlation coefficient would be low. Thus correlation between the two different images—input and segmented—can be an useful measure to evaluate the quality of segmentation. The correlation coefficient can be calculated in the following way.

The coefficient of correlation $\rho_{xy}$ for two sets of data $X = \{x_1, x_2, \cdots, x_N\}$ and $Y = \{y_1, y_2, \cdots, y_N\}$ is given by

$$\rho_{xy} = \frac{\frac{1}{N} \sum_{i=1}^{N} x_i y_i - \bar{x}\bar{y}}{\sqrt{\frac{1}{N} \sum_{i=1}^{N} x_i^2 - \bar{x}^2} \sqrt{\frac{1}{N} \sum_{i=1}^{N} y_i^2 - \bar{y}^2}}, \qquad (2.29)$$

where $\bar{x} = \frac{1}{N} \sum_{i=1}^{N} x_i$ and $\bar{y} = \frac{1}{N} \sum_{i=1}^{N} y_i$. The correlation coefficient, $\rho_{xy}$ takes on values from +1 to -1, depending on the type and extent of correlation between the sets of data.

b. *Contrast*

Another requirement for a good segmentation is that the contrast at inter-region boundaries must be very high compared to that for the interior points. This criterion immediately suggests that the average contrast, i.e., contrast per pixel, say $\bar{K}_b$, of all inter-region boundary points in all subimages should be high compared to that (say, $\bar{K}_\Omega$) over all points enclosed within the bound-aries. Therefore,

$$\bar{K}_b >> \bar{K}_\Omega.$$

The contrast $c_{ij}$, at the pixel position $(i, j)$ can be computed as in equation (2.21), which we repeat here as

$$c_{ij} = \frac{|B - B_{ij}|}{B} = \frac{|\triangle B|}{B}, \qquad (2.30)$$

where $B$ is the immediate surrounding luminance of the $(i, j)$th pixel with intensity $B_{ij}$.

Let SB be the set of all boundary points and SI be the set of all interior points ($SB \cup SI = F$, $SB \cap SI = null$ set). Contrast of all boundary points, $K_b$ and that of interior points, $K_\Omega$ are, therefore,

$$K_b = \sum_{(i,j) \,\in\, SB} c_{ij} \text{ and } K_\Omega = \sum_{(i,j) \,\in\, SI} c_{ij}.$$

Note that $K_\Omega$ is an indicant of homogeneity within regions—lower the value of $K_\Omega$, higher is the homogeneity. The contrast per pixel, $\bar{K}_b$, of all inter-region boundary points and that over all points enclosed within the boundaries, $\bar{K}_\Omega$ can be obtained by dividing $K_b$ by the number of boundary points and $K_\Omega$ by the number of interior points.

## 2.6 Comparison with Multilevel Thresholding Algorithms

Since the co-occurrence matrix contains information regarding the spatial distribution of graylevels in the image, several workers have used it for segmentation. For thresholding at graylevel $s$, Weszka and Rosenfeld [174] defined the busyness measure as follows:

$$Busy(s) = \sum_{i=0}^{s} \sum_{j=s+1}^{L-1} t_{ij} + \sum_{i=s+1}^{L-1} \sum_{j=0}^{s} t_{ij}. \tag{2.31}$$

The co-occurrence matrix used in (2.31) is symmetric. For an image with only two types of regions, say, object and background, the value of $s$ which minimizes Busy(s), gives the threshold. Similarly, for an image having more than two regions, the busyness measure provides a set of minima corresponding to different thresholds.

Deravi and Pal [58] gave a measure that they called "conditional probability of transition" from one region to another as follows. If the threshold is at $s$, the conditional probability of transition from the region $[0, s]$ to $[s+1, L-1]$ is

$$P_1 = \frac{\displaystyle\sum_{i=0}^{s} \sum_{j=s+1}^{L-1} t_{ij}}{\displaystyle\sum_{i=1}^{s} \sum_{j=0}^{s} t_{ij} + \sum_{i=0}^{s} \sum_{j=s+1}^{L-1} t_{ij}} \tag{2.32}$$

and the conditional probability of transition from the region $[(s+1), (L-1)]$ to $[0, s]$ is

$$P_2 = \frac{\displaystyle\sum_{i=s+1}^{L-1}\sum_{j=0}^{s} t_{ij}}{\displaystyle\sum_{i=s+1}^{L-1}\sum_{j=s+1}^{L-1} t_{ij} + \sum_{i=s+1}^{L-1}\sum_{j=0}^{s} t_{ij}}. \tag{2.33}$$

$p_c(s)$, the conditional probability of transition across the boundary, is then defined as

$$p_c(s) = (P_1 + P_2)/2. \tag{2.34}$$

Expressions (2.32)–(2.34) suggest that a minimum of $p_c(s)$ will correspond to a threshold such that most of the transitions are within the class and few are across the boundary. Therefore, a set of minima of $p_c(s)$ would be obtained corresponding to different thresholds in F.

Chanda et al. [35] also used the co-occurrence matrix for thresholding. They defined an average contrast measure as

$$AVC(s) = \frac{\displaystyle\sum_{i=0}^{s}\sum_{j=s+1}^{L-1} t_{ij} * (i-j)^2}{\displaystyle\sum_{i=0}^{s}\sum_{j=s+1}^{L-1} t_{ij}} + \frac{\displaystyle\sum_{i=s+1}^{L-1}\sum_{j=0}^{s} t_{ij} * (i-j)^2}{\displaystyle\sum_{i=s+1}^{L-1}\sum_{j=0}^{s} t_{ij}}. \tag{2.35}$$

AVC(s) shows a set of maxima corresponding to the thresholds between various regions in F. In the computation of $t_{ij}$, they considered only vertical transitions in the downward direction.

## 2.6.1 Results and Discussion

Table 2.1 shows some objective measures, which we have already discussed in the previous sections. Consider two 32-level images (Figure 2.3 and Figure 2.4), each of size 64 × 64. Figure 2.3(a) is the Lincoln image while Figure 2.4(a) is the biplane image. Table 2.1 shows the values of different objective measures in conjunction with the total number of regions or patches, say $N_\Omega$, produced by different segmentation techniques for the images. Note that the number of regions is an important parameter to justify goodness of segmentation. For the Lincoln image, the number of segmented regions obtained by the discussed algorithm is almost one-fourth of those obtained by the other algorithms and for biplane image, the number of regions is roughly half of those produced by the algorithms of Rosenfeld, Pal-Deravi, and Chanda et al., respectively.

Usually, with the increase in number of regions, correlation is expected to increase. The segmentation of both Lincoln and biplane images supports this fact. But even with a much smaller number of regions for both the images produced by the proposed scheme, the correlation values are comparable to those for the segmented images obtained from other algorithms. This indicates successful merging of small regions to the proper neighboring regions.

**Table 2.1.** Evaluation of different segmentation algorithms.

| Lincoln image | | | | |
|---|---|---|---|---|
| Objective measure | described | [174] | [58] | [35] |
| Number of regions $N_\Omega$ | 52 | 187 | 192 | 189 |
| Correlation | 0.9788 | 0.9879 | 0.9873 | 0.9908 |
| Boundary contrast/pixel $\bar{K}_b$ | 0.204 | 0.202 | 0.200 | 0.194 |
| Region contrast/pixel $\bar{K}_\Omega$ | 0.0294 | 0.0257 | 0.0258 | 0.0293 |
| Biplane image | | | | |
| Number of regions $N_\Omega$ | 35 | 59 | 59 | 76 |
| Correlation | 0.9886 | 0.9892 | 0.9892 | 0.9884 |
| Boundary contrast/pixel $\bar{K}_b$ | 0.1499 | 0.1866 | 0.1866 | 0.1782 |
| Region contrast/pixel $\bar{K}_\Omega$ | 0.0151 | 0.0144 | 0.0144 | 0.0150 |

Also, due to merging, the homogeneity of the segmented regions is expected to increase. For good segmentation, this homogeneity should be very high. This means that the average contrast $\bar{K}_\Omega$ within a region should be low. The parameter region contrast/pixel, $\bar{K}_\Omega$, shows that the average homogeneity is reasonably good. Finally, the average boundary contrast $\bar{K}_b$, for both images is very much comparable to all the cases. Different segmented images along with the input are shown in Figures 2.3((a)–(e)) and 2.4((a)–(e)). For a better display of segmented regions, all segmented images are stretched over a gray scale of 0–255.

## 2.7 Some Justifications for Image Data Compression

The segmentation scheme, discussed in this chapter, is well suited for image data compression. It exploits the benefit of the multilevel thresholding based on conditional entropy, and partitions an image hierarchically. It also merges small regions efficiently.

The algorithm shows the possibility of globally approximating many segmented regions or patches by a single polynomial function. In other words, one can think to model different regions in an image by a single polynomial surface. For this, all such regions should have similar graylevels. The segmented regions to be approximated by a single polynomial can be extracted under a single threshold. Thresholding based segmentation thus provides an advantage over the split and merge technique of segmentation [133]. The latter does not provide any group of patches or regions of similar gray levels located at different places in an image at a time. It is, therefore, preferable to choose a thresholding technique of segmentation for coding application because, under such segmentation, a set of approximation parameters can represent many regions. This set of parameters represents a single surface on which different regions are situated at different locations. Hence, one need not code all

**Fig. 2.3.** (a) Input Lincoln image; (b) segmented image by the proposed method; (c) segmented image by Chanda et al. [35]; (d) segmented image by Weska and Rosenfeld [174]; (e) segmented image by Deravi and Pal [58].

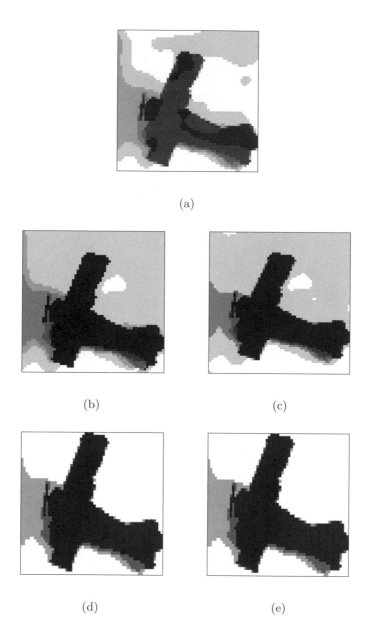

**Fig. 2.4.** (a) Input image of biplane; (b) segmented image by the proposed method; (c) segmented image by Chanda et al. [35]; (d) segmented image by Weska and Rosenfeld [174]; (e) Segmented image by Deravi and Pal [58].

the regions separately for their gray information. This is an important reason, responsible for providing advantage to image compression. However, the
graylevel distribution over some of the image surface patches may be such
that the global approximation is not adequate for them. One can call such
patches, under a given threshold, *busy* patches. To overcome this difficulty, a
lower order (compared to that of the global approximation) polynomial function can be used for local approximation of each of the residual surface patches
in the subimage. Therefore, a subimage can be reconstructed using the global
surface, along with the local residual surfaces for the busy patches if they are
really present. Such a hybrid approximation scheme helps to improve the compression ratio. Note that exactly the same kind of approximation is used to
guide the segmentation process, which ensures that the extracted subimages
can be modeled by low order polynomials resulting in better compression.

To more clearly visualize the advantage of the algorithm to image compression, one can consider the following example.

Suppose in a threshold band limited subimage $F_{(x,y)}$ we have $N$ surface
patches, then for the local quadratic approximation one requires $6N$ coefficients. On the other hand, if we have the global quadratic approximation of
the subimage and local planar approximation of the residual surface patches,
the total number of coefficients is $3N + 6$. For an improvement in compression
ratio of the global–local approximation over the conventional local approximation, we must have $6N > 3N + 6$, i.e., $N > 2$. This implies a positive gain
in storage if the subimage has more than two surface patches, which is usually
the case. Thus, it is evident that for polynomial approximation, we need fewer
numbers of bits for any segmentation based lossy image compression technique
where regions or patches are approximated separately. Compression factor, as
a result, would improve (assuming the same contour coding scheme as in the
concerned method).

## 2.8 Concluding Remarks

It is always desirable to break up an image into different regions. Later on,
these regions can be processed either separately or collectively. We must always keep in mind that segmentation should fulfill our purpose. One segmentation technique may be found to be very good in one application while it may
be completely unsuitable for the other. However, a knowledge based segmentation is expected to yield semantically meaningful regions, which can find
many new applications in a wider scale. Such segmentation can be viewed as
an intelligent segmentation.

# 1-d B-B Spline Polynomial and Hilbert Scan for Graylevel Image Coding

## 3.1 Introduction

Chapter 3 examines the use of one dimensional Bézier-Bernstein (B-B) polynomial function in image segmentation and image compression. The approximation used here can be viewed as a modification of the standard B-B approximation. We shall explain the way of approximation in the one dimensional case using graylevel image pixel values. Later on, we shall examine its feasibility in the area of image coding. To find the justification of such an approach of approximation, we shall first examine if the conventional way of approximating an image by Bézier-Bernstein polynomial, in a raster scan, provides any advantage from the data compression standpoint. For this, one can consider an entire row (or column) of an image as a single segment for its approximation. From the approximation theorem of Bernstein [113] it is evident that, for a given error, the order of the polynomial increases with the maximum gray value present in the segment. Therefore, if the maximum gray value in an image is very large, the order of the polynomial also becomes large. Consequently, it introduces a large number of control or guiding pixels for approximation. As a result, approximation becomes computationally expensive and the segment generation also becomes slow. This makes it inconvenient to use the conventional way of approximating an image for its compression.

We emphasize on the local control of data points (pixels) instead of minimizing the global squared error. We can think of an absolute error criterion to keep the absolute error within a bound during approximation of image segments. And, for the sake of data compression, of course, one can choose the second order polynomial function. Approximation is seen to be more effective on Hilbert scanned images rather than on raster scanned images. This is because due to the neighborhood property of the Hilbert scan, long homogeneous segments are found to be approximated; resulting in fewer numbers of segments for encoding than that for a raster scanned image. Consequently, the compression ratio is found to be higher.

## 3.2 Hilbert Scanned Image

Hilbert curve is one of the space filling curves, published by G. Peano in 1890. The Hilbert curve has a one-to-one mapping between an n-dimensional space and a one dimensional space, which preserves point neighborhoods as much as possible. There are many applications of this curve. A review on the applications of Hilbert curve can be found in [137, 155]. Some of the researchers have already used this curve in the area of image processing. Reported works in the area of image compression can be found in [5, 4, 45, 83, 84, 85, 86, 126, 154, 153].

Let $R^n$ be an n-dimensional space. The Peano curve published in 1890 is a locus of points $(y_1, y_2, \cdots y_n) \in R^n$ defined by continuous functions $y_1 = \chi_1(\nu), y_2 = \chi_2(\nu) \cdots y_n = \chi_n(\nu), (\nu \in R^1)$ where $0 \leq y_1, y_2, \cdots y_n < 1$ and $0 \leq \nu < 1$. It was an analytical solution of a space filling curve. In 1891, Hilbert drew a curve having the space filling property in $R^2$. Hilbert found a one-to-one mapping between segments on the line and quadrants on the square. Figure 3.1 shows the Hilbert curve with different resolutions. Hilbert scan considers the positions on the square through which the curve passes. Therefore, a Hilbert scanned image or simply a Hilbert image is a one dimensional image with its pixels identical to those through which the curve passes. Thus, it maintains the neighborhood property.

A Hilbert image or a Hilbert scanned image is a set of ordered pixels that can be obtained by scanning the positions of pixels through which this curve passes.

### 3.2.1 Construction of Hilbert Curve

Construction of Hilbert curve, following Hilbert's ideas, considers a square that is filled by the curve. Since our objective is to scan a gray tone image and produce a Hilbert scanned image for the study of image compression, we shall explain the basic philosophy behind construction of the curve and provide a scheme through which real life images can be converted into Hilbert scanned images. We also provide a scheme for inverse mapping to get back gray tone images from the Hilbert scanned images.

First of all, we divide the square as shown in Figure 3.2 into four quarters. The construction starts with a curve $H_0$, which connects the centers of the quadrants by three line segments. Let us assume the size of the segments to be 1. In the next step, we produce four copies (reduced by 1/2) of this initial stage and place the copies into the quarters as shown. Thereby we rotate the first copy clockwise and the last one counterclockwise by 90 degrees. Then we connect the start and end points of these four curves using three line segments (of size 1/2) as shown and call the resulting curve $H_1$. In the next step, we scale $H_1$ by 1/2 and place four copies into the quadrants of the square as in step one. Again we connect using three line segments (now of size 1/4) and obtain $H_2$. This curve contains 16 copies of $H_0$, each of size 1/4. As a general

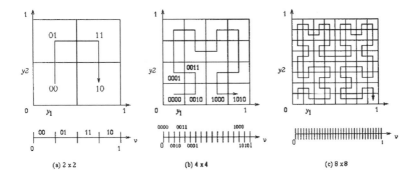

**Fig. 3.1.** Hilbert curve with different resolutions.

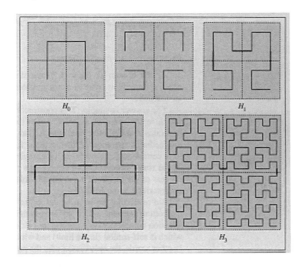

**Fig. 3.2.** Four stages of the Hilbert curve.

rule, in step $n$ we obtain $H_n$ from four copies of $H_{n-1}$, which are connected by three line segments of length $1/2^n$ and this curve contains $4n$ copies of $H_0$ (scaled by $1/2^n$). A different approach (normally known as the L-system approach) for construction of the Hilbert curve can be found in [134]. Since in image compression problem we are concerned with mapping gray tone images of different sizes into corresponding Hilbert scanned images, we construct Hilbert curve with different resolutions using Freeman's four connected chain code. The chain code is shown in Figure 3.3. Using this chain code, the curves $H_0$, $H_1$, and $H_2$ are respectively given below:

$H_0$: 123.
$H_1$: 214,1,123,2,123,3,432.

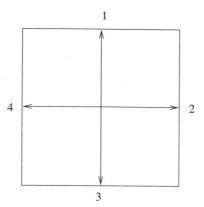

**Fig. 3.3.** 4-connected chain code.

$H_2$: 123221412144341,1,214112321233432,2,214112321233432,
3,341443234322123.

Below we present a c-program fragment that provides four connected chain
codes for different resolutions of a Hilbert curve and the corresponding Hilbert
scanned image.

```
printf("Enter resolution of the Hilbert curve : ");
scanf("%d",&k);
l=1;
p=(int)pow(4.0,(double) l);
for (i=1; i < p; i++);
x2[i]=i;
printf("The curve H0, seed pattern, is : ");
for (i=1; i < p; i++)
printf("%d",x2[i]);
while (l <=k){
/*_____find first copy_____*/
for (i=1; i < p; i++){
x1[i]=x2[i]+1;
if (x1[i] > 4)
x1[i]=x1[i] - 4;
}
for (i=1; i < p; i++){
x1[i]=x1[i]+2;
if (x1[i] > 4)
x1[i]=x1[i] - 4;
}
j=0;
for (i=p-1; i > 0; i-){
++j;
```

```
y[j] =x1[i];
}
for (i=1; i < p; i++)
x1[i]=y[i];
/*————————seed filling———————-*/
for (i=1; i < p; i++)
x3[i]=x2[i];
/*————————find last copy————————-*/
for (i=1; i < p; i++){
x4[i]=x2[i] -1;
if (x4[i] < 1)
x4[i]=x4[i]+4;
}
for (i=1; i < p; i++){
x4[i]=x4[i] + 2;
if (x4[i] > 4)
x4[i]=x4[i] - 4;
}
j=0;
for (i=p-1; i > 0; i–){
++j;
y[j]=x4[i];
}
for (i=1; i < p; i++)
x4[i]=y[i];
/*————————-substitution—  ————————-*/
x1[p]=1;
x2[p]=2;
x3[p]=3;
printf("H-scan for level l = %d is: ",l);
for (i=1; i<=p; i++)
printf("%d",x1[i]);
for (i=1; i<=p; i++)
printf("%d",x2[i]);
for (i=1; i<=p; i++)
printf("%d",x3[i]);
for (i=1; i < p; i++)
printf("%d",x4[i]);
/* ————————-seed for the higher level————*/
for (i=1; i<=p; i++)
y[i]=x1[i];
j=p;
for (i=1; i<= p; i++){
++j;
y[j]=x2[i];
```

```
}
j=2*p;
for (i=1; i<=p; i++){
++j;
y[j]=x3[i];
}
j=3*p;
for (i=1; i< p; i++){
++j;
y[j]=x4[i];
}
l++;
p=(int)pow(4.0,(double)l);
for (i=1; i < p; i++)
x2[i]=y[i];
}
```

Thus, we see for a fixed resolution, the program fragment provides a representation of the Hilbert curve in terms of 4-connected chain codes. This chain codes provide the scan directions in an image for the corresponding Hilbert image. Below, we show how the Hilbert scanned image can be obtained.

```
/*————pixel arrangement according to H-scan————*/
/* pixel can be arranged using the coded Hilbert curve or its mirror */
/* image. Below we give one example.————————*/
/* Array y contains the Hilbert image for an image in img array.——*/
i=1; j=1;
y[1]=img[i][j];
for (k1=1; k1 < p; k1++){
if (x2[k1] ==1)
i=i+1;
if (x2[k1] ==2)
j=j+1;
if (x2[k1] ==3)
i=i-1;
if (x2[k1] ==4)
j=j-1;
y[k1+1]=img[i][j];
}
```

The inverse mapping of the Hilbert scanned image is straightforward. We have the 1-d Hilbert scanned image and the corresponding 4-connected chain codes. From these two factors, one can quickly get back the original image.

## 3.3 Shortcomings of Bernstein Polynomial and Error of Approximation

Bernstein polynomial is a powerful tool to approximate a continuous function within any degree of accuracy. It uses the global information while approximating a function and the order of the polynomial increases with accuracy in approximation. The Bernstein polynomial of degree $p$ from is

$$B_{ip}(t) = \sum_{i=0}^{p} f(\frac{i}{p}) \, \phi_{ip}(t) \tag{3.1}$$

for approximating a function $f(t)$. Here $f(t)$ is defined and finite on the closed interval $[0, 1]$. Also,

$$\phi_{ip}(t) = \binom{p}{i} t^i \, (1-t)^{p-i}$$

and

$$\binom{p}{i} = \frac{p!}{(p-i)!(i)!}$$

with $i = 1, 2, \cdots p$.
The order $p$ of the Bernstein polynomial $B_{ip}(t)$ satisfies the inequality

$$\frac{k_m}{\epsilon \, \delta^2} < p \tag{3.2}$$

in order to have the error of approximation less than $\epsilon$, where $k_m$ is the maximum value of the approximating function $f(t)$ in the interval $[0, 1]$. $\delta$ is a positive number such that for points $t_1, t_2 \in (0, 1)$

$$| f(t_1) - f(t_2) | < \frac{\epsilon}{2},$$

whenever $| t_1 - t_2 | < \delta$.
   Since a graylevel image in a raster scan can be approximated either row wise or column wise, it appears from the inequality (3.2) that the order of the approximating polynomial may be different for different rows (or columns) depending on the value of $k_m$ (assuming $\epsilon$ and $\delta$ do not change appreciably). As an illustration, let us consider the case of approximating, row wise, a 32 level $(0, 1, \cdots 31)$ image of size $32 \times 32$. If a row has its maximum value $k_m = 31$, then for $\epsilon = 1$, (i.e., one unit error in gray value) $p > \frac{31 \times 31 \times 31}{29 \times 29} \approx 35.42$, i.e., 36. Note that the maximum value of $\delta = \frac{29}{31}$, because $|t_1 - t_2| = 1/31 - 30/31$ $(t_1, t_2 \in (0, 1))$. Therefore, for $k_m = 31$, one can choose $p$ to be equal to 36.
   On the other hand, if $k_m = 2$, then $m \approx 1.06$, i.e., $p = 2$. $k_m = 2$ means some of the graylevel values in the row are same and is equal to 1. Since in a gray image it is very likely to have the maximum value anywhere in each row, the order may be as high as the maximum graylevel in the image. This makes the method ineffective.

## 3.4 Approximation Technique

It is seen in the previous section that to approximate a raster scanned gray tone image row wise (or column wise), the order of the Bernstein polynomial varies from row to row (or column to column), and for an image with one unit error in approximation ($\epsilon = 1$) this order becomes close to the maximum value present in each row (or column). The large order of the polynomial, in turn, makes the approximation time as well as the reconstruction time relatively high. Again, the variation in order of the polynomial from row to row (or column to column) makes the coding scheme complicated.

An attempt is made in this chapter to develop an approximation scheme that keeps the order of the polynomial equal to two. Since the order is chosen two, the amount of error $\epsilon$, as expected, will be significantly high. In order to circumvent this, a modification of the conventional approximation scheme based on Bézier-Bernstein polynomial is proposed. This leads to the formulation of a new scheme by which it is also possible to obtain any degree of accuracy in approximation.

Given $n$ points, the approximation algorithm requires $n$-2 unique quadratic B-B spline functions for their representation. Unlike the method described in section 3.3, the scheme, proposed here, decomposes a row (column) either into a single gray segment or into a number of segments so as to enable them to be approximated properly. An error bound has been defined that guides the process of segmentation.

### 3.4.1 Bézier-Bernstein (B-B) Polynomial

Equation (3.1), which represents a $p$-th degree Bernstein polynomial for approximating a function $f(t)$, $0 \leq t \leq 1$ can be written as

$$B_{ip}(t) = \phi_{op}(t)f(0) + \phi_{1p}(t) \ f(\frac{1}{p}) + \phi_{2p}(t) \ f(\frac{2}{p}) + \cdot + \phi_{pp}(t)f(1).$$

$B_{ip}(t)$ is seen to consider a set of weights $\phi_{ip}(t)$ $(0 \leq t \leq 1)$ along with some fixed points of the function $f(t)$ in $[0, 1]$ for its approximation. With the choice of some arbitrary points for $f(\frac{i}{p})$, one can determine $B_{ip}(t)$ for each value of t.

Let $v_i$ represent a point in a multi-dimensional space and that $v_i = f(\frac{i}{p})$. Thus $B_{ip}(t)$ becomes,

$$B_{ip}(t) = \sum_{i=0}^{p} \phi_{ip}(t) \ v_i. \tag{3.3}$$

Equation (3.3) can be viewed as a vector valued Bernstein polynomial and it approximates a polygon with vertices $v_i$ and t in $[0, 1]$. $B_{ip}(t)$ is thus seen to generate a space curve. Equation (3.3) is known as $p$-th degree Bézier-Bernstein (B-B) polynomial. For $p = 2$, the quadratic B-B polynomial (dropping the index i in $B_{ip}$) is

$$B_2(t) = \sum_{i=0}^{2} \phi_{i2}(t)v_i$$

$$= \phi_{02}(t)\ v_o\ + \phi_{12}(t)\ v_1\ + \phi_{22}(t)\ v_2$$

$$= (1-t)^2\ v_o\ + 2\ t\ (1-t)\ v_1 +\ t^2\ v_2. \tag{3.4}$$

### 3.4.2 Algorithm 1: Approximation Criteria of $f(t)$

In order to develop an approximation technique, let us first formulate the key criteria associated with this technique.

Let us assume $n$-2 quadratic B-B polynomials for the representation of $n$ data points such that

$$f(t_i) = B_2{}^i(t_i) \qquad\qquad i = 1,\ 2,\ 3, \cdots,\ n - 2$$

where $B_2{}^i(t_i)$ is the value of the $i$th quadratic B-B polynomial at the point $t_i$ and is given by

$$B_2{}^i(t_i) = (1 - t_i)^2 v_o + 2t_i(1 - t_i)v_1{}^i + t_i{}^2 v_2. \tag{3.5}$$

Let

$$B_2{}^1(0) = B_2{}^2(0) = \cdots = B_2{}^{n-2}(0) = v_o$$

and

$$B_2{}^1(1) = B_2{}^2(1) = \cdots = B_2{}^{n-2}(1) = v_2.$$

In other words, at the end supports all the quadratic B-B polynomials are assumed to be identical. The points at end supports are also the vertices of the underlying $n$-2 polygons. The second vertex (also called the control point) $v_1{}^i$ of the $n$-2 polynomials are all different. This is shown in Figure 3.4.

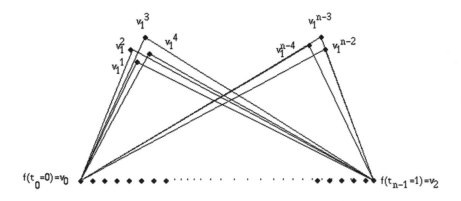

**Fig. 3.4.** Second control points due to a sequence of quadratic polynomials.

From equation (3.5), the second control point of the $i$th polynomial can be computed as

$$v_1{}^i = \frac{B_2{}^i(t_i) - (1 - t_i)^2 \, v_o - t_i{}^2 \, v_2}{2 \, t_i \, (1 - t_i)}. \tag{3.6}$$

Let $\overline{v_1} = \frac{1}{n-2} \sum_{i=1}^{n-2} v_1{}^i$ be the average value of the second control points for $(n-2)$ polynomials and let the corresponding B-B polynomial with control points $v_o$, $\overline{v_1}$, and $v_2$ be $\overline{B_2}(t_i)$. The discrete form of $\overline{B_2}(t_i)$ can be written as

$$\overline{B_2}(t_i) = (1 - t_i)^2 \, v_o + 2 \, t_i \, (1 - t_i)\overline{v_1} + t_i{}^2 \, v_2. \tag{3.7}$$

From equations (3.5) and (3.7),

$$| \, \overline{B_2}(t_i) - B_2{}^i(t_i) \, | = | \, \overline{v_1} - v_1{}^i \, | \times 2 \, t_i \, (1 - t_i). \tag{3.8}$$

This equation denotes the absolute difference between the polynomial $\overline{B_2}(t_i)$ and an arbitrary $i$th quadratic B-B polynomial $B_2{}^i(t_i)$ at an instant $t_i$. The maximum absolute difference of $\overline{B_2}\,(t_i)$ and $B_2{}^i\,(t_i)$ is

$$\begin{aligned} | \, \overline{B_2} - B_2{}^i \, |_{max} &= | \, \overline{v_1} - v_1{}^i \, |_{max} \times [2 \, t_i \, (1 - t_i) \,]_{max} \\ &= | \, \overline{v_1} - v_1{}^i \, |_{max} \times \tfrac{1}{2}. \end{aligned} \tag{3.9}$$

Note that $t_i(1 - t_i)$ is always positive. Similarly,

$$| \, \overline{B_2} - B_2{}^i \, |_{min} = | \, \overline{v_1} - v_2{}^i \, |_{min} \times [ \, 2 \, t_i \, (1 - t_i)]_{min}. \tag{3.10}$$

The expression $t_i \, (1 - t_i)$ has maximum at $t = \tfrac{1}{2}$ and the value falls symmetrically either side as $t$ moves away from $\tfrac{1}{2}$. Since $t_i \in (0, 1)$, the expression $2 \, t_i \, (1 - t_i)$ is minimum for the possible minimum/maximum value of $t_i$. For equally spaced data points, the minimum possible value of $t_i$ is $\frac{1}{(n-1)}$ and the maximum possible value of $t_i$ is $\frac{n-2}{n-1}$. In either case, $[ \, 2t_i(1 - t_i)]_{min} = \frac{2(n-2)}{(n-1)^2}$. With this,

$$\begin{aligned} | \, \overline{v_1} - v_1{}^i \, |_{min} &= \tfrac{(n-1)^2}{2 \, (n-2)} | \, \overline{B_2} - B_2{}^i \, |_{min} \\ &= \tfrac{(n-1)^2}{2 \, (n-2)} \, \epsilon_{min} \end{aligned} \tag{3.11}$$

and

$$\begin{aligned} | \, \overline{v_1} - v_1{}^i \, |_{max} &= 2 \, | \, \overline{B_2} - B_2{}^i \, |_{max} \\ &= 2 \, \epsilon_{max} \end{aligned} \tag{3.12}$$

where $| \, \overline{B_2} - B_2{}^i \, |_{min} = \epsilon_{min}$ and $| \, \overline{B_2} - B_2{}^i \, |_{max} = \epsilon_{max}$ are respectively the minimum and maximum absolute errors in approximating a function $f(t)$ and $t_i \, (1 - t_i)$ is maximum at $t_i = \tfrac{1}{2}$. It is straightforward to observe from equation (3.11) and (3.12) that

$$| \, \overline{v_1} - v_1{}^i \, |_{min} \leq | \, \overline{v_1} - v_1{}^i \, | \leq | \, \overline{v_1} - v_1{}^i \, |_{max}, \tag{3.13}$$

or,

$$\frac{2(n-2)}{(n-1)^2} \leq |\overline{v_1} - v_1{}^i| \leq 2\epsilon_{max}. \tag{3.14}$$

Similarly,

$$\epsilon_{min} \leq |\overline{B_2} - B_2{}^i| \leq \epsilon_{max}. \tag{3.15}$$

Therefore, the inequality (3.13) tells that the function $f(t_i) = B_2{}^i(t_i), i = 1, 2, \cdots n-2$ can be approximated by $\overline{B_2}(t)$ with an error inequality expressed in equation (3.15).

### 3.4.3 Implementation Strategy

It is seen from the previous section that the inequality (3.13) and (3.15) can be used to approximate a gray tone image segment. During approximation, it may be the case that the inequality (3.13) does not hold for all values of $i$ associated with a segment of the image, representing either a row (or a column) or the entire Hilbert scanned image. Let us consider that the inequality is true for $n_o$ pixels out of n in the segment. Thus the remaining $(n\text{-}n_o)$ pixels can again be approximated over the interval $[0, 1]$. Approximation technique for a raster scanned image thus may involve decomposition of all the rows (or columns) into a number of gray segments, while for a Hilbert scanned image, it may decompose the single piece of segment into segments of different sizes. The approximation always starts, in either case, with a fixed size, which may be 16, 32, 64, 128, or 256. Note that the inequality (3.13) is always true for a segment having three pixels irrespective of the inequality (3.15). The 3-pixel approximation is, therefore, the smallest segment for approximation. For a raster scanned image, either the last two pixels or the last pixel of the row (or column) may remain free. In this case, the same pixels/pixel may be left as it is or the same pixel may be considered once or twice to ensure approximation. This is the undesired situation for approximation at the end point. For a raster scanned image of size $M \times M$, the undesired situation may happen at most M times (worst case) due to row or column wise approximation while for a Hilbert scanned image, this undesired situation may happen only once.
Example:

In order to illustrate the method of approximation, let us consider a sequence of 38 data points as shown in Table 3.1. The maximum and minimum errors, $\epsilon_{max}$ and $\epsilon_{min}$, for approximation are 10.0 and 0.000001, respectively. The approximation partitions the data set into three segments. The beginning and end point of each partitioned segment are approximated with zero error, whereas all other data points are approximated with errors between $\epsilon_{min}$ and $\epsilon_{max}$. Note that the approximation may have much lower error than $\epsilon_{max}$. The partition of data points in Table 3.1 into three segments is controlled by the equation (3.13). Length of the first partition of the data segment is 11, whereas the second and third partitions have lengths 7 and 20, respectively.

**Table 3.1.** Illustration of approximation techniques.

| No. of segments | Original data data | Approx. values | Error in approximation | $\bar{v}_1$ |
|---|---|---|---|---|
| | 140 | 140.0000 | 0.0000 | |
| | 140 | 143.1117 | -3.1117 | |
| | 140 | 146.1098 | -6.1098 | |
| | 157 | 148.9941 | 8.0059 | |
| 1 | 157 | 151.7647 | 5.2353 | 155.8432 |
| | 162 | 154.4216 | 7.5784 | |
| | 157 | 156.9647 | 0.0353 | |
| | 157 | 159.3941 | -2.3941 | |
| | 157 | 161.7098 | -4.7098 | |
| | 166 | 163.9117 | 2.0883 | |
| | 166 | 166.0000 | 0.0000 | |
| | 166 | 166.0000 | 0.0000 | |
| | 174 | 170.3444 | 3.6556 | |
| 2 | 174 | 172.6844 | 1.3156 | 182.0400 |
| | 174 | 173.0200 | 0.9800 | |
| | 166 | 171.3511 | -5.3511 | |
| | 166 | 167.6777 | -1.6777 | |
| | 162 | 162.0000 | 0.0000 | |
| | 166 | 166.0000 | 0.0000 | |
| | 166 | 165.4410 | 0.5590 | |
| | 162 | 164.8388 | -2.8388 | |
| | 162 | 164.1936 | -2.1936 | |
| | 166 | 163.5051 | 2.4949 | |
| | 162 | 162.7735 | -0.7735 | |
| | 162 | 161.9988 | 0.0012 | |
| | 162 | 161.1808 | 0.8192 | |
| | 162 | 160.3198 | 1.6802 | |
| | 157 | 159.4156 | -2.4156 | |
| 3 | 157 | 158.4682 | -1.4682 | 160.8947 |
| | 157 | 157.4777 | -0.4777 | |
| | 157 | 156.4440 | 0.5560 | |
| | 157 | 155.3672 | 1.6328 | |
| | 157 | 154.2472 | 2.7528 | |
| | 157 | 153.0841 | 3.9159 | |
| | 157 | 151.8778 | 5.1222 | |
| | 148 | 150.6283 | -2.6283 | |
| | 148 | 149.3357 | -1.3357 | |
| | 148 | 148.0000 | 0.0000 | |

### 3.4.4 Algorithm 2

Here each row (column) of pixels has been viewed as a space curve and is segmented depending on the homogeneity among the pixels. Each segment is then approximated by the modified approximation scheme. Here, we consider

$$\overline{v_1} = \frac{1}{n} \sum_{i=1}^{n} v_1{}^i, \tag{3.16}$$

where $v_1^i$s are computed using equation (3.6).

Since the segments are all homogeneous, approximation for coding depends on the homogeneity parameter and not on any external approximation parameter as required in the case of Algorithm 1. The approximation is faster. Since for each homogeneous segment $v_1^i$s are averaged for $\overline{v}_1$, every approximation has its own $\epsilon_{max}$ that varies from segment to segment.

**Small deformation space curve and the concept of homogeneity**

An image may be considered as an intensity surface with surface contours representing the space curves along the rows and columns of the image. Note that for any curve $\Gamma$, the amount of information contained in it can be represented by its curvature vector $\mathbf{k_v}$ or by any other related quantity. The curvature vector $\mathbf{k_v}$ is defined as

$$\mathbf{k_v} = \frac{d\mathbf{t}}{d\mathbf{s}},$$

$t$ being the tangent vector and $s$ being the arc length. For a curve $\Gamma$, with given end points, its bending energy $B_e$ can be written as

$$B_e = \int_{\Gamma} k_v{}^2 \ ds.$$

Here the deformation of the curve is in the direction normal to the axis of the equilibrium position. Therefore, when the x-axis is along the axis of equilibrium position, the deformation may be represented by $z(x)$ and consequently we have

$$\begin{aligned} B_e &= \int_{\Gamma} k_v{}^2 \ dx \\ &= \int_{\Gamma} \frac{[z''(x)]^2}{[1 + (z'(x))^2]^3} \ dx. \end{aligned} \tag{3.17}$$

For small deformation, $z'(x) \approx 0$ and $B_e \approx \int_{\Gamma} [z''(x)]^2 \ dx$. Since $B_e$ represents the total energy of the curve, $k_v{}^2$ or $(z'')^2$ represents the energy of the curve at an arbitrary point. Therefore, in an image plane, $k_v{}^2$ will represent the energy of the image space curve at a pixel position.

With the above principle, a curve (a set of pixels along a row or a column) can be considered to be perfectly homogeneous if the bending energy is zero at every pixel position. This is obviously the most stable state of the curve (i.e., without any deformation). Homogeneity decreases with the increase of deformation. For the purpose of image compression, we are interested in finding the homogeneous segments of pixels in an image because such segments can be approximated with a small amount of error and they do not significantly produce any smearing effect. From the space curve analogy, homogeneous segments of pixels are segments with $z'(x) \approx 0$. However, in practice, it is very difficult to obtain long segments of pixels with zero gradient everywhere. In order to circumvent this difficulty, we consider the average of the first order derivative values for a segment of pixels and compute the variance of these derivative values. Since small value of $z'(x)$ corresponds to small deformation of the image space curve at a pixel position, its average value should correspond to average deformation and hence, the square root of the variance, i.e., the standard error provides a measure for the deformation.

## 3.5 Image Data Compression

Since we are restricted to one dimensional approximation, we consider both the Hilbert and raster scanned images for compression. Among the space-filling curves, note that the Hilbert/Peanno scanned images have already received attention in image compression due to its neighborhood scanning behavior.

A. Coding Scheme

An image on a raster scan can be approximated either row wise or column wise. The one that needs fewer number of segments is selected for coding. For a Hilbert scanned image, the approximation is along the length of the curve. We basically encode the approximation parameters of a segment along with the length of the segment. In the following section, we will be explaining the bit requirement for the proposed methods of coding.

B. Bit Requirement

Let us consider an image of size $M \times M$ with $L$ number of gray levels $\{0, 1, 2, \cdots, (L-1)\}$. Since there may be a number of gray segments resulting in the process of approximation, each of them can be coded with their corresponding approximation parameters, namely $v_o$, $v_1$, $v_2$, and the length of the segment, $n$. Since the positional information of approximation (control parameters of the Bézier curve) parameters is not taken into account for coding, the size of the gray segments plays an important part for regeneration of the image. As the maximum possible size of a segment on a raster scan is M, the maximum number of bits required for encoding the size of a segment is $\log_2 M$. In particular, the number of bits required to encode the size of a segment, satisfying the approximation criterion, depends on the maximum value for a segment chosen for approximation. In practice, the size of segments is found to be much less than the length of the raster. The segments, in fact, are found to occur frequently with the same length. As a result, the probability of occurrence for

the segments of same size is noticeable. Each of the gray segments is a Bézier arc and is represented by its three parameters, namely $v_o$, $\bar{v}_1$ and $v_2$. Of them, $\bar{v}_1$ may not be an integer. So, instead of $\bar{v}_1$, we consider the integer part of the reconstructed data point $d_1$ (say) at $t = \frac{1}{2}$ for the segment. We designate this pixel by $v_d$. Thus, $v_o$, $v_d$, $v_2$, and $n$ completely specifies an approximated data segment, where $v_o$, $v_d$, and $v_2$ are the three pixel brightness values on the arc. These brightness values (approximation parameters) in an image are found to frequently occur for different segments. Consequently, Huffman coding for all the parameters provide good results for compression of images. Furthermore, $v_o$, $v_d$, and $v_2$ being the brightness values, they are found to be indistinguishable from their neighboring values when they differ by small values. This fact can be used to reduce the number of independent brightness values to be encoded. The number of parameters drastically decreases when all the arcs are replaced by horizontal line segments. This increases the compression ratio at the cost of quality of the reconstructed image in terms of PSNR value. We, therefore, have the following two different situations for compression:
(a) when the segments are all quadratic arc segments,
(b) when the segments are all replaced by horizontal line segments.

Let $\theta_l$, $\theta_{v_o}$, $\theta_{v_d}$, and $\theta_{v_2}$ be the average number of bits/pixel for the length of segments, and the parameters $v_o$, $v_d$, and $v_2$, respectively. The total number of bits $N_b$, when the segments are all arcs, is given by,

$$(N_b)_A = N_s(\theta_l + \theta_{v_o} + \theta_{v_2} + \theta_{v_d}), \tag{3.18}$$

where, $N_s$=number of segments.
When all the segments are lines, the number of bits reduces to

$$(N_b)_L = N_s(\theta_l + \theta_{bl}) \tag{3.19}$$

where $\theta_{bl}$ is the average number of bits/pixel for the pixel values on line segments.

### 3.5.1 Discriminating Features of the Algorithms

Below we provide the discriminating features of the two proposed algorithms. For Algorithm 1:

- Segmentation of pixels does not need any separate algorithm. The approximation scheme itself selects the specific segments.
- The method of approximation depends on the selection of $\epsilon_{max}$ and $\epsilon_{min}$. The values of these parameters are the same for all segments in the image. The resulting performance in reconstruction, therefore, is parameter dependent.
- For large $\epsilon_{max}$, the possibility of long homogeneous segments of pixels for satisfying the approximation criterion increases. This may introduce visual disparity (smearing effect) between the original and the reconstructed segments. This, in turn, may affect the overall picture quality. For a raster

scanned image, this effect may become formidable if $\epsilon_{max}$ exceeds a certain value. However, for a Hilbert scanned image, this effect is almost negligible even for a very high value $\epsilon_{max}$.

For Algorithm 2:

- A separate algorithm selects only those segments that are homogeneous in some sense. For this, an image is considered as an intensity surface and the homogeneity concept of pixels over segments is viewed as a small deformation space curve on this intensity surface.
- Length of a homogeneous segment of pixels depends on the standard error of deformation of the segment from its equilibrium position.
- Different homogeneous segments in an image are approximated with different values of $\epsilon_{max}$, which are automatically determined in the process of approximation. The performance of the algorithm, therefore, does not depend on $\epsilon_{max}$ as in algorithm 1, but on the chosen value for the standard error.

## 3.6 Regeneration

Reconstruction of the image during decoding is done using quadratic B-B polynomial. We use here the recursive computation algorithm based on Newton's forward difference scheme as described in [27, 26]. Let $y = at^2 + bt + c$ be a polynomial representation of the equation (3.4) where the constant parameters a, b, and c are determined by the three pixels (two end pixels and one mid pixel) of the arc segment. The usual Newton's method for evaluating the polynomial results in multiplications and does not make use of the previously computed values to compute new values.

Assume the parameter $t$ ranges from 0 to 1. Let the incremental value be $q$. Then the corresponding $y$ values will be $c$, $aq^2 + bq + c$, $4aq^2 + 2bq + c$, $9aq^2 + 3aq + c$, $\cdots$. It is observed from [27, 26] that

$$\Delta^2 y_j = 2aq^2 \quad and \quad y_{j+2} - 2y_{j+1} + y_j = 2aq^2 \quad j \geq 0.$$

This leads to the recurrence formula

$$y_2 = 2y_1 - y_o + 2aq^2 \tag{3.20}$$

that involves just three additions to get the next value from the two preceding values at hand. Since the gray segment size is known, the increment $q$ can be obtained from $q = \frac{1}{segment\ size\ -1}$ The regenerated gray value $y_2$ can therefore be determined from equation (3.20).

## 3.7 Results and Discussion

Here, we have made an attempt to demonstrate an application of 1-dimensional quadratic Bézier-Bernstein polynomial approximation in coding gray tone Hilbert and raster scanned images. Drawbacks in using the conventional way of approximation were examined and a modification was then introduced in order to make it useful for image data compression. Based on the modified concept, two different algorithms have been formulated. Both the algorithms have been examined to compress 256×256 (8 bits) gray tone images following the Hilbert and raster scan. The performance of the algorithms on the Hilbert scanned images is found to be better than that on the raster scanned images. This is due to the neighborhood property of the Hilbert scan. More precisely, the Hilbert curve always passes through the neighborhood pixels, and since the neighborhood pixels are, in general, strongly correlated, the approximation is done over longer segments. Over such long segments, the variation in pixel intensity is low. As a result, arc approximation is not as economical as the line segment approximation (in terms of approximation parameters). Consequently, lower compression ratio or larger number of bits/pixel is required. But the line segment approximation reduces the PSNR value compared to that for arc segment approximation. On the other hand, for raster scanned images, the quality of the reconstructed images is disturbed when the maximum length of segment exceeds a certain value. Short segments, in general, are found to produce better quality for the reconstructed images. Table 3.2 shows the results on compression and quality for 256×256 8-bit raster scanned images for Algorithm 1, while Table 3.3 provides the results for the corresponding Hilbert scanned images. The approximation uses both the line and arc segments. Tables 3.4 and 3.5 indicate the performance of Algorithm 2 for the raster and Hilbert scanned images. Finally, the comparison for the algorithm due to Kamata et al. [86] is shown in Table 3.6.

Note that Algorithm 1 in the raster scan mode may produce smearing for large values of $\epsilon_{max}$ , because with the increase in the value of $\epsilon_{max}$ , the possibility of long homogeneous segments of pixels satisfying the approximation criterion increases. As a result, visual disparity may arise. This fact is also true for Algorithm 2 in the raster mode for larger values of the standard error. Figure 3.5 shows this smearing effect for Algorithm 1 and Algorithm 2 in the raster scan mode. The line segment approximation in the raster mode also affects the reconstructed quality for high values of $\epsilon_{max}$.

For the 8-bit Lena and Girl images, compression is found to be higher in the Hilbert scan mode compared to that in the raster scan mode. From the Tables 3.4, and 3.5, it is seen that Algorithm 2 also behaves in the same way as Algorithm 1. Higher compression is found to occur in the Hilbert scan mode. Figure 3.6 shows two different decoded images for Lena and Girl images for Algorithm 1, while Figure 3.7 shows the results of the decoded images for Algorithm 2 due to Hilbert scan. Comparison with Kamata's algorithm (Figures 3.8 and 3.9) shows that the proposed algorithms perform better for

(a)
(b)
(c)
(d)
(e)
(f)

**Fig. 3.5.** Results for Algorithm 1 ((c), (d)) and Algorithm 2 ((e)), (f)) due to raster scan: (a) Input Lena image; (b) input Girl image; (c) bpp = 1.47, PSNR = 30.574; (d) bpp = 1.40, PSNR = 28.075; (e) bpp = 1.71, PSNR = 30.020; (f) bpp = 1.539, PSNR = 30.169.

**Table 3.2.** Performance of Algorithm 1 on raster scanned images.

| Image | Mode of approx. | $\epsilon_{max}$ | Max length for segment | Compression rate in bpp | MSQ | PSNR in db |
|-------|-----------------|------------------|------------------------|-------------------------|-----|------------|
| Lena | line | 7 | 128 | 1.231 | 211.817 | 24.871 |
|      | segment | 10 | 64 | 1.084 | 244.087 | 24.255 |
|      |         |    |    |       |         |        |
| Girl |         | 5 | 128 | 1.347 | 84.673 | 28.853 |
|      |         | 7 | 64 | 1.215 | 99.526 | 28.151 |
| Lena | arc | 20 | 256 | 1.767 | 25.763 | 34.020 |
|      | segment | 25 | 256 | 1.602 | 38.745 | 32.248 |
|      |         | 30 | 256 | 1.477 | 56.967 | 30.574 |
|      |         |    |     |       |        |        |
| Girl |         | 20 | 256 | 1.839 | 53.287 | 30.864 |
|      |         | 25 | 256 | 1.590 | 77.102 | 29.260 |
|      |         | 30 | 256 | 1.404 | 101.274 | 28.075 |

**Table 3.3.** Performance of Algorithm 1 on Hilbert scanned images.

| Image | Mode of approx. | $\epsilon_{max}$ | Max length for segment | Compression rate in bpp | MSQ | PSNR in db |
|-------|-----------------|------------------|------------------------|-------------------------|-----|------------|
| Lena | line | 8 | 256 | 1.122 | 104.865 | 27.924 |
|      | segment | 10 | 256 | 1.027 | 110.625 | 27.692 |
|      |         | 15 | 256 | 0.846 | 124.338 | 27.184 |
|      |         | 18 | 256 | 0.692 | 131.624 | 26.937 |
|      |         |    |     |       |        |        |
| Girl |         | 18 | 128 | 0.768 | 99.579 | 28.149 |
|      |         | 20 | 128 | 0.720 | 105.089 | 27.915 |
|      |         | 25 | 128 | 0.607 | 119.794 | 27.346 |
| Lena | arc | 25 | 256 | 1.644 | 48.765 | 31.249 |
|      | segment | 30 | 256 | 1.443 | 56.924 | 30.577 |
|      |         | 35 | 256 | 1.286 | 68.758 | 29.757 |
|      |         |    |     |       |        |        |
| Girl |         | 35 | 256 | 1.094 | 81.878 | 28.999 |
|      |         | 38 | 256 | 1.007 | 86.545 | 28.758 |
|      |         | 40 | 256 | 0.974 | 104.883 | 27.923 |

the Lena image, in terms of PSNR value at the same compression rate. At the compression rate of 1.44 bit/pixel, Algorithm 1 provides a PSNR value of 30.57 db, while the algorithm due to Kamata et al. provides 30.01 db, and Algorithm 2 provides 31.22 db. At the compression rate of approximately 1.28 bpp, the PSNR due to Algorithm 1 is 29.75 db; the PSNR due to Kamata's algorithm is 29.16 db, while Algorithm 2 provides a PSNR of 30.82 db at a slightly higher compression rate of 1.34 bpp. For the Girl image, Algorithm 2 provides a PSNR value of 28.81 db at the compression rate of 0.68 bpp, compared to 28.44 db as provided by the algorithm due to Kamata et al.

**Table 3.4.** Performance of Algorithm 2 on raster scanned images.

| Image | Mode of approx. | Standard error | Max length for segment | Compression in bpp | MSQ | PSNR in db |
|---|---|---|---|---|---|---|
| Lena | line | 4 | 64 | 1.897 | 190.19 | 25.33 |
| | segment | 6 | 64 | 1.609 | 232.55 | 24.46 |
| Girl | | 6 | 64 | 1.952 | 111.57 | 27.65 |
| | | 7 | 64 | 1.785 | 128.79 | 27.03 |
| Lena | arc | 15 | 64 | 1.933 | 40.27 | 32.08 |
| | segment | 17 | 64 | 1.819 | 50.71 | 31.07 |
| | | 19 | 64 | 1.713 | 64.71 | 30.02 |
| Girl | | 15 | 64 | 1.827 | 42.64 | 31.83 |
| | | 17 | 64 | 1.627 | 54.80 | 30.74 |
| | | 18 | 64 | 1.539 | 62.53 | 30.16 |

**Table 3.5.** Performance of Algorithm 2 on Hilbert scanned images.

| Image | Mode of approx. | Standard error | Max length for segment | Compression in bpp | MSQ | PSNR in db |
|---|---|---|---|---|---|---|
| Lena | line | 16 | 64 | 0.78 | 87.09 | 28.73 |
| | segment | 18 | 64 | 0.72 | 92.98 | 28.44 |
| | | 20 | 64 | 0.66 | 101.51 | 28.06 |
| Girl | | 16 | 64 | 0.76 | 77.52 | 29.23 |
| | | 17 | 64 | 0.71 | 81.20 | 29.03 |
| | | 18 | 64 | 0.67 | 85.49 | 28.81 |
| Lena | arc | 17 | 64 | 1.44 | 49.07 | 31.22 |
| | segment | 19 | 64 | 1.34 | 53.81 | 30.82 |
| Girl | | 18 | 64 | 1.48 | 101.42 | 28.06 |
| | | 20 | 64 | 1.33 | 114.48 | 27.54 |

**Table 3.6.** Comparison between three different algorithms.

| image | Algorithm 1 | | Algorithm 2 | | Algorithm[86] | |
|---|---|---|---|---|---|---|
| | bpp | PSNR in db | bpp | PSNR in db | bpp | PSNR in db |
| Lena | 1.44 | 30.577 | 1.44 | 31.222 | 1.45 | 30.019 |
| | 1.28 | 29.757 | 1.34 | 30.821 | 1.20 | 29.163 |
| Girl | 1.09 | 28.999 | 1.07 | 30.436 | 1.01 | 30.361 |
| | 0.67 | 27.692 | 0.68 | 28.811 | 0.68 | 28.442 |

(a)  (b)

(c)  (d)

**Fig. 3.6.** Results for Algorithm 1 due to Hilbert scan: (a) bpp = 0.69, PSNR =26.937; (b) bpp = 0.60, PSNR = 27.346; (c) bpp = 1.28, PSNR = 29.757; (d) bpp = 0.97, PSNR = 27.923.

The approximation technique described is different from the conventional least square method of approximation. Instead of minimizing the global squared sum of errors, it controls an absolute maximum error for each data point. It should be noticed in this context that if the pixels of a segment have low intensity variation, then the techniques based on conventional quadratic least square and the quadratic B-B polynomial approximation will produce the same result. Since the proposed method of approximation controls an absolute local error instead of global sum of errors, it is expected that even for moderate variation of intensity within data points, the proposed method will produce better results. Also, given an error term, the conventional least

(a)                                    (b)

(c)                                    (d)

**Fig. 3.7.** Results for Algorithm 2 due to Hilbert scan: (a) bpp = 0.72, PSNR = 28.446; (b) bpp = 0.67, PSNR = 28.811; (c) bpp = 1.34, PSNR = 30.821; (d) bpp = 1.33, PSNR = 27.543.

square technique does not ensure that all the data points will satisfy the error criterion, whereas in the proposed method this is not the case. Furthermore, it is not needed to compute any functional distance to justify the goodness of approximation because the error term itself quantifies this.

Note further that our intention here is to demonstrate, through an application, the effectiveness of one-dimensional B-B spline function in image data compression for both the raster and Hilbert scanned images. The algorithms are efficient for the Hilbert scanned images because of strong correlation between pixels over long segments. Both the schemes are fast and simple in hardware implementation. However, it is needless to mention that the two-

**Fig. 3.8.** Comparison of Lena image: (a) Algorithm 1: bpp = 1.44, PSNR = 30.577; (b) Kamata: bpp = 1.45, PSNR = 30.019; (c) Algorithm 2: bpp = 1.44, PSNR = 31.222; (d) Algorithm 1: bpp = 1.28, PSNR = 29.757; (e) Kamata: bpp = 1.20, PSNR = 29.163; (f) Algorithm 2: bpp = 1.34, PSNR = 30.821.

**Fig. 3.9.** Comparison of Girl image: (a) Algorithm 1: bpp = 1.09, PSNR = 28.999; (b) Kamata: bpp = 1.01, PSNR = 30.361; (c) Algorithm 2: bpp = 1.07, PSNR = 30.436; (d) Algorithm 1: bpp = 0.60, PSNR = 27.346; (e) Kamata: bpp = 0.68, PSNR = 28.442; (f) Algorithm 2: bpp = 0.68, PSNR = 28.811.

dimensional approximation always provides a better compression ratio than the corresponding one-dimensional approximation.

## 3.8 Concluding Remarks

The modified approach for approximation of one-dimensional data using B-B spline function is very efficient both in making the approximation as well as in generating the approximated data values. Depending on the specified error, the method itself chooses the data segment and the approximation is done simultaneously. The combination of two such important steps is a unique feature of the approximation as described in Algorithm 1.

# 4

---

# Image Compression

## 4.1 Introduction

Image compression is a process where we are mainly concerned with minimizing the number of bits to represent an image. It has applications primarily in the areas of transmission, storage of information, and reduced data processing. All the compression techniques can, in general, be grouped into four different categories, namely pixel coding, predictive coding, transform coding, and other methods. Between the four different categories, three deal with the spatial domain techniques, while the transform coding category mainly deals with various transform domain techniques. Under the pixel coding category, the prominent methods are pulse code modulation (PCM), run length, and bit plane coding. The predictive coding category includes delta modulation (DM), line by line differential pulse code modulation or line by line DPCM, two dimensional DPCM, interpolative technique, and adaptive technique. The other methods include hybrid coding, two tone/graphics coding, vector quantization, second generation coding, and fractal coding. Transform coding plays a very significant role and includes zonal coding, threshold coding, multidimensional techniques, and adaptive techniques. In transform coding, discrete Fourier transform (DFT), Karhunen-Loeve transform KLT (also known as Hotelling transform), Walsh-Hadamard transform, Harr transform, Slant transform, discrete cosine transform (DCT), and various wavelet tranforms are frequently used.

During the last two decades, various image compression techniques have been developed. Each of these methods has its own merits and demerits, and each has its own compression ratio. The segmentation based technique is relatively easy to understand and belongs to second generation coding. We shall, therefore, consider an image compression algorithm that uses 2-d Bézier-Bernstein function to encode gray values in segmented subimages. The algorithm is known as SLIC (subimage based lossy image compression). SLIC encodes images through approximation of segmented regions by 2-d

Bézier-Bernstein polynomial, contours by 1-d Bézier-Bernstein polynomial, and texture by Huffman coding scheme using Hilbert scan on texture blocks.

## 4.2 SLIC: Subimage-based Lossy Image Compression

In the approximate coding of digital still images, one is mainly concerned with the compression ratio and the fidelity of the reconstructed images. We show how compression can be made by globally approximating many segmented patches by a single polynomial function together with local correction, if needed. For this, all such patches should have similar graylevels, and one can extract the segmented patches under approximation by a single polynomial using a single threshold. Such segmented patches can be viewed as different surface patches of almost similar gray values, and the collection of all such patches under a single threshold is defined as a subimage. The segmentation scheme [24] recursively uses an object/background thresholding algorithm based on conditional entropy. Thresholding based segmentation strategy provides an advantage over that done by the split and merge technique [133]. The latter does not provide any group of patches or regions of similar graylevels at a time. It is, therefore, preferable to choose a thresholding based segmentation strategy for coding application. However, the graylevel distribution over some of the image surface patches may be such that the global approximation is not adequate for them. We call such patches, under a given threshold, *busy* patches. To overcome this difficulty under such circumstances, a lower order (compared to that of the global approximation) polynomial function is used for local approximation of each of the residual surface patches in the subimage. Therefore, the subimage is reconstructed using the global surface along with the local residual surfaces for the busy patches, if they are really present. Such a hybrid approximation scheme helps to improve the compression ratio. Note that this is exactly the same kind of approximation one can use during segmentation of an image [24]. Thus, compression can use necessary information of approximation from the segmentation of images. Contours can be coded by line and arc segments. Sometimes very small regions are found in images in the form of a texture, and region contours are found to fluctuate very rapidly so that a large number of knots or key pixels is required on contours for approximation. Under such conditions, encoding of contours by line and arc segments is not economical. Such regions can be separated out in the form of blocks from images, if they are really present. These blocks are then suitably encoded. Figure 4.1 shows the 8-bit Lena image of size 256 × 256 and its segmentation without and with texture regions. Contour images for some hierarchical thresholds are shown in Figure 4.2. In Figure 4.1(b), all the gray values in thresholded regions are replaced by the corresponding threshold value. This approach is simple and straightforward, and displays the segmented image noticeably well, provided the difference of gray values at respective pixel positions between the two images is adequate to be visually perceived. However, to perceive difference between the two images, one can use completely different values as we have done for Figure 4.1(c). Here, we have chosen zero gray values (completely dark) for textured regions. To get segmented images with texture regions, we first found the textured regions, and then the non-textured segmented regions from the rest of the regions. Their gray values have been replaced by respective threshold values. For an

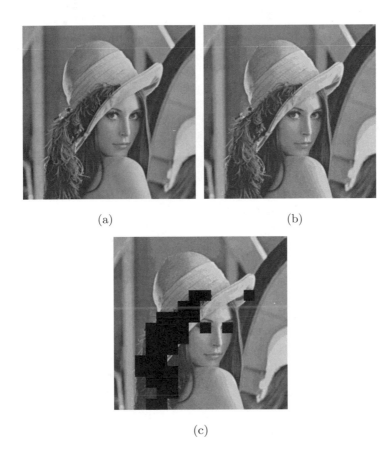

(a)                                    (b)

(c)

**Fig. 4.1.** (a) Input Lena image; (b) segmentation without texture region; (c) segmentation with texture region.

input image of $k$-1 thresholds, we have $k$ subimages. If $N_1, N_2, \cdots N_k$ are the number of sparse image surface patches in them, then considering variable order global approximation of $k$ subimages and variable order approximation for sparse residual surface patches, the compression ratio for an M×M image with $L$ graylevels becomes

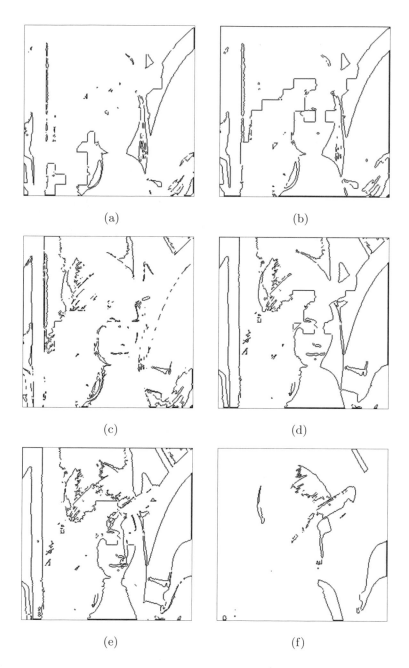

(a)                                    (b)

(c)                                    (d)

(e)                                    (f)

**Fig. 4.2.** Contours of Lena image for some hierarchical thresholds.

$$R_c = \frac{\alpha(\sum\limits_{i=1}^{k} C_{gi} + \sum\limits_{i=1}^{k} C_{ie}) + \beta_c + \beta + \gamma}{M^2 \log_2 L}, \tag{4.1}$$

where $C_{g,i}, i = 1, 2, \cdots, k$ is the number of coefficients required for the $i$th subimage for variable order global approximation and $C_{ie}$ is the number of coefficients for regions that require residual approximation. We assign $\alpha$ number of bits for each coefficient. $\beta_c$ is the overhead for all patches due to such correction. $\beta$ is the overhead due to different orders of approximation of subimages and $\gamma$ is the number of bits for contour representation of the image.

If $\nu$ is the number of bits required for encoding texture blocks, then the equation (4.1) becomes

$$R_c = \frac{\alpha(\sum\limits_{i=1}^{k} C_{gi} + \sum\limits_{i=1}^{k} C_{ie}) + \beta_c + \beta + \nu + \gamma}{M^2 \log_2 L}. \tag{4.2}$$

Note that the number of bits for graylevel approximation, in general, is

$$\beta_{gr} = \alpha \left(\sum\limits_{i=1}^{k} C_{gi} + \sum\limits_{i=1}^{k} C_{ie}\right) + \beta_c + \beta + \nu. \tag{4.3}$$

If the global approximation itself is sufficient to meet the desired error criterion so that the approximation of residual error is not needed, then the term containing $C_{ie}$ and hence $\beta_c$ in equation (4.2) do not contribute anything and under such conditions, equation (4.2) reduces to

$$R_c = \frac{\alpha \sum\limits_{i=1}^{k} C_{gi} + \beta + \nu + \gamma}{M^2 \log_2 L}. \tag{4.4}$$

Further, when all global approximations are seen to be of fixed order and local residual approximations are also of fixed order, we get the total number $N_c$ of coefficients as

$$N_c = C_g k + C_l (N_1 + N_2 + \cdots + N_k), \tag{4.5}$$

where $C_g$ is the number of coefficients required for global approximation of a subimage and $C_l$ is the number of coefficients for local residual surface approximation of each of the $N_1, N_2, \cdots, N_k$ patches. Compression ratio $R_c$ in this case reduces to

$$R_c = \frac{\alpha N_c + \nu + \gamma}{M^2 \log_2 L}. \tag{4.6}$$

Note that when all the regions $N_1, N_2, \cdots N_k$ in all subimages are locally approximated for their residual surface, we do not need to store information for $\beta$ and $\beta_c$. So these two terms do not contribute anything. Kunt et al. [97] observed small errors in data approximation when each surface is represented by its $r$ pixels. These $r$ pixels on the surface are used to recompute the coefficients. The only possible error appears in the quantization of each pixel. We followed the same strategy and examined both the cases in our work. Since each pixel can be represented by $\log_2 L$ bits, the equation (4.2) can be rewritten as

$$R_c = \frac{\log_2 LN_{pix} + \beta_c + \beta + \nu + \gamma}{M^2 \log_2 L}, \tag{4.7}$$

where $N_{pix}$ is the total number of surface pixels. The number of bits required for graylevel approximation in this case is

$$\beta_{gr} = \log_2 LN_{pix} + \beta_c + \beta + \nu. \tag{4.8}$$

In the following section, we discuss the choice of weights in the least square approximation for the proposed coding scheme.

### 4.2.1 Approximation and Choice of Weights

Subimages obtained through the segmentation scheme as described in Chapter 1 were used for compression. Readers interested in details can consult [24]. The approximation algorithms are exactly the same as used for segmentation, but the weights are different from unity. For compression, weights are chosen in a way described below. For completeness and clear understanding, we first briefly state the approximation problem. Bézier-Bernstein polynomial has been used because our segmentation algorithm was basically designed for image compression, and Bézier-Bernstein polynomial provides a number of merits in compression and reconstruction. The Bézier-Bernstein surface is a tensor product surface and is given by

$$
\begin{aligned}
s_{pq}(u, v) &= \sum_{r=0}^{p} \sum_{z=0}^{q} \phi_{rp}(u)\phi'_{zq}(v)V_{rz} \\
&= \sum_{r=0}^{p} \sum_{z=o}^{q} B_{rp}D_{zq}u^r(1-u)^{p-r}v^z(1-v)^{q-z}V_{rz},
\end{aligned}
\tag{4.9}
$$

where $u, v \in [0, 1]$ and $B_{rp} = \frac{p!}{(p-r)!r!}$, $D_{zq} = \frac{q!}{(q-z)!z!}$. p and q define the order of the Bézier-Bernstein surface.

To approximate an arbitrary image surface $f(x, y)$ of size M×M, $f(x, y)$ should be defined in terms of a parametric surface (here $s_{pq}$ with the parameters $u$ and $v$ both in $[0, 1]$. Therefore, the function $f(x, y)$ can be thought in terms of $g(u, v)$ where $u = \frac{(i-1)}{(M-1)}$; $i = 1, 2, .. \cdots M$ and $v = \frac{(j-1)}{(M-1)}$; $j = 1, 2, .. \cdots M$.

We choose the weighted least square technique for estimation of parameters $V_{rz}$ to be used for reconstruction of the decoded surface. Although the total square error for the conventional unweighted least square approximation may be less than that for the weighted least square, the approximation produced by the latter may be psychovisually more appealing than that by the former, provided weights are chosen judiciously. For an image, edge points are more informative than the homogeneous regions because edges are the distinct features of an image. Thus, edges should be given more emphasis while approximating an image patch and this can be done through weighted least square. Thus, the weighted squared error can be written as

$$
\begin{aligned}
E^2 &= \sum_u \sum_v [W(u,\ v)(g(u,\ v) - s_{pq}(u,\ v))]^2 \\
&= \sum_u \sum_v [W(u,\ v)(g(u,\ v) - \sum_{r=0}^{p} \sum_{z=0}^{q} \phi_{rp}(u)\phi'_{zq}(v)V_{rz}]^2,
\end{aligned}
\tag{4.10}
$$

where $W(u,\ v)$ is the weight associated with the pixel corresponding to $(u,\ v)$. For $p = q$, the surface $s_{pq}(u,\ v)$ is defined on a square support. Since $W(u,\ v)$ is the weight associated with each pixel, it can be considered constant for that pixel. Therefore, one needs to find out the weight matrix before solving equations for the weighted least square. Once $W(u,\ v)$ is known, these equations reduce to a system of linear equations and can be solved by any conventional technique.

We emphasize that for order determination, we use the unweighted approximation scheme. In the weighted least square approximation of regions, special weights are given to boundary pixels so that the error, in the mean square sense, over the boundary is less than that in the unweighted least square approximation. For this, we have considered the gradients of boundary pixels as their weights. One can also consider higher power of gradients. The gradients of the boundary pixels, $G(u,v)$ and hence the weights $W(u,v)$ in equation (4.10), can be calculated using the following equation.

$$
W(u,v) = (G_v{}^2 + G_u{}^2)^{1/2},
\tag{4.11}
$$

where $G_u = g(u+1,v) - 2g(u,v) + g(u-1,v)$ and $G_v = g(u,v+1) - 2g(u,v) + g(u,v-1)$.

Image compression in our scheme is a two-stage process. In stage 2, for encoding we approximate the subimages minimizing a *weighted* least square error with a polynomial of the same order as determined in stage 1 (for segmentation). The same order is used because the order (global and also local) of a subimage or the nature of approximation is not expected to change due to merging of small regions. However, one can once again find the order of approximation before encoding. The reason is, the best fit surface does not necessarily psychovisually represent the most appealing (informative) surface. If we try to find the optimal order of the polynomial using weighted least square, then that optimal order is expected to be more than that for the unweighted least square. Consequently, the compression ratio will go down. Of course, the two orders cannot be widely different. Thus, there is a need to compromise.

We have to find a polynomial that can approximate the surface satisfactorily, and at the same time, preserve information that is psychovisually important. That is exactly what we attempted to achieve with the proposed scheme.

Note that the order of the polynomial can be determined exactly in the same way as we did in 2.4.3

### 4.2.2 Texture Coding

To encode the texture blocks we, first of all, Hilbert scan [134] each block. A Hilbert scanned image or simply a Hilbert image corresponding to a graylevel image is a 1-d image with its pixels identical to those in the graylevel image through which the Hilbert curve passes. Hilbert drew a curve having the space filling property in $R^2$ and he found a one-to-one mapping between segments on the line and quadrants on the square. The merit of the curve is to pass through all points on a quadrant and move to the neighboring quadrant. Hilbert curves with different resolutions are shown in Figure 4.3 The efficiency

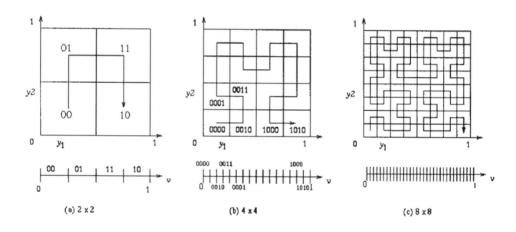

**Fig. 4.3.** Hilbert curve with different resolutions.

of Hilbert scan has already been reported in 1-d image compression [86]. In our texture compression scheme, Hilbert scan converts each texture block into its corresponding 1-d Hilbert image. Line segments are then extracted from these Hilbert images in a straightforward way because texture blocks are all labeled by the threshold values. Also, since the blocks are textured in nature, we get tiny line segments in large number. Repetition of line segments of identical size and identical labels is very frequent. Huffman coding, therefore, provides good compression for them. Since Hilbert scan is used for texture blocks, one must be able to express the block size compatible to Hilbert image. Therefore, the choice of the window size for extraction of texture blocks can be made very easily. We have chosen the block size equal to 16. The number of bits for texture coding is the total number of bits required for all the blocks, i.e., $\nu$ in equation (4.4) is given by

$$\nu = \sum_{i=1}^{N_{tb}} \nu_i, \tag{4.12}$$

where $\nu_i$ is the number of bits for the $i$th texture block and $N_{tb}$ is the total number of texture blocks.

### 4.2.3 Contour Coding

Contours of segmented regions are coded using the methodologies described in [26] and [23]. [26] uses 1-dimensional Bézier-Bernstein polynomial while [23] uses stretched discrete circular arcs for encoding contour images. In encoding contours of segmented regions, they are processed once again, as described below, to remove redundancy. Regions in each of the $k$ subimages ($k$-1 being the number of thresholds) have their own contours labeled respectively from 1 to $k$. All these contours need not be coded because of redundancy. We have reduced this redundancy in two stages. In the first stage, we remove the contours of all regions in the subimage with maximum boundary or contour length compared to those in other subimages. The reason behind this removal is that the contours of ($k$-1) subimages uniquely define the contour geometry for the remaining subimage. In the second stage, the contour map for ($k$-1) subimages is examined to get a representation suitable for coding. Since the regions are adjacent to each other and each region is defined by its own boundary, we have "double contouring" in the contour map of an image. Note that the contour of one region defines part of other adjacent regions. In order to remove double contouring, we consider the following contour processing scheme. The part of a contour, which is defined by contour of some other regions, is deleted and the non-deleted contour fragments are encoded. Let us now elaborate on it.

**Removal of double contouring**:

Let us first consider a particular region (say, the $j$th region of $l$th subimage) $\Omega_{lj}$ of a fixed label $l$ and examine if the regions of other labels are adjacent to $\Omega_{lj}$. We call the contour of $\Omega_{lj}$ the primary contour and contours of the adjacent regions the adjacent contours. The primary contour is first encoded. The part of adjacent contours defined by the primary contour is then examined and deleted. Also, different parts of a higher labeled contour defined by its adjacent lower labeled contours are deleted, provided the deleted segments are all connected. Thus, the deletion is always done by lower labeled adjacent contours. Non-deleted contour fragments are then encoded. Lower labeled contours are encoded first. The process is repeated until all contours of different labels adjacent to a primary contour are examined for deletion and encoded. Note that the same primary contour may be considered more than once to examine and encode all adjacent contours, but the primary contour is to be encoded only once. This happens if a primary contour has more than one adjacent contour of the same label. All other primary contours having the same label are then sequentially considered. The entire process is repeated for regions of different labels. To explain the contour processing scheme more clearly, we consider a $(k+1)$ bit status word $W_s = X_s,\ X_1 X_2 \cdots X_k$. It indicates the status of the primary and adjacent contours. The first bit, $X_s$ in $W_s$, always shows the status of the primary contour. $X_s = 1$ indicates that the primary contour is to be encoded along with adjacent contours but $X_s = 0$ indicates the primary contour is already encoded and only the adjacent contours need to be examined and encoded. The position of the first non-zero bit in $X_1 X_2 \cdots X_k$ denotes the label of the primary contour. For example, consider $W_s = 1,\ 111101101$. According to the status word, the primary contour has label 1 and adjacent contours have labels 2, 3, 4, 6, 7, and 9. Further, the adjacent contours with labels 2, 3, 4, 6, 7, and 9 must have some part of their contours defined by the primary contour. The defined part must be deleted in each case. Since $X_s = 1$, the primary contour must also be encoded. Similarly, $W_s = 0,\ 101100101$ indicates that the primary contour has label 1. The primary contour must not be encoded because it has the status word $X_s = 0$. Contours with labels 3, 4, 7, and 9 are to be examined for deletion and encoded if required. Note that we consider, sequentially, all the primary contours of a fixed label. As a result, when we move on to a primary contour of label $k$, all the bits in $W_s$ from 2 to $(k-1)$ are zeros. Therefore, if $N_p$ is the number of primary contours, the number of bits $N_{bp}$, required to preserve the region adjacency information, is given by

$$N_{bp} = (k+1)N_p \ . \tag{4.13}$$

**Encoding of primary and adjacent contours using 1-d Bézier-Bernstein polynomial**:

Key pixels are detected on the primary contour as well as on the non-deleted contour fragments to serve as knots. Key pixels are basically points of high curvature and inflexion points. The key pixels on contours are such that an arc between any two key pixels always remains confined within a right triangle, with its base as the line joining the two key pixels. As a result, between two consecutive key pixels, contour fragments are decomposed either into straight line or arc segments [26, 27]. Each of the arcs is approximated by a 1-d Bézier-Bernstein polynomial and so can be viewed as a Bézier-Bernstein arc. We consider the parametric representation of arcs because it is axis independent. Given the starting point, each line segment requires one point while an arc needs two points for their description. Since the selection of key pixels depend on high curvature, any segment with rapid changes of curvature will have more number of key points (dense) than a segment with less curvature change. Note that line and arc segments between knots, therefore, are of variable sizes. Obviously, the line and arc segments between key pixels have smaller length where the key pixels are dense. Thus, key pixels (dense and non-dense) captures the structure of the contour and helps to maintain curvature of the entire contour at the time of reconstruction. Now, to encode an arc we first consider the end pixel of the arc. Next, we encode the difference of coordinates ($\triangle x$, $\triangle y$) of the pixel on the arc at the parameter value, $t=1/2$ and the mid pixel of the base of the arc. Since an arc between two key pixels may or may not be approximated by a single quadratic Bézier-Bernstein polynomial, to ensure good approximation and encoding, we restrict the minimum and the maximum number of pixels on an arc. For a $64 \times 64$ image, these numbers are taken 12 and 30, respectively, while for a $256 \times 256$ image, these numbers are assumed to be 20 and 40, respectively. In other words, for a $64 \times 64$ image, the length of every arc is restricted to lie between 12 and 30, while for a $256 \times 256$ image, the length of every arc is assumed to lie between 20 and 40. To find out the number of bits required to encode $\triangle x$ and $\triangle y$, we consider a few steps from 1-dimensional quadratic B-B polynomial. Position coordinates of the point on the arc at $t=1/2$ are

$$
\begin{aligned}
x_a &= (1-t)^2 x_o + 2t(1-t)x_1 + t^2 x_2 \\
&= \tfrac{x_o}{4} + \tfrac{x_1}{2} + \tfrac{x_2}{4} \\
y_a &= (1-t)^2 y_o + 2t(1-t)y_1 + t^2 y_2 \\
&= \tfrac{y_o}{4} + \tfrac{y_1}{2} + \tfrac{y_2}{4} .
\end{aligned} \tag{4.14}
$$

Here, $(x_o, y_o)$ and $(x_2, y_2)$ are respectively the start and end pixels of an arc, and at these two points, tangents to the reconstructed arc have their point of intersection at $(x_1, y_1)$. Since we are using relative coordinates, $(x_o, y_o)$ is always the origin of the running frame of axes and hence, we take $x_o = 0$ and $y_o = 0$. Therefore, equation (4.14) reduces to

$$
\begin{aligned}
x_a &= \tfrac{x_1}{2} + \tfrac{x_2}{4} \\
y_a &= \tfrac{y_1}{2} + \tfrac{y_2}{4} .
\end{aligned} \tag{4.15}
$$

The midpoint of the base of the arc is given by $(x_m = x_2/2, y_m = y_2/2)$. The difference thus becomes

$$
\begin{aligned}
\triangle x &= x_a - x_m \\
&= \tfrac{x_1}{2} + \tfrac{x_2}{4} - x_m \\
\triangle y &= y_a - y_m \\
&= \tfrac{y_1}{2} + \tfrac{y_2}{4} - y_m .
\end{aligned}
$$

Since an arc between any two key pixels remains always confined within a right triangle with its base as the line joining the two key pixels, the point of intersection of tangents at two ends of the arc also remains within this right triangle. Therefore, $x_1$ can take on its position anywhere between 0 and $x_2$, and $y_1$ between 0 and $y_2$ with respect to the running axes of coordinates. Thus, we get three different cases as given below.

case I: $x_1 = 0$,

$$\triangle x = \frac{x_2}{4} - x_m$$
$$= -\frac{x_2}{4}, \quad since \; x_m = x_2/2;$$

case II: $x_1 = x_2$

$$\triangle x = \frac{x_1}{2} + \frac{x_2}{4} - x_m$$
$$= \frac{x_2}{4};$$

case III: $x_1 = x_m$

$$\triangle x = \frac{x_m}{2} + \frac{x_2}{4} - x_m$$
$$= 0.$$

Thus, we see that $|\triangle x|$ has its maximum equal to $x_2/4$ while its minimum equals zero. For odd $x_2$, we take $\lceil \frac{x_2}{2} \rceil$ or $\lfloor \frac{x_2}{2} \rfloor$, depending on whether $x_1$ is greater or less than $x_m$ so that their difference remains small. The same is the case for $y_2$. Therefore, the number of bits required to encode $\triangle x$ and $\triangle y$ can be dynamically decided based on $x_2$ and $y_2$, respectively (end pixel of the arc). For a $64 \times 64$ image, the maximum number of pixels on an arc, we have assumed, is 30. Hence, its base is always less than 30. So the end pixel can always be encoded by 5 bits. Therefore, $\triangle x < 30/4$, which is 7.5. Similarly, $\triangle y < 7.5$. In the discrete case, we consider $\triangle x \leq 8$ and $\triangle y \leq 8$. Thus, we get the following bit requirements for an arc as follows:

| $64 \times 64$ image | $256 \times 256$ image |
| --- | --- |
| identity (line or arc): 1 bit. | identity (line or arc): 1 bit. |
| $x_d$: 5 bits; | $x_d$: 6 bits; |
| $y_d$: 5 bits; | $y_d$: 6 bits; |
| quadrant information: 2 bits; | quadrant information: 2 bits; |
| $\triangle x$: $log_2 \lceil x_2/4 \rceil$ bits; | $\triangle x$: $log_2 \lceil x_2/4 \rceil$ bits; |
| $\triangle y$: $log_2 \lceil y_2/4 \rceil$ bits; | $\triangle y$: $log_2 \lceil y_2/4 \rceil$; bits |
| sign for $\triangle x$: 1 bit; | sign for $\triangle x$: 1 bit; |
| sign for $\triangle y$: 1 bit; | sign for $\triangle y$: 1 bit; |

Note that the number of bits used to encode of $\triangle x$ and $\triangle y$ varies with the number of pixels on arcs. Thus, for a $256 \times 256$ image, we need 25 bits for an arc of length 33 to 40 pixels and 23 bits for an arc of length less than or equal to 32. Number of types of arcs of 33 to 40 pixels is 40-33+1=8 and of 20 to 32 pixels is 32-20+1=13. The total number of bits for these types of arcs is $8 * 25 + 13 * 23 = 499$ and the total number of pixels on these types of arcs is $4 * 73 + 13 * 26 = 630$. Assuming arcs of all possible lengths are equally probable, the average bit per contour pixel on arc in a $256 \times 256$ image is $499/630 = 0.79$ bits/pixel.

For a $64 \times 64$ image, an arc of length 17 to 30 pixels needs 21 bits while 19 bits are needed for an arc of length less than or equal to 16. This gives an average of 0.97 bits/contour pixel on arc. The number of types of arcs less than or equal to 16 is 16-12+1=5 and that greater than 16 is 30-17+1=14.

For a line segment, we set the minimum and maximum number of pixels to 4 and 8 respectively for both $64 \times 64$ and $256 \times 256$ images. Chosen length for a line segment is small enough to maintain high accuracy of the curvature of contour lines. Here, we encode straightaway the absolute difference $(x_d, y_d)$ between the start and end points of the line segment. Thus, we need the following bits for images of two different sizes.

| 64 × 64 image | 256 × 256 image |
|---|---|

identity (line or arc): 1 bit.          identity (line or arc): 1 bit.

$x_d$: 3 bits;                              $x_d$: 3 bits;

$y_d$: 3 bits;                              $y_d$: 3 bits;

quadrant information: 2 bits;          quadrant information: 2 bits;

This gives a total of 9 bits, i.e., a maximum of (9/4) or 2.25 bits/pixel and a minimum of (9/8) or 1.125 bits/pixel. One can also find the number of bits for line segments of all possible lengths. Here, the number of types of line segments of different lengths is 8-4+1=5. The total number of pixels for these types of line segments is 4+5+6+⋯ +8=5/2(8+4)=30. Considering all such types of line segments are equally probable, we have an average of 5*9/30 bits or 1.5 bits for a contour pixel on line segments.

**Starting pixels**

For a 64 × 64 image, we consider 12 bits and for a 256 × 256 image, 16 bits per starting pixel. Therefore, the number of bits for contour pixels can be computed using the following equations:

$$\gamma_{64\times64} = N_{bp} + 12N_{sp} + 0.97N_{ca} + 1.5N_{cl} \tag{4.16}$$

$$\gamma_{256\times256} = N_{bp} + 16N_{sp} + 0.79N_{ca} + 1.5N_{cl} \tag{4.17}$$

where $N_{sp}$ is the number of starting pixels on contours. The number of contour pixels on arc and line segments are represented respectively by $N_{ca}$ and $N_{cl}$.

## 4.3 Quantitative Assessment for Reconstructed Images

In order to check the quality of the reconstructed images, most of the authors compute the mean squared error (MSE), although it is clear that MSE does not always reflect the quality of visual images. A reconstructed image with low MSE may psychovisually appear to be distorted compared to another one with high MSE. For this reason, many authors have felt the need of some other measures for the image quality assessment. Since the mechanism of understanding image quality is not yet fully known, it is very hard to devise a perfectly complete quantitative measure for quality judgment. But one can always consider a measure that depends on some important attributes (depending on local and global properties) present in the input image. We have, therefore, proposed in our investigation, a fidelity vector $F_v$ whose components are indices of different measures. Here, in addition to MSE and PSNR, we use image correlation, homogeneity, contrast, and fractal dimension to assess the quality of the reconstructed image.

We classify the quality assessment indices into two categories: (say) x and y. The classification is based on mathematical and physical features. The indices based on mathematical features take care of accuracy in approximation while the indices based on physical features take care of the preservation of physical features present in the reconstructed image. In x, we compute indices taking into account both the images (input and reconstructed) together. MSE and PSNR are in this category. Image correlation between the input and reconstructed images is also included in the category of x. In y, we compute various indices, each characterizing a different image attribute such as homogeneity, contrast, and fractal dimension for the two images separately. The above indices are all concerned with pixel intensities of the image.

A good quality reconstructed image should preserve all these components in the fidelity vector of the input image. Thus, the closeness between two such fidelity vectors for the input and reconstructed images indicates the closeness between them.

Different components of the fidelity vector $F_v$ are given below.

**MSE**

The mean squared error

$$MSE = \frac{Total\ squared\ error}{Number\ of\ data\ points}. \tag{4.18}$$

**PSNR**

The normal procedure to evaluate the image quality is to compute the peak signal to noise ratio (PSNR) value of the original as well as of the reconstructed image. PSNR value is defined as

$$PSNR(dB) = 10\log_{10}\frac{(L-1)^2}{MSE}. \tag{4.19}$$

**Correlation**

The coefficient of correlation $\rho_{xy}$ for two sets of data $X = \{x_1, x_2, \cdots, x_N\}$ and $Y = \{y_1, y_2, \cdots, y_N\}$ is given by

$$\rho_{xy} = \frac{\frac{1}{N}\sum_{i=1}^{N} x_i y_i - \bar{x}\bar{y}}{\sqrt{\frac{1}{N}\sum_{i=1}^{N} x_i^2 - \bar{x}^2}\sqrt{\frac{1}{N}\sum_{i=1}^{N} y_i^2 - \bar{y}^2}}, \tag{4.20}$$

where $\bar{x} = \frac{1}{N}\sum_{i=1}^{N} x_i$ and $\bar{y} = \frac{1}{N}\sum_{i=1}^{N} y_i$. The correlation coefficient $\rho_{xy}$ takes on values from +1 to -1, depending on the type and extent of correlation between the sets of data. We use correlation measure between the input and reconstructed image. This provides a measure of nearness of two images.

**Homogeneity Index**

As a measure of homogeneity, we compute an homogeneity index. This index simply calculates the second order entropy because it provides local information about the behavior of pixel intensity change. The graylevel values in an image are not independent of each other. One can consider the sequences of pixels to incorporate the dependency of pixel intensities in estimating the entropy. In order to compute the entropy of an image, the following theorem due to Shannon [151, 73] can be stated.

**Theorem**

Let $p(s_i)$ be the probability of a sequence $s_i$ of graylevels of length $l$, where a sequence $s_i$ of length $l$ is defined as a permutation of $l$ graylevels. Let us define

$$H^{(l)} = -\frac{1}{l} \sum_i p(s_i) \log_2 p(s_i), \qquad (4.21)$$

where the summation is taken over all graylevel sequences of length $l$. Then $H^{(l)}$ is a monotonic decreasing function of $l$ and $H^{(l)}_{\lim l \to \infty} = H$, the entropy of the image. For different values of $l$, we get different orders of entropy.

Case 1: $l = 1$, i.e., sequence of length one. If $l = 1$, we get

$$H^{(1)} = -\sum_{i=0}^{L-1} p_i \log_2 p_i,$$

where $p_i$ is the probability of occurrence of the graylevel $i$. Such an entropy is a function of the histogram only and it may be called *global entropy* of the image. Therefore, different images with identical histograms would have the same $H^{(1)}$ value, irrespective of their content.

Case 2: $l = 2$, i.e., sequence of length two. Hence,

$$H^{(2)} = -\frac{1}{2} \sum_i p(s_i) \log_2 p(s_i)$$
$$= -\frac{1}{2} \sum_i \sum_j p_{ij} \log_2 p_{ij}, \qquad (4.22)$$

where $s_i$ is a sequence of length two and $p_{ij}$ is the probability of occurrence of the graylevels $i$ and $j$. Therefore, $H^{(2)}$ can be obtained from the co-occurrence matrix. $H^{(2)}$ takes into account the spatial distribution of graylevels. Therefore, two images with identical histograms but different spatial distributions will result in different entropy, $H^{(i)}$ values. $H^{(i)}$, $i \geq 2$ may be called local entropy. Since the second order entropy reflects the local behavior of image, it is expected that for a homogeneous region/patch, this measure should be low.

**Contrast Measure**

Image quality index (IQI) from equation (2.25) is used as a measure of contrast.

$$IQI = \frac{\sum\limits_{i=1}^{M}\sum\limits_{j=1}^{N} |\triangle B_{ij}|/B}{MN - \sum\sum h_{ij}}.$$

**Texture Measure**

To compare the texturedness of the reconstructed image with the original image, we examine the fractal dimension $(FD)$ of the reconstructed as well as of the original images. In general, fractal dimension provides a measure of irregularities and, therefore, it can be used very effectively as one of the means to compare the texture quality of two images, provided one of them is obtained after some operation on the other. This is because two images having the same fractal dimension does not necessarily mean that they have the same surface irregularities. In our case, the change in fractal dimension of the reconstructed image from that of the original image indicates the extent of damage in texture of the input image due to approximation. The concept of self-similarity can be used to estimate the fractal dimension. A bounded set $A$ in Euclidian n-space is self-similar if $A$ is the union of $N_r$ distinct (non-overlapping) copies of itself scaled up or down by a ratio $r$. The fractal dimension $D$ of $A$ is given by the relation [117] $1 = N_r r^D$, i.e.,

$$D = \frac{\log(N_r)}{\log(1/r)}. \tag{4.23}$$

There exist several approaches to estimate the $FD$ of an image. We have used [36] to compute the fractal dimension.

Thus, we get the fidelity vector,

$$F_v = [MSE, PSNR, \rho_{xy}, H^{(1)}, H^{(2)}, IQI, FD]^T. \tag{4.24}$$

## 4.4 Results and Discussion

In the SLIC algorithm, subimages obtained through segmentation have been used for gray encoding while their contour maps are encoded after removing redundancy. For each subimage, the order of the approximating Bézier-Bernstein polynomial is computed. We have followed the IQI based approach for order computation because of psychovisual reasons. For the Lincoln image, local correction is not needed for the residual surface of any region in any subimage, while for both Lena and Girl images, local corrections are required. The Girl image is found to have local correction for 18 patches while the Lena image requires local correction for 31 patches. For the Lincoln image, we have obtained eight subimages corresponding to seven thresholds. Orders of the polynomials for these subimages, computed by the IQI based approach, were found to be 2, 2, 2, 2, 2, 0, 2, 2, respectively. Determination of the orders of polynomials using the classical method requires a search for $\delta$ in equation (1.10) from the data set, corresponding to an $\epsilon$ that is twice the error of approximation (in fact, for graylevel images, we require a 2-d version of the equation (1.10) and hence a search for $\delta_1$ and $\delta_2$ is required). We have seen that the orders computed by the classical approach for the subimages of Lincoln are more or less the same to those computed by the IQI based approach. However, this order may sometimes be higher than that computed by the IQI based approach. This is because of the hard constraint of $\epsilon$ on $\delta$ in equation (1.10).

After removing contour redundancy, knots or key pixels were detected from the contours, and segments between two key pixels were approximated by line or arc segments. A line or arc segment greater than the pre-assumed length was suitably broken up and was approximated accordingly. For the reconstruction of coded images, we followed two different ways using the same polynomial order for each of the subimages. The main reason behind these two reconstructions is to examine how different they are from each other as well as from the original input. Reconstructions are based on:

(1) the estimated (in the weighted least square sense) control points for each subimage resulting in a Bézier-Bernstein surface;

(2) equally spaced points on the estimated Bézier-Bernstein surface obtained in (1).

Contour encoding in the two different cases of reconstruction of the image remains the same. Only the gray values in subimages are encoded using the above two different ways. In the first case, each control point (coefficient) has been encoded by 12 bits whereas in the second case, equally spaced gray points are coded using the graylevel information of the image. The number of gray points (pixels) are exactly equal to the number of control points. Assuming these points to lie on a Bézier-Bernstein surface patch, we have solved $(p+1)*(p+1)$ equations to get $(p+1)*(p+1)$ control points of the surface. The Bézier-Bernstein surfaces in two cases are not exactly identical, but they are very close.

The experiments have been performed using a Silicon Graphics Indy workstation running IRIX 5.3. The workstation has MIPS RS4600, 96 MB memory, and 132 MHz speed. The JPEG algorithm used is of version 6a (7 Feb. 96). All the images in our experiments have been printed by a HP LaserJet printer 5P with a resolution of 600 dpi.

### 4.4.1 Results of SLIC Algorithm for 64 X 64 Images

Table 4.1 shows the number of bits and the compression ratio required to encode the 5-bit Lincoln image when contours are encoded by 1-d B-B polynomial. Since this image does not have any texture blocks, the number of bits are mainly due to graylevel and contour encoding. The number of bits, $\beta_{gr}$ for graylevel encoding, can be computed using equations (4.3) and (4.8) for reconstruction 1 and reconstruction 2, while the number of bits, $\gamma_{64\times64}$ for contour encoding, can be computed using the equation (4.16). The Lincoln image was found to have 442 contour pixels on line segments and 348 contour pixels on arc segments. Nine status words, each 9 bits long, provided region adjacency information during decoding of the Lincoln image, and the number of starting pixels was found to be 38. So, the overhead due to contour encoding is $9*9+12*38$ bits or 537 bits. For gray encoding, the overhead due to order of approximation from equation (4.3) is $\beta = 8*2 = 16$ bits (since, $\beta_c = 0$). The number of coefficients for approximation of Lincoln image is 64. Thus, we get the total bit requirements and compression ratio as shown in Table 4.1. From Table 4.1, it is seen that for reconstruction 2, the gain

**Table 4.1.** Bit requirements.

| Image | $\beta_{gr}$ | | $\gamma_{64\times64}$ | Total no. of bits | | C.R | C.R |
|-------|------------|-----------|------------------|-----------|-----------|-----|-----|
| | Recon. 1 from eq.(4.3) | Recon. 2 from eq.(4.8) | from eq.(4.16) | Recon. 1 | Recon. 2 | 1 | 2 |
| Lincoln | 784 | 336 | 1537.56 | 2321.56 | 1873.56 | 8.82 | 10.93 |

in compression ratio is higher than that for reconstruction 1 by roughly 25 percent. One can notice the total number of bits for contour coding is not an integer. This is because we computed an average estimate for them instead of actual number of bits. Hence the total number of bits is also not an integer. For the quality of reconstructed images, we consider the following tables for different values of the components of the fidelity vectors. From the evaluation

**Table 4.2.** Evaluation of reconstructed image.

| Components of $F_v$ | Lincoln image | | |
|---------------------|---------------|---------------|---------------|
| | Input | *Approach* 1 | |
| | | recons. 1 | recons. 2 |
| MSE | 0 | 7.438 | 7.884 |
| PSNR | $\infty$ | 21.388 | 21.135 |
| $\rho xy$ | 1.0 | 0.958 | 0.958 |
| $H^{(1)}$ | 3.432 | 2.693 | 2.646 |
| $H^{(2)}$ | 0.1005 | 0.144 | 0.054 |
| IQI | 6959.24 | 6973.53 | 6985.07 |
| FD | 2.577 | 2.547 | 2.555 |

Table 4.2, it is clear that the coefficient based reconstructions for the two different approaches are very close to each other, though the PSNR value when the contours are encoded and reconstructed by 1-d B-B polynomial is slightly

higher. Other components of the fidelity vector are practically the same. This is also true for the reconstructions based on equispaced surface pixels. All the reconstructed images have different values in entropy from that of the input image. This change is due to merging of small regions in the segmentation procedure before encoding of the input image and polynomial approximation in the reconstruction process. Fractal dimension of the reconstructed images differ slightly from that of the input. This is probably due to the reason that contours of the reconstructed images are not as smooth as that of the input. Below in Figure 4.4, we present reconstructed Lincoln image along with the input for visual comparison.

(a)                                    (b)

(c)

**Fig. 4.4.** Reconstruction of Lincoln image: (a) input Lincoln image; (b) reconstruction from coefficients; (c) reconstruction from surface points.

### 4.4.2 Results of SLIC Algorithm for 256 X 256 Images

We now discuss the results of the compression algorithm on two famous 8-bit images (Lena and Girl) where each one is of size $256 \times 256$. These two images are more complicated than the previous $64 \times 64$ Lincoln image, because these images have texture regions in them and the texture blocks as seen from Table 4.3 have taken a considerably large number of bits, lowering the compression ratio. The number of contour pixels on line and arc segments for the Lena image are, respectively 7398 and 3538. The number of bits for starting pixels were found to be 5328 for 333 pixels while 600 bits were required for status words. Graylevel values altogether needed 111 coefficients for global approximation and 124 coefficients for local corrections. An overhead of 198 bits were required for graylevel approximation. Figures 4.5(a), 4.5(b), and 4.5(c) show the reconstructed Lena images for the input image as shown in Figure 1.1(a). For the Girl image (Figure 4.6(a)), the number of pixels approximated by line and arc segments were 6041 and 4016, respectively. 4720 bits were required for the starting pixels, while 912 bits were required for the status words. For the local corrections of 18 patches, 72 coefficients or 576 bits were required. The reconstructed images due to two different approaches are shown in Figures 4.6(b), 4.6(c), and 4.6(d), respectively.

To examine the performance of the proposed algorithm on a $256 \times 256$ image, we examined the compression ratio as well as compared the result with that of JPEG algorithm [169]. Note that due to different versions of JPEG algorithm, results may slightly vary. In order to compute the compression ratio by the JPEG algorithm, we chose the quality factor in such a way that the PSNR value of the decompressed images remains as close as possible to that of the reconstructed images due to our proposed algorithm. For the Lena image, the quality factors are 50 and 30, respectively, for the JPEG result 1 and JPEG result 2 (Figures 4.5(b) and (c)); for the Girl image, the quality factors are 32 and 30 (Figures 4.6(c) and 4.6(d)).

**Table 4.3.** Bit requirements.

| Image | $\beta_{gr}$ | $\nu$ | $\gamma_{256 \times 256}$ | Total no. of bits |
|-------|--------------|-------|---------------------------|-------------------|
|       | from eqn.(4.8) | from eqn.(4.12) | from eqn.(4.17) | |
| Lena  | 2238 | 26122 | 19820.02 | 48180.02 |
| Girl  | 1742 | 20123 | 17866.14 | 39731.14 |

**Table 4.4.** Comparison of compression ratio.

| Image | compression ratio | | |
|-------|------------|---------------|---------------|
|       | Approach 1 | JPEG result 1 | JPEG result 2 |
| Lena  | 10.88 | 8.86 | 10.92 |
| Girl  | 13.20 | 13.12 | 13.63 |

In order to evaluate the quality of the reconstructed images, we present below the values of the different indices of the fidelity vector $F_v$. To compare the performance of our method we used the JPEG algorithm. Table 4.5 shows

(a)

(b)                                          (c)

**Fig. 4.5.** Reconstruction of Lena image: (a) Using surface points; (b) JPEG result 1; (c) JPEG result 2.

that the result of the described algorithm is better than the JPEG result 1 because it has lower MSE and higher PSNR values. The correlation values are comparable for all the images, which means that all the images are almost alike. The index FD for the texture measure is the same for all of them, which means texture in all the images is maintained in the same way (on the average basis).

### 4.4.3 Effect of the Increase of Spatial Resolution on Compression and Quality

For the 8-bit Lena image, some of the researchers have used an image size of $256 \times 256$ while some others have used the size of $512 \times 512$. These two

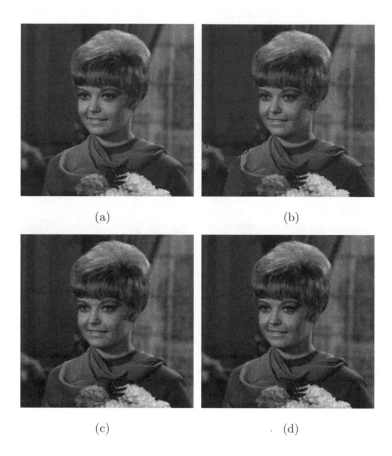

(a)                         (b)

(c)                       .  (d)

**Fig. 4.6.** Reconstruction of Girl image: (a) Input; (b) using surface points; (c) JPEG result 1; (d) JPEG result 2.

different sizes are widely found in the literature. Due to this variation in size, compression is, also, found to be widely different. To get an idea how the compression and quality are affected by the increase of spatial resolution, we provide some of the results on the Lena image from the recent articles.

In [145], two different compression ratios correspond to two different sizes of the structuring element used in the work. The compression ratio is 31.00 when the structuring element has the size 6 × 6 and 20.00 when the size is 4 × 4. PSNR values for the reconstructed images have not been mentioned. From Table 4.7, it is found that except in one case [160], the quality (PSNR value) of the reconstructed images, due to different methods, are almost the same. In some of the articles, the PSNR value is not mentioned (N.M). From the work of Fisher et al. [61], the compression ratio is found to be 3.10 times

**Table 4.5.** Evaluation of reconstructed Lena images.

| Components of $F_v$ | Lena image | | | |
|---|---|---|---|---|
| | For input | For output | JPEG result 1 | JPEG result 2 |
| MSE | 0 | 96.953 | 129.638 | 142.574 |
| PSNR | $\infty$ | 28.265 | 27.003 | 26.590 |
| $\rho_{xy}$ | 1.0 | 0.977 | 0.992 | 0.989 |
| $H^{(1)}$ | 2.529 | 1.909 | 2.639 | 2.528 |
| $H^{(2)}$ | 0.0021 | 0.0009 | 0.00007 | 0.00046 |
| IQI | 27.616 | 35.700 | 30.197 | 30.372 |
| FD | 2.619 | 2.620 | 2.624 | 2.593 |

**Table 4.6.** Evaluation of reconstructed Girl images.

| Components of $F_v$ | Girl image | | | |
|---|---|---|---|---|
| | For input | For output | JPEG result 1 | JPEG result 2 |
| MSE | 0 | 52.848 | 37.236 | 38.497 |
| PSNR | $\infty$ | 31.457 | 32.421 | 32.27 |
| $\rho_{xy}$ | 1.0 | 0.987 | 0.991 | 0.991 |
| $H^{(1)}$ | 1.956 | 1.591 | 2.268 | 2.264 |
| $H^{(2)}$ | 0.043 | 0.018 | 0.144 | 0.197 |
| IQI | 85.952 | 115.263 | 90.619 | 89.553 |
| FD | 2.607 | 2.577 | 2.531 | 2.529 |

**Table 4.7.** Some results on Lena image due to increase in spatial resolution.

| Image size | Article | Principle of coding | Compression ratio | PSNR in db |
|---|---|---|---|---|
| $512 \times 512$ | [139] | vector quantization | 12.30 | 29.95 |
| $256 \times 256$ | [33] | sketch based | 5.30 | N.M |
| $256 \times 256$ | [61] | fractal | 11.85 | 30.58 |
| $512 \times 512$ | [61] | fractal | 36.78 | 30.71 |
| $512 \times 512$ | [107] | fractal | 40.00 | 30.20 |
| $512 \times 512$ | [145] | segmentation using morphology | 31.00 | N.M |
| | | | 20.00 | N.M |
| $512 \times 512$ | [141] | block prediction | 30.76 | 32.78 |
| $512 \times 512$ | [160] | region based fractal | 41.00 | 26.56 |
| $512 \times 512$ | [108] | fractal | 44.00 | 29.10 |
| $512 \times 512$ | [159] | fractal | 44.44 | 29.10 |
| $256 \times 256$ | [75] | fractal | 10.60 | 30.72 |
| $512 \times 512$ | [52] | wavelet based fractal | 65.60 | 29.90 |

larger for the size of $512 \times 512$, while from the work of [75] and [108], we see that an increase of 4.15 times is possible. In our opinion, one can obtain a compression ratio larger by a factor between 3.5 and 4.0 simply by increasing the size of an image from $256 \times 256$ to $512 \times 512$. Thus, it is expected that our developed method will provide a compression ratio in the range 38.0–43.52 for the Lena and 46.2–52.8 for the Girl image, respectively.

## 4.5 Concluding Remarks

The algorithm, SLIC, uses a segmentation scheme that is suitable for image compression. The segmentation scheme provides a number of similar gray regions corresponding to each threshold, instead of a single region. Consequently, a global surface fit (high possibility due to similar gray regions) becomes most economical. When the order of a polynomial for approximating a subimage goes beyond a preassigned positive integer, say q (which may happen due to the physical configuration of regions or large variation on region boundaries), we need to compute local corrections over the residual surfaces for which the mean squared error with respect to the global surface of order q exceeds a certain limit. Computing the order of the polynomial by the IQI based approach is simple as well as effective. A remarkable gain in compression ratio is found when encoded in terms of surface points, with the quality of reconstructed images almost the same as that found for reconstruction from control points. It is seen that texture regions require the largest number of bits during their encoding (Lena and Girl images). Examination of the quality of reconstructed images through the fidelity vector is to quantitatively determine the fidelity of images.

The approximation for hierarchical segmentation is different from approximation of subimages for their encoding. The former examines the segmentation of subimages, with the assurance that more psychovisually appealing reconstruction can be made while the latter actually does the approximation. The components of the fidelity vector are different objective measures that examine different important features of images. Thus, the smaller the values of the components of the fidelity vectors of two images, the larger the resemblance between the two images.

# Part II

Intermediate Steps

# 5

# B-Splines and Its Applications

## 5.1 Introduction

Though Bézier-Bernstein (B-B) splines are very similar to B-splines in designing a curve or a surface, the latter provides more flexibility during interactions. Consequently, B-splines are more effective and more efficient, and hence are more widely used. Since B-B splines use the Bernstein basis, we cannot deny its influence over the design of B-B curves and surfaces. Any point on a B-B curve is the weighted average of all the control points, of course, excepting the end control points. Therefore, the effect of a change in one control point is transmitted over the entire curve. Thus, any change in one control point globally affects the curve. We cannot make a local change within a curve, even when we are badly in need of one. The other limitation of the B-B spline is the degree of the polynomial. For a cubic B-B spline, the number of control points is always four while for an $m$th degree curve, the number of control points is m+1, or in other words, the degree of the spline function is always one less than the number of control points. Hence, the degree of the B-B spline curve is restricted by the number of control points. The lack of local control and the hard relation of degree of the polynomial function with the number of control points are the major drawbacks of B-B splines.

To design curves and surfaces in a more versatile way, Schoenberg [146] formulated the B-spline theory. He introduced a unique non-global basis function associated with each control point. This basis is called the B-spline basis. Here, each control point is capable of controlling the curve over a range of parameter values. Within this range of parameter values, the associated basis function is non-zero and is zero beyond the parameter values. As a result, B-spline basis functions are found to introduce better interactive flexibility in curve and surface design. One of the great advantages of B-spline basis is that one can change the order of the basis function without changing the number of the control points in the control graph of an object.

In a special situation, B-spline contains the Bernstein basis.

## 5.2 B-Spline Function

Cox [46] and de Boor [54] independently put forward a recursive definition for numerical computation of normalized B-spline basis function. An $(m-1)th$ degree B-spline curve $P(u)$ is defined as

$$P(u) = \sum_{i=0}^{n} B_{i,m}(u)V_i \qquad 2 \leq m \leq n+1, \qquad (5.1)$$

where $V_i$ is the $i$th control point of the $(n+1)$th point control polygon vertices and $B_{i,m}$ are the B-spline blending functions, which are basically polynomials of degree m-1. $B_{i,m}$ are also called the B-spline basis functions. The order $m$ can be chosen from 2 to $n+1$. The basis function $B_{i,m}(u)$ is defined by the recursion formula of Cox-de Boor.

$$B_{i,m}(u) = \frac{(u - t_i)}{t_{i+m-1} - t_i} B_{i,m-1}(u) + \frac{(t_{i+m} - u)}{t_{i+m} - t_{i+1}} B_{i+1,m-1}(u), \qquad (5.2)$$

where, $t_i \leq u \leq t_{i+m}$ and

$$B_{i,1}(u) = \begin{cases} 1 & if\ t_i \leq u \leq t_{i+1} \\ 0 & otherwise. \end{cases} \qquad (5.3)$$

The $t_i$s in equation (5.2) are elements of a knot vector. From the equation (5.2), it is clear that the basis function $B_{i,m}(u)$ is non-zero in the interval $[t_i, t_{i+m}]$. For a cubic B-spline, $m = 4$ and $B_{i,4}$ is non-zero in the interval $[t_i, t_{i+4}]$. The basis function spans the knots $t_i$, $t_{i+1}$, $t_{i+2}$, $t_{i+3}$, $t_{i+4}$. Note that when knots are not repeated, B-spline is zero at the end-knots $t_i$ and $t_{i+m}$, i.e.,

$$B_{i,m}(u = t_i) = 0, \qquad B_{i,m}(u = t_{i+m}) = 0.$$

But in B-splines, we use repeated knots (i.e., $t_i = t_{i+1} = \cdots$). Therefore, $B_{i,m}$ can have the form $\frac{0}{0}$. Hence, we assume $\frac{0}{0} = 0$ to incorporate repeated knots.

To trace an $(m-1)$th degree curve, $P(u)$, in equation (5.1) the parameter $u$ ranges from 0 to $n - m + 2$. It can be shown that for any value of the parameter $u$, the sum of the basis functions is

$$\sum_{i=0}^{n} B_{i,m}(u) = 1. \qquad (5.4)$$

Therefore, the B-spline curve lies within the convex hull defined by its control polygon, which is a similar property exhibited by the B-B curve.

### 5.2.1 B-Spline Knot Structure for Uniform, Open Uniform, and Nonuniform Basis

The equation (5.2) shows that we need to choose a set of knots , $t_i$, which relate the parameter $u$ to the control points. This relation, together with the

# Color Figures

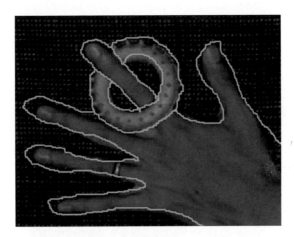

Fig. 9.17.

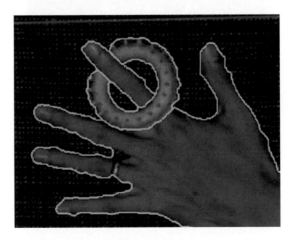

Fig. 9.19.

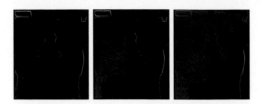

Fig. 10.9.

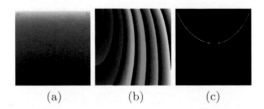

(a)                      (b)

Fig. 10.13.

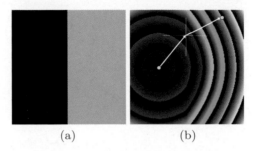

(a)              (b)              (c)

Fig. 10.14.

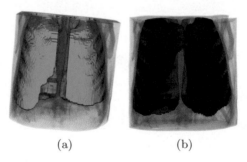

(a)                      (b)

Fig. 10.17.

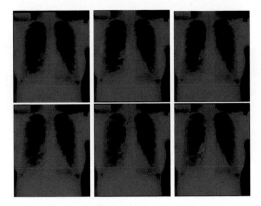

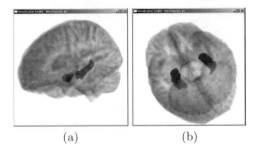

Fig. 10.18.

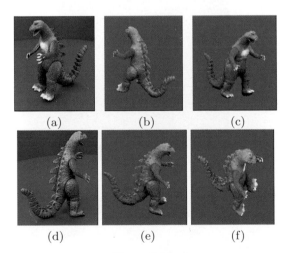

(a)        (b)

Fig. 10.19.

(a)      (b)      (c)

(d)      (e)      (f)

Fig. 10.20.

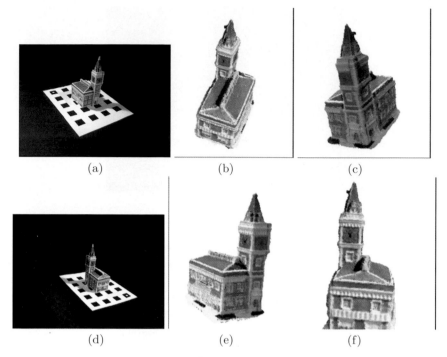

Fig. 10.21.

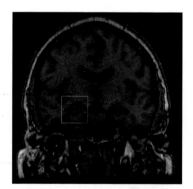

Fig. 10.22.

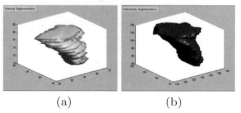

(a)                    (b)

Fig. 10.23.

location of the control points, provides control over the shape of the curve to be drawn. In B-spline, we have three different choices for knot values: the uniform non-periodic B-spline knots, uniform periodic knots, and nonuniform knots. Open curves are modeled by uniform non-periodic knots, while closed curves are modeled by uniform periodic knots. Similarly, nonuniform knots can also be of two different types: nonuniform non-periodic and nonuniform periodic to model respectively open and closed curves.

## Uniform Non-Periodic Knot Structure

The $m$th order or (m-1 degree) B-spline $B_{i,m}(u)$, $i = 0, 1, \cdots, n$ is defined for the parameter $u \in [0, n - m + 2]$. $B_{i,m}$ represents a curve, known as the B-spline curve. When the curve is a uniform open curve (non-periodic), its uniform non-periodic knots $t_0$ to $t_{n+m}$ are chosen according to the following rule:

$$
\begin{aligned}
t_i &= 0 & if && 0 \leq i < m \\
&= i - m + 1 & if && m \leq i \leq n \\
&= n - m + 2 & if && n < i \leq n + m.
\end{aligned}
\tag{5.5}
$$

Example: Find the uniform non-periodic knot vector for a b-spline open curve for which $n = 5$ and $m = 3$.

We can note that knots range from $t_0$ to $t_{n+m} = t_8$. According to equation (5.5), $t_0 = t_1 = t_2 = 0$ and $t_6 = t_7 = t_8 = 4$. Besides, we have $t_3 = 1$, $t_4 = 2$, and $t_5 = 3$. The knot vector is, therefore, $[0, 0, 0, 1, 2, 3, 4, 4, 4]$.

In general, the choice of knots according to the equation (5.5) is found to provide the following knot structure for uniform non-periodic open curves,

$$
\underbrace{0, 0, \cdots 0}_{m \text{ knots}}, 1, 2, \cdots, n - m + 1, \underbrace{n - m + 2, n - m + 2, \cdots, n - m + 2}_{m \text{ knots}}.
$$

The use of repeated knots ensures that the end points of the spline coincide with the end points of the control polygon. Note that in the beginning, we have $m$ knots, at the end we have $m$ knots, and in between we have $n - m + 1$ knots. Therefore, the total number of knots for any open control polygon is $m + (n - m + 1) + m$ or $n + m + 1$.

## Uniform Periodic Knot Structure

When the B-spline curve is closed (periodic) and the spacing between the knot values is fixed, the resulting curve is called a uniform periodic B-spline curve. In other words, uniform periodic B-spline is used to model closed curves. Some of the uniform knot vectors, for example, are shown below.

A knot vector with uniform spacing looks like

$$
[-1.5, -1.0, -0.5, 0.0, 0.5, 1.0, 1.5, 2.0].
$$

Sometimes, knot values are normalized in the range between 0 and 1. An example for this is

$$[0.0, 0.2, 0.4, 0.6, 0.8, 1.0].$$

In many applications, we need a knot vector with a separation of unity and starting value of 0. We take an example for this as

$$[0, 1, 2, 3, 4, 5, 6, 7].$$

In general, the total number of knots in this case is one less than that for the open curves, i,e., $n + m$, since the initial and starting knots are identical. The knot values $t_0, t_1, \cdots, t_{n+m}$ are cyclic, i.e., $0, 1, \cdots, n, 0, 1, \cdots$. Hence,

$$t_m = 0, \ t_{m+1} = 1, \ t_{m+i} = t_i.$$

This means we choose the knot values $t_i = i$, and reduce all basis functions to one.

**Nonuniform Knot Structure**

Nonuniform knot vectors may be unequally spaced together with or without multiple internal knots. Some of the knot vectors are $[0, 0, 0, 1, 1, 1, 2, 2, 2, 3, 3]$, $[0, 1, 2, 2, 3, 3, 4]$, and $[0, 0.22, 0.48, 0.75, 1]$.

## 5.3 Computation of B-Spline Basis Functions

Given the knot structure, one can easily compute the B-spline basis functions recursively using the equation (5.2) to design a curve. All these basis functions in the recursive computation defines a triangular structure as shown below.

$$
\begin{aligned}
&B_{i,m} \\
&B_{i,m-1} \ B_{i+1,m-1} \\
&B_{i,m-2} \ B_{i+1,m-2} \ B_{i+2,m-3} \\
&\ \vdots \qquad\quad \vdots \qquad\quad \vdots \\
&B_{i,1} \qquad B_{i+1,1} \qquad B_{i+2,1} \qquad B_{i+3,1} \cdots B_{i+m-1,1}.
\end{aligned}
\tag{5.6}
$$

The inverse structure shows how the first order basis function $B_{i,1}$ depends on higher order basis functions.

$$
\begin{aligned}
&B_{i-m+1,m} \cdots B_{i-1,m} \ B_{i,m} \ B_{i+1,m} \cdots B_{i+m-1,m} \\
&\quad \vdots \ \vdots \qquad\quad \vdots \quad \vdots \qquad \vdots \ \vdots \\
&\qquad\qquad B_{i-1,2} \ B_{i,2} \ B_{i+1,2} \\
&\qquad\qquad\qquad\quad B_{i,1}.
\end{aligned}
\tag{5.7}
$$

We shall now consider a few examples so that readers get a complete understanding of the computation of the basis functions.

Example: Compute the quadratic periodic basis functions.

Since the degree $= 2$, we have $m = 3$. Also, let us choose, $n = 3$ in equation (5.1); i.e., we consider four control points: $V_0$, $V_1$, $V_2$, and $V_3$. Hence, we need to compute four basis functions, namely $B_{0,3}$, $B_{1,3}$, $B_{2,3}$, and $B_{3,3}$.

We can compute using equation (5.6)

$$B_{0,3} \; B_{1,3} \; B_{2,3} \; B_{3,3}$$
$$B_{0,2} \; B_{1,2} \; B_{2,2} \; B_{3,2} \; B_{4,2}$$
$$B_{0,1} \; B_{1,1} \; B_{2,1} \; B_{3,1} \; B_{4,1} \; B_{5,1}.$$

The inverse functions can be written using equation (5.7):

$$B_{0,3} \; B_{1,3} \; B_{2,3} \; B_{3,3} \; B_{4,3} \; B_{5,3}$$
$$B_{0,2} \; B_{1,2} \; B_{2,2} \; B_{3,2} \; B_{4,2}$$
$$B_{0,1} \; B_{1,1} \; B_{2,1} \; B_{3,1}.$$

Let us now find out the knot vector. From equation (5.2), it is clear that $B_{5,1}$ needs the knots $t_5$ and $t_6$. The total number of knots is, therefore, $n+m+1 = 3 + 3 + 1 = 7$. Hence, the knot vector is $t = [0123456]$, i.e., $t_0 = 0$, $\cdots$ $t_{n+m} = t3 + 3 = t_6$.

### 5.3.1 Computation of Uniform Periodic B-spline Basis

The blending functions for a uniform periodic B-splines are also periodic. This means for all values of $n$ and $m$, all the blending functions have the same shape. Each successive blending function is a shifted version of the previous function. Hence,

$$\begin{aligned}
B_{i,m}(u) &= B_{i+1,m}(u + \triangle u)\\
&= B_{i+2,m}(u + 2\triangle u),
\end{aligned} \tag{5.8}$$

where $\triangle u$ is the interval between adjacent knot values.
Example: Computation of a uniform quadratic B-spline basis functions.

Let us now compute the blending functions corresponding to a uniform quadratic B-spline. For a quadratic B-spline, the order is 3. Hence we choose n=3. This means we have four control points. We, therefore, have four basis or blending functions, e.g., $B_{0,3}$, $B_{1,3}$, $B_{2,3}$, and $B_{3,3}$. Each of these blending functions is defined over $m$ subintervals. The total number of knots is $n + m + 1$, which is 7 in the present case $[0, 1, 2, 3, 4, 5, 6, 7]$. The total number of subintervals is, therefore, 6. The parameter $u$ ranges from 0 to $n + m$ or 6.

Now,

$$\begin{aligned}
B_{0,3}(u) &= \tfrac{u-t_0}{t_2-t_0} B_{0,2} + \tfrac{t_3-u}{t_3-t_1} B_{1,2}\\
&= \tfrac{1}{2}u B_{0,2} + \tfrac{1}{2}(3 - u)B_{1,2}\\
&= \tfrac{1}{2}u\tfrac{u-t_0}{t_1-t_0} B_{0,1} + \tfrac{1}{2}u\tfrac{t_2-u}{t_2-t_1} B_{1,1}\\
&\quad + \tfrac{1}{2}(3 - u)\tfrac{u-t_1}{t_2-t_1}B_{1,1} + \tfrac{1}{2}(3 - u)\tfrac{t_3-u}{t_3-t_2} B_{2,1}\\
&= \tfrac{1}{2}u^2 B_{0,1} + \{\tfrac{1}{2}u(2 - u)\\
&\quad + \tfrac{1}{2}(3 - u)(u - 1)\}B_{1,1}\\
&\quad + \tfrac{1}{2}(3 - u)^2 B_{2,1}.
\end{aligned} \tag{5.9}$$

Equation (5.9) provides the basis functions over the $m$ subintervals. It can be decomposed as follows.

$$B_{0,3}(u) = \begin{cases} \frac{1}{2}u^2 & 0 \le u < 1 \\ \frac{1}{2}u(2-u) + \frac{1}{2}(u-1)(3-u) & 1 \le u < 2 \\ \frac{1}{2}(3-u)^2 & 2 \le u < 3. \end{cases} \qquad (5.10)$$

Computing $B_{0,3}(u)$, we can get the other periodic basis functions by subtracting a shift of one unit from $u$. Thus,

$$B_{1,3}(u) = \begin{cases} \frac{1}{2}(u-1)^2 & 1 \le u < 2 \\ \frac{1}{2}(u-1)(3-u) + \frac{1}{2}(u-2)(4-u) & 2 \le u < 3 \\ \frac{1}{2}(4-u)^2 & 3 \le u < 4 \end{cases} \qquad (5.11)$$

$$B_{2,3}(u) = \begin{cases} \frac{1}{2}(u-2)^2 & 2 \le u < 3 \\ \frac{1}{2}(u-2)(4-u) + \frac{1}{2}(u-3)(5-u) & 3 \le u < 4 \\ \frac{1}{2}(5-u)^2 & 4 \le u < 5 \end{cases} \qquad (5.12)$$

$$B_{3,3}(u) = \begin{cases} \frac{1}{2}(u-3)^2 & 3 \le u < 4 \\ \frac{1}{2}(u-3)(5-u) + \frac{1}{2}(u-4)(6-u) & 4 \le u < 5 \\ \frac{1}{2}(6-u)^2 & 5 \le u < 6. \end{cases} \qquad (5.13)$$

With all the basis functions in hand, we can draw the uniform periodic quadratic B-spline curve.

## 5.4 B-Spline Curves on Unit Interval

We now want to examine the periodic B-spline curves on a unit interval, instead of considering different intervals because for the periodic B-splines, the blending functions in different intervals are translates of one another. Therefore, we need to reparameterize the B-spline parameter on the unit interval. We have already seen that the influence of a given blending function is limited to $m$ intervals. Hence, considering these facts, we can write a periodic B-spline curve on the unit interval as

$$P_j(s) = \sum_{i=0}^{m-1} N_{i+1,m}(s)V_{j+i} \qquad 1 \le j \le n - m + 1 \qquad (5.14)$$

$$and, \quad 0 \le s < 1.$$

In equation (5.14), $s$ is the reparameterized form of the parameter $u$ and $N_{i,m}(s)$ is the reparameterized blending function corresponding to the blending function $B_{i,m}(u)$; $j$ gives the number of curve segments and $n$ is one less than the number of vertices of the control polygon. Equation (5.14) can be extended as

$$P_j(s) = N_{1,k}(s)V_j + N_{2,k}(s)V_{j+1} + \cdots + N_{m,m}(s)V_{j+m-1}. \tag{5.15}$$

For $m = 3$, the re-parameterized blending functions on the unit interval $0 \leq s < 1$ are as follows:

$$\begin{aligned}
N_{1,3}(s) &= \frac{(1-s)^2}{2} \\
N_{2,3}(s) &= \frac{-2s^2+2s+1}{2} \\
N_{3,3}(s) &= \frac{s^2}{2}.
\end{aligned} \tag{5.16}$$

Substituting all these blending functions, the periodic quadratic B-spline curve on the unit interval is then

$$\begin{aligned}
2\,P_j(s) &= (1 - 2s + s^2)V_j + (-2s^2 + 2s + 1)V_{j+1} + s^2 V_{j+2} \\
&= s^2(V_j - 2V_{j+1} + V_{j+2}) \\
&\quad + s(-2V_j + 2V_{j+1} + 0.V_{j+2} \\
&\quad + 1(V_j + V_{j+1} + 0.V_{j+2}
\end{aligned} \tag{5.17}$$

or, in the matrix form

$$\begin{aligned}
P_j(s) &= (\,S\,)(\,N\,)(\,V\,) \\
&= \tfrac{1}{2}\,(\,s^2 \quad s \quad 1\,) \begin{pmatrix} 1 & -2 & 1 \\ -2 & 2 & 0 \\ 1 & 1 & 0 \end{pmatrix} \begin{pmatrix} V_j \\ V_{j+1} \\ V_{j+2} \end{pmatrix}.
\end{aligned} \tag{5.18}$$

Likewise for periodic cubic B-spline, $m = 4$ and the reparameterized blending functions on the unit interval are as follows :

$$\begin{aligned}
N_{1,4}(s) &= \frac{-s^3+3s^2-3s+1}{6} \\
N_{2,4}(s) &= \frac{-3s^3+6s^2+4}{6} \\
N_{3,4}(s) &= \frac{-s^3+3s^2+3s+1}{6} \\
N_{4,4}(s) &= \frac{s^3}{6}.
\end{aligned} \tag{5.19}$$

The curve in the matrix form is, therefore,

$$\begin{aligned}
P_j(s) &= (\,S\,)(\,N\,)(\,V\,) \\
&= \tfrac{1}{6}\,(\,s^3 \quad s^2 \quad s \quad 1\,) \begin{pmatrix} -1 & 3 & -3 & 1 \\ 3 & -6 & 3 & 0 \\ -3 & 0 & 3 & 0 \\ 1 & 4 & 1 & 0 \end{pmatrix} \begin{pmatrix} V_j \\ V_{j+1} \\ V_{j+2} \\ V_{j+3} \end{pmatrix}.
\end{aligned} \tag{5.20}$$

Note that for any $m$,

$$(\,S\,) = (\,s^{m-1} \quad s^{m-2} \quad \cdots \quad 1\,) \quad 0 \leq s < 1. \tag{5.21}$$

Cohen and Risenfeld [42] have shown the generalized form of $N$ for periodic B-spline curves, as given by

$$N_{i+1,j+1} = \frac{1}{(m-1)!} \binom{m-1}{i} \sum_{r=j}^{m-1} (m-(r+1))^i (-1)^{r-j} \binom{m}{r-j} \tag{5.22}$$

where $0 \leq i,\ j \leq m - 1$.

**Closed Periodic B-Spline Curves**

For closed periodic B-spline curves, we need to repeat some of the control polygon vertices. The curve in this case is given by

$$P_{j+1}(s) = \sum_{i=0}^{m-1} N_{i+1,m}(s)V_{((j+i)\ mod(n+1))+1} \quad 0 \le j \le n. \quad (5.23)$$

In the matrix form, this can be written as

$$P_{j+1}(s) = (S)(N) \begin{pmatrix} V_{(j\ mod\ (n+1))+1} \\ V_{((j+1)\ mod\ (n+1))+1} \\ \vdots \\ V_{((j+1+n-m)\ mod\ (n+1))+1} \end{pmatrix}. \quad (5.24)$$

Here, mod is the modulo or remainder function, e.g., $5\ mod\ 3 = 2$ (mod is the remainder function).

Example:

Find the 4th order closed B-spline curve whose control polygon is a square with 8 vertices, say, $V_1 = (2,0)$, $V_2 = (4,0)$, $V_3 = (4,2)$, $V_4 = (4,4)$, $V_5 = (2,4)$, $V_6 = (0,4), V\ 7 = (0,2)$, and $V_8 = (0,0)$.

Answer: Since the curve has order $= 4$, we have $m = 4$. The number of polygon vertices is $n = 8$. Obviously here, $V_9 = V_1 = (2,0)$, since the curve is closed. The first curve segment, $P_1$ from equation (5.24) is, therefore,

$$P_1 = (S)(N) \begin{pmatrix} -1 & 3 & -3 & 1 \\ 3 & -6 & 3 & 0 \\ -3 & 0 & 3 & 0 \\ 1 & 4 & 1 & 0 \end{pmatrix} \begin{pmatrix} V_1 \\ V_2 \\ V_3 \\ V_4 \end{pmatrix}$$

$$= (S)(N) \begin{pmatrix} 2 & 0 \\ 4 & 0 \\ 4 & 2 \\ 4 & 4 \end{pmatrix}.$$

From equation (5.21), the $S$ matrix is

$$(S) = \begin{pmatrix} s^3 \\ s^2 \\ s \\ 1 \end{pmatrix},$$

and the reparameterized $N$ matrix can be obtained from equation (5.22):

$$N_{1,4} = \tfrac{1}{3!} \binom{3}{0}\binom{4}{0}$$
$$= \tfrac{1}{6}.$$

Therefore, the first segment can be computed using the following matrix equation;

$$P_1 = \tfrac{1}{6} \begin{pmatrix} s^3 & s^2 & s & 1 \end{pmatrix} \begin{pmatrix} -1 & 3 & -3 & 1 \\ 3 & -6 & 3 & 0 \\ -3 & 0 & 3 & 0 \\ 1 & 4 & 1 & 0 \end{pmatrix} \begin{pmatrix} 2 & 0 \\ 4 & 0 \\ 4 & 2 \\ 4 & 4 \end{pmatrix}.$$

### 5.4.1 Properties of B-Spline Curves

A B-spline curve, $P(t)$ is a polynomial spline function of degree $m - 1$ such that in each interval $t_i \leq t < t_{i+1}$, $P(t)$ is a polynomial of degree $m - 1$, and $P(t)$ and its derivatives of order $1, 2, 3 \cdot m - 2$ are all continuous over the entire curve. When $m = 4$, we get a cubic B-spline curve. This means in each interval, the curve is a cubic polynomial. Since for any parameter u, the sum of all the basis functions is one, i.e.,

$$\sum_{i=0}^{n} B_{i,m}(u) = 1,$$

the B-spline curve lies within the convex hull defined by the control points. We can note in this context that the B-spline convex hull is different from the Bézier convex hull. Any point on a B-spline curve lies within a convex hull of $m$ neighboring points. Hence,

(1) The entire curve lies within the union of all such convex hulls formed by taking $m$ successive defining polygon vertices.

(2) The curve has variation diminishing property, i.e., the curve does not oscillate about any straight line more often than its defining polygon.

(3) The curve is affine invariant.

(4) The curve follows the shape of the defining polygon.

### 5.4.2 Effect of Multiplicity

Sometimes we need to insert corner points on a curve to depict a realistic shape. Corner points are the locations of high curvature regions. This may be effected by increasing the multiplicity of one or more control points. Multiplicity of a control point means counting it more than once. Thus, multiplicity of a control point by 2 means the same control point is considered twice, while multiplicity of 4 means it is considered 4 times, and so on. The effect is that the curve is pulled on and on, and finally passes through it. Readers interested in details can consult the book [142]

### 5.4.3 End Condition

Sometimes, we have difficulty in designing closed or periodic B-spline curves. The curve does not pass through the extreme end or control points of the guiding polygons. Barsky [16] has examined the conditions of the end control points for cubic B-splines. David and Rogers provided a generalized treatment in their book [142]. For quadratic periodic B-spline curves, we have $m = 3$ and it can be shown that the starting and end points are given by

$$P_s = \tfrac{1}{2}(V_0 + V_1)$$
$$P_e = \tfrac{1}{2}(V_{n_1} + V_n),$$

and for cubic curves ($m = 4$)

$$P_s = \tfrac{1}{6}(V_0 + 4V_1 + V_2)$$
$$P_e = \tfrac{1}{6}(V_{n_2} + 4V_{n-1} + V_n).$$

The first derivative at these points for $m = 3$ is

$$P_s' = V_1 - V_0$$
$$P_e' = V_n - V_{n-1},$$

while for cubic periodic B-spline ($m = 4$), first and second order derivatives are

$$P_s' = \tfrac{1}{2}(V_2 - V_0) \quad P_s'' V_0 - 2V_1 + V_2$$
$$P_e' = \tfrac{1}{2}(V_n - V_{n-2}) \quad P_e'' V_{n-2} - 2V_{n-1} + V_n.$$

Multiple coincident vertices at one end of a periodic B-spline curve pulls the starting and end points of the curve nearer to the vertex. For $m - 1$ multiple coincident vertices, the end point of the curve coincides with the vertices and the tangent vector of the curve.

## 5.5 Rational B-Spline Curve

Adams and Rogers nicely explained the rational B-spline curves in their book [142]. We shall slightly review it so that the image processing and machine vision community can examine the possibility of using it in their area. Before we explain rational B-spline curve, we would like to explain homogeneous coordinates in some detail.

### 5.5.1 Homogeneous Coordinates

In order to study the geometric relationships of figures under perspective transformations, projective planes were introduced by geometers. The two dimensional projective plane is defined as follows:

In a three dimensional Cartesian space, consider the set of all lines through the origin and the set of all panes through the origin. In the projective plane, a line through the origin is called a point, while a plane through the origin is called a line of the projective plane. This is so, because if we consider the perspective projection onto the plane $z = 1$ using the origin as the center of projection, then a line through the origin always projects onto a point on the plane $z = 1$ and a plane through the origin projects onto line on the plane $z = 1$.

If $(a, b, c)$ is any point in Cartesian 3-dimensional space, then this point determines a line through the origin whose equations are

$$x = at$$
$$y = bt$$
$$z = ct,$$

where $t$ is a parameter. Any other point $(at, bt, ct)$ determines the same line. So, two points, $(a_1, b_1, c_1)$ and $(a_2, b_2, c_2)$, are on the same line through the origin if

$$a_2 = a_1 t$$
$$b_2 = b_1 t$$
$$c_2 = c_1 t.$$

We say $(a_1, b_1, c_1)$ $(a_2, b_2, c_2)$. The equivalence classes of all triples equivalent to $(a, b, c)$, written as $[(a, b, c)]$, are the points of the projective plane. Any representative $(a_1, b_1, c_1)$ equivalent to $(a, b, c)$ is called the homogeneous coordinates of the point $[a, b, c]$ in the projective plane.

The points of the form $(a, b, 0)$ are called ideal points of the projective plane. This comes from the fact that lines in the plane $z = 0$ project to infinity. In a similar way, any plane through the origin has an equation $n_1 x + n_2 y + n_3 z = 0$. We can observe that $kn_x + kn_2 y + kn_3 z = 0$, where $k$ is a multiple, also defines the same plane.

Any triple of numbers $(n_1, n_2, n_3)$ defines a plane through the origin. Now, $(n_1, n_2, n_3)$ $(d_1, d_2, d_3)$ if there is a number $k$ such that $d_1 = kn_1$, $d_2 = kn_2$, and $d_3 = kn_3$. The equivalence classes of all triples $[n_1, n_2, n_3]$ are the lines of the projective plane. Any representative $(d_1, d_2, d_3)$ of the equivalence classes $[n_1, n_2, n_3]$ is called the homogeneous line coordinate in the projective plane.

If $(x_1, y_1, z_1)$, $z_1 \neq 0$ are the homogeneous coordinates of a point of the projective plane, the equations $x = \frac{x_1}{z_1}$ and $y = \frac{y_1}{z_1}$ define a correspondence between points $P_1(x_1, y_1, z_1)$ of the projective plane and points $P(x, y)$ of the Cartesian plane. There is no Cartesian point corresponding to the ideal point $(x_1, y_1, 0)$. But it is convenient to consider it as defining an infinitely distant point.

Also, it is clear that any Cartesian point $P(x, y)$ corresponds to a projective point $P(x_1, y_1, z_1)$ whose homogeneous coordinates are $x_1 = x$, $y_1 = y$, and $z_1 = 1$. This correspondence between Cartesian coordinates and homogeneous coordinates is exploited in graphics transformations. Note that even though there is a correspondence between the points of the projective plane and those of the Cartesian plane, these planes have different topological properties and these properties should be taken into account while working with homogeneous coordinates. Finally, if $P_1(x_1, y_1, z_1, w_1)$ are the homogeneous coordinates of a point in the three dimensional projective plane, then the corresponding three dimensional Cartesian point $P(x, y, z)$ for $w \neq 0$ is as follows:

$$x = \frac{x_1}{w_1}, \ y = \frac{y_1}{w_1}, \ z = \frac{z_1}{w_1}.$$

On the other hand if $P(x, y, z)$ is a Cartesian point, it corresponds to the projective point $P(x, y, z, 1)$. Hence, the homogeneous representation of an object in n-space can be viewed as an object in (n+1)-space. The coordinates in n-space are called ordinary coordinates and those in (n+1)-space are called homogeneous coordinates. The mapping from n-space to (n+1)-space is one-to-many, i.e., there is an infinite number of equivalent representations of n-space object in (n+1)-space. The inverse mapping from (n+1)-space to n-space is many-to-one. The homogeneous representation of $(x, y, z)$ is $(wx, wy, wz, w)$ for any $w \neq 0$ and a homogeneous point $(a, b, c, d)$ has a three dimensional image $(a/d, b/d, c/d)$.

### 5.5.2 Essentials of Rational B-Spline Curves

With the concept of homogeneous coordinates discussed above, a rational B-spline curve is defined in 3-d Cartesian space as a projection of a nonrational B-spline in 4-d homogeneous coordinate space by

$$P_r(u) = \sum_{i=o}^{n} R_{i,m}(u) V_i, \tag{5.25}$$

where $V_i$s are the 3-d control polygon vertices and $R_{i,m}$ is the rational B-spline basis functions, and are connected to nonrational B-spline basis functions in the way as

$$R_{i,m}(u) = \frac{w_i B_{i,m}(u)}{\sum\limits_{i=0}^{n} w_i B_{i,m}(u)}, \tag{5.26}$$

where $w_i \geq 0$ for $\forall i$. Thus, $R_{i,m}(u)V_i$ is the projection in 3-space from $B_{i,m}(u) V_i^w$ in homogeneous 4-space. Hence, the rational B-spline basis functions and curves are generalizations of nonrational B-spline basis functions and curves.

For rational B-spline basis functions, it is also true that

$$\sum_{i=0}^{n} R_{i,m}(t) = 1, \tag{5.27}$$

where $t$ is any parameter. About the properties of rational B-spline curve, we can say that:

(1) It is also variation diminishing like the B-spline curve.

(2) It also lies within the union of convex hulls formed by $m$ successive defining polygon vertices like the B-spline curve.

(3) Like B-spline, it also follows the shape of the defining polygon.

(4) The curve is invariant with projective transformation. Thus, it follows a stronger condition compared to B-spline curves, which are affine invariant.

## 5.6 B-Spline Surface

B-spline surface is defined exactly in the same way as the Bézier surface. It is the Cartesian product surface and is given by

$$S(u, v) = \sum_{i=0}^{n} \sum_{j=0}^{q} B_{i,m} B_{j,p} V_{i,j}. \tag{5.28}$$

## 5.7 Application

Roberto Cipolla and Andrew Blake [39] used B-spline to measure the differential invariants of the image velocity field by computing average values from the integral of normal image velocities around image contours. They showed how an active observer making small, deliberate motions can use the estimate of the divergence and deformation of the image velocity field to determine the orientation of the object surface and time to contact. They tracked arbitrary image shapes using B-spline control snakes and computed efficiently the invariants as closed-form functions of the B-spline snake control points. Subsequently, they used this information to guide a robot manipulator in obstacle collision avoidance, object manipulation, and navigation.

### 5.7.1 Differential Invariants of Image Velocity Fields

Differential invariants of image velocity fields were originally introduced by Koenderink and Van Doorn [92, 94, 93] in the context of computational vision and analysis of visual motion. The image velocity of a point in space due to motion between the observer and scene [121] is

$$\mathbf{Q}_t = \frac{(\mathbf{U} \wedge \mathbf{Q}) \wedge \mathbf{Q}}{\lambda} - \Omega \wedge \mathbf{Q}, \tag{5.29}$$

where $\mathbf{U}$ =translational velocity, $\Omega$ =rotational velocity around the viewer center, and $\lambda$ is the distance to the point. Let us now look at the local variation of image velocities in the vicinity of the ray $\mathbf{Q}$, and consider an arbitrary co-ordinary system with the $x - y$ plane spanning the image plane. We assume that the z-axis is aligned with the ray. With respect to this coordinate system, let the translational and angular velocity have respectively the components as shown, $U = \{U_1, U_2, U_3\}$ and $\Omega = \{\Omega_1, \Omega_2, \Omega_3\}$. Assume the image velocity field at a point $(x, y)$ in the vicinity of $\mathbf{Q}$ is $\mathbf{v}(x, y)$ with $(u, v)$ as $x$ and $y$ components. The image velocity field for a sufficiently small field of view can be described by $(u_0, v_0)$ and by the first order partial derivatives of the image velocity, i.e., by $u_x, u_y, v_x, v_y$ [171, 122] as

$$u_0 = -\frac{U_1}{\lambda} - \Omega_2. \tag{5.30}$$

$$v_0 = -\frac{U_2}{\lambda} + \Omega_1. \tag{5.31}$$

$$u_x = \frac{U_3}{\lambda} + \frac{U_1 \lambda_x}{\lambda^2}. \tag{5.32}$$

$$u_y = \Omega_3 + \frac{U_1 \lambda_y}{\lambda^2}. \tag{5.33}$$

$$v_x = -\Omega_3 + \frac{U_2 \lambda_x}{\lambda^2} \tag{5.34}$$

$$v_y = \frac{U_3}{\lambda} + \frac{U_2 \lambda_y}{\lambda^2}. \tag{5.35}$$

The system of equations is underconstrained as there are fewer number of equations than there are number of unknowns. $\lambda$ determines the structure of the scene.

An image feature or shape will undergo a transformation for the image velocity field. The transformation from a shape at time $t$ to the deformed shape at time $t + \delta t$ can be approximated by an affine transformation. We can write as the first order approximation

$$\begin{pmatrix} u \\ v \end{pmatrix} = \begin{pmatrix} u_0 \\ v_0 \end{pmatrix} + \begin{pmatrix} u_x & u_y \\ v_x & v_y \end{pmatrix} \begin{pmatrix} x \\ y \end{pmatrix} + O(x^2, xy, y^2). \tag{5.36}$$

Cipolla and Blake neglected the non-linear term $O(x^2, xy, y^2)$ in their analysis. One can decompose the velocity gradient term into three components with each term having a simple geometric significance, invariant under the transformation of the image coordinate system.

$$\begin{aligned} \begin{pmatrix} u_x & u_y \\ v_x & v_y \end{pmatrix} &= \frac{curl\mathbf{v}}{2} \begin{pmatrix} 0 & -1 \\ 1 & 0 \end{pmatrix} + \frac{div\mathbf{v}}{2} \begin{pmatrix} 1 & 0 \\ 0 & 1 \end{pmatrix} + \\ &\quad \frac{def\mathbf{v}}{2} \begin{pmatrix} \cos\mu & -\sin\mu \\ \sin\mu & \cos\mu \end{pmatrix} \begin{pmatrix} 1 & 0 \\ 0 & -1 \end{pmatrix} \begin{pmatrix} \cos\mu & \sin\mu \\ -\sin\mu & \cos\mu \end{pmatrix} \\ &= \frac{curl\mathbf{v}}{2} \begin{pmatrix} 0 & -1 \\ 1 & 0 \end{pmatrix} + \frac{div\mathbf{v}}{2} \begin{pmatrix} 1 & 0 \\ 0 & 1 \end{pmatrix} \\ &\quad + \frac{def\mathbf{v}}{2} \begin{pmatrix} \cos 2\mu & \sin 2\mu \\ \sin 2\mu & -\cos 2\mu \end{pmatrix}, \end{aligned} \tag{5.37}$$

where

$$\begin{aligned} div\mathbf{v} &= (u_x + v_y) \\ curl\mathbf{v} &= -(u_y - v_x) \\ (def\mathbf{v})\cos 2\mu &= (u_x - v_y) \\ (def\mathbf{v})\sin 2\mu &= (u_y + v_x). \end{aligned} \tag{5.38}$$

The curl, divergence, and magnitude of deformation are scalar invariants and do not depend on a particular choice of coordinate system. The axes of maximum extension and compression rotate with rotations of the image plane axes. The curl component measures the change in orientation of patches in the image, while the divergence term indicates scale or change in size. The deformation term indicates the distortion of the image shape as a shear. Use of differential invariants of the image velocity field is significant in the sense that the deformation component provides information about the orientation of surface and the divergence component can provide an estimate of the time to contact or collision.

We shall now check the conditions under which the image velocity field can be well approximated by its first order terms. The requirement is transformation that should be locally equivalent to an affine transformation, i.e., parallel lines remain parallel. In other words, transformation from a plane in the world to the image must be described by an affine mapping. This is what we call weak perspective. One can establish after an examination of the quadratic terms in the equation of image velocity about the vicinity of a point in the image,

$$\frac{\triangle \lambda}{\lambda} << 1, \tag{5.39}$$

and

$$\frac{\Omega.\delta}{\Omega.Q} << 1. \tag{5.40}$$

We note that $\delta$, the difference between two rays, defines the field of view in radians and $\triangle \lambda$ is the depth of relief in the field of view. An empirical result says that if the distance to the object is greater than the depth of relief by an order of magnitude [161], then the assumption of weak perspective is a good approximation to perspective projection. It is true that at close distances "looming" or "fanning" effects will become prominent and the affine transformation is not sufficient to describe the changes in the image. In many practical cases, it is possible to restrict our attention to small fields of view in which the weak perspective model is valid.

### 5.7.2 3D Shape and Viewer Ego-motion

In the above section, we have seen the differential invariants expressed in terms of viewer's translation $(U_1/\lambda, U_2/\lambda, U_3/\lambda)$ and surface orientation $(\lambda_x/\lambda, \lambda_y/\lambda)$. From the previous equations through some algebraic manipulations one can write,

$$curl\mathbf{v} = -2\Omega_3 + \frac{(-U_1\lambda_y+U_2\lambda_x)}{\lambda^2} \tag{5.41}$$

$$div\mathbf{v} = 2\frac{U_3}{\lambda} + \frac{(U_1\lambda_x+U_2\lambda_y)}{\lambda^2} \tag{5.42}$$

$$(def\mathbf{v})\cos 2\mu = \frac{(U_1\lambda_x-U_2\lambda_y)}{\lambda^2} \tag{5.43}$$

$$(def\mathbf{v})\sin 2\mu = \frac{(U_1\lambda_y + U_2\lambda_x)}{\lambda^2}. \tag{5.44}$$

The average image translation $(u_0, v_0)$ can always be canceled out by appropriate camera rotations, while divergence and deformation remain unaffected by viewer rotation, such as panning or tilting of the camera or eye movements, whereas these rotations could lead to considerable changes in image point velocities or disparities.

Differential invariants depend on the viewer motion, depth, and surface orientation. When the translations are scaled by depth, $\lambda$, we get a 2-D vector, say $\mathbf{A}$, given by

$$\begin{aligned}\mathbf{A} &= \left(\frac{U_1}{\lambda}, \frac{U_2}{\lambda}\right) \\ &= \frac{U - (U.Q)Q}{\lambda}.\end{aligned} \tag{5.45}$$

Similarly, when the depth gradient is scaled by depth, $\lambda$, we get a 2-D vector, say $\mathbf{F}$ to represent the surface orientation, given by

$$\begin{aligned}\mathbf{F} &= \left(\frac{\lambda_x}{\lambda}, \frac{\lambda_y}{\lambda}\right) \\ &= \frac{grad\lambda}{\lambda}.\end{aligned} \tag{5.46}$$

$|\mathbf{F}|$ provides the tangent of the slant of the surface, i.e., tangent of the angle between the surface normal and visual direction. It is zero for a frontal view and infinite when the viewer is in the tangent plane of the surface. Direction of $\mathbf{F}$ provides the direction in the image of increasing distance and this is equal to the tilt, $\tau$, of the surface tangent plane. Hence,

$$|\mathbf{F}| = \tan\sigma, \qquad \angle\mathbf{F} = \tau.$$

Relation between the differential invariants, motion parameters, and surface orientation can, therefore, be shown as

$$curl\mathbf{v} = -2\Omega.Q + |\mathbf{F} \wedge \mathbf{A}|. \tag{5.47}$$

$$div\mathbf{v} = \frac{2U.Q}{\lambda} + \mathbf{F}.\mathbf{A}. \tag{5.48}$$

$$def\mathbf{v} = |\mathbf{F}||\mathbf{A}|, \tag{5.49}$$

and

$$\mu = \frac{\angle\mathbf{A} + \angle\mathbf{F}}{2}. \tag{5.50}$$

Note that $\mu$ bisects the sum of the angles of $\mathbf{F}$ and $\mathbf{A}$.

### 5.7.3 Geometric Significance

Formulation in the preceding section clearly shows the speed-scale ambiguity and the bas-relief ambiguity. Translational velocities appear scaled by depth. So, we note that a nearby object moving slowly or a far-away object moving quickly have the same effects and, therefore, introduces an ambiguity known as speed-scale ambiguity. Similarly, increasing the slant of the surface $\mathbf{F}$ while scaling the movement by the same amount will leave the local image velocity field unchanged. As a result, the ambiguity, viz. the bas-relief ambiguity, arises. Therefore, we conclude that from two weak perspective views and with no knowledge of the viewer translation, it is impossible to determine whether the deformation in the image is due to a large $|\mathbf{A}|$ and a small slant or due to a small rotation and a large slant. So, a nearby "shallow" object will produce the same effect as a far-away "deep" structure. As a consequence, we can only recover the depth gradient $\mathbf{F}$ up to an unknown scale.

it is interesting to note the similarity between motion parallax [109, 140, 38] which relate the relative image velocity between two nearby points $\mathbf{Q}_t^{(1)}$ and $\mathbf{Q}_t^{(2)}$ to their relative inverse depths,

$$\mathbf{Q}_t^{(2)} - \mathbf{Q}_t^{(1)} = [(\mathbf{U} \wedge \mathbf{Q}) \wedge \mathbf{Q}] \left[ \frac{1}{\lambda^{(2)}} - \frac{1}{\lambda^{(1)}} \right], \qquad (5.51)$$

and the equation relating image deformation to surface orientation

$$def\mathbf{Q}_t = |(\mathbf{U} \wedge \mathbf{Q}) \wedge \mathbf{Q}| \left[ grad(\frac{1}{\lambda}) \right]. \qquad (5.52)$$

The results are essentially the same, relating local measurements of relative image velocities to scene structure in a simple way which is uncorrupted by the rotational image velocity component. In the first case, the depths are discontinuous and differences of discrete velocities are related to the difference of inverse depths. In the latter case, the surface is assumed smooth and continuous and derivatives of image velocities are related to derivatives of inverse depth.

### 5.7.4 Constraints

It is difficult to completely solve for the structure and motion due to insufficient information. We have six equations in eight unknowns of the scene structure and motion. For a complete solution in a single neighborhood we need to compute second order derivatives to get more equations [109, 171].

### Case: Known Translation and Arbitrary Rotation

In this case, we can use equations (5.48), (5.49) and (5.50) to unambiguously recover the surface orientation and the distance to the object in temporal units. For the speed-scale ambiguity, we can express the latter as a time to contact. The axis of expansion ($\mu$) of the deformation component and the projection in the image of the direction of translation ($\angle\mathbf{A}$) allow the recovery of the tilt of the surface equation (5.50). Now subtract the contribution due to the surface orientation and viewer translation parallel to the image axis from the image divergence equation (5.48). This equals $|def\mathbf{v}|\cos(\tau - \angle\mathbf{A})$. The remaining component of divergence is due to movement towards or away from the object. This can be used to recover the time to contact $t^c$ as

$$t^c = \frac{\lambda}{\mathbf{U}.\mathbf{Q}}. \tag{5.53}$$

The time to contact fixes the viewer translation in temporal units. It allows the specification of the magnitude of translation parallel to the image plane $\mathbf{A}$, up to the same speed-scale ambiguity. The magnitude of deformation can be used to recover the slant $\sigma$ of the surface from equation (5.49).

The advantage of this formulation is that camera rotations do not affect the estimation of shape and distance. Effects of errors in the direction of translation are evident as scalings in depth or by a relief transformation [92].

If the cameras or eye rotate to keep the object of interest in the middle of the image, the eight unknowns reduce to six. The magnitude of rotations needed to bring the object back to the center of the image determines $\mathbf{A}$ and hence allows us to solve for these unknowns. The major effect of any error in the estimate of rotation is to scale depth and orientations.

Even without any additional assumptions, we can get useful information from the first order differential invariants. Inspection of equations (5.48) and (5.49) shows that the time to contact must lie in an interval given by

$$\frac{1}{t^c} = \frac{div\mathbf{v}}{2} \pm \frac{def\mathbf{v}}{2}. \tag{5.54}$$

The upper bound on time to contact occurs when the component of viewer translation parallel to the image plane is in the opposite direction to the depth gradient. The lower bound occurs when the translation is parallel to the depth gradient. The upper and lower estimates of time to contact are equal when there is no deformation component. This is the case in which the viewer translation is along the ray. The estimate of time to contact is then exact. A similar equation has been described by [157]. Subbarao's result suggests the curl and deformation components can be used to estimate bounds on the rotational component about the ray,

$$\mathbf{\Omega}.\mathbf{Q} = -\frac{curl\mathbf{v}}{2} \pm \frac{def\mathbf{v}}{2}. \tag{5.55}$$

Koenderink and Van Doorn [95] showed that when weak perspective is a valid approximation, the deformation component alone in a small field of view can provide surface shape information. As a result, recovery of a 3D shape can be made up to a scale and relief transformation.

Two different cases are described next.

## 5.7.5 Extraction of Differential Invariants

There are a number of ways to extract differential invariants from the image. Differential invariants of the image velocity field characterize the changes in apparent shape due to relative motion between the viewer and scene. It is possible to recover the normal image velocity component from local measurements at a curve [163, 76]. It is shown that this information is sufficient to estimate differential invariants within closed curves. The moments of area of a contour are defined in terms of an area integral with boundaries defined by the contour in the image plane;

$$I_f = \int_{a(t)} f \, dx dy, \tag{5.56}$$

where $a(t)$ is the area of a contour of interest at time $t$ and $f$ is a scalar function of image position $(x, y)$. For example, $f = 1$ gives the zero order moment of area (labeled as $I_o$). This is the area of the contour. Similarly, when $f = x$ or $f = y$, we get first order moments about the $x$ or $y$ axis in the image plane. Moments of area can be measured through their temporal derivatives in the following way:

$$\frac{d}{dt}(I_f) = \frac{d}{dt} \left[ \int_{a(t)} f \, dx dy \right] \\ = \oint_{c(t)} [f \mathbf{v}.\mathbf{n}^p] \, ds. \tag{5.57}$$

$\mathbf{v}.\mathbf{n}^p$ is the normal component of the image velocity $\mathbf{v}$ at a point on the contour. We, therefore, note that the temporal derivatives of moments of area are simply the effect of integration of the normal image velocities at a contour weighted by a scalar $f(x, y)$. By Green's theorem, an integral over the contour $c(t)$ can be expressed as an integral over the area enclosed by the contour $a(t)$. Therefore,

$$\frac{d}{dt}(I_f) = \int_{a(t)} div(f\mathbf{v})] dx dy \\ = \int_{a(t)} [f div \mathbf{v} + \mathbf{v}.grad f] dx dy \\ = \int_{a(t)} [f div \mathbf{v} + f_x u + f_y v] dx dy \tag{5.58} \\ = u_0 \int_{a(t)} f_x dx dy + u_x \int_{a(t)} [x f_x + f] dx dy + u_y \int_{(t)} y f_x dx dy \\ + v_0 \int_{a(t)} f_y dx dy + v_x \int_{a(t)} [x f_y + f] dx dy + v_y \int_{a(t)} [y f_y + f] dx dy,$$

where we get the last line using equation (5.36). We, therefore, see that the image velocity field deforms the shape of contours in the image and the shape of contours can be described by moments of area. Thus, the change in moments of area can be used in terms of the affine transformation parameters.

With the origin at the centroid of the contour of interest so that the first moments are zero, the above equation with $f = x$ and $f = y$ shows that the centroid of the deformed shape specifies the mean translation $[u_0, v_0]$. $f = 1$ shows that the divergence of the image velocity field can be estimated as the derivative of scaled area,

$$\frac{dI_0}{dt} = I_0(u_x + v_y) \tag{5.59}$$

and

$$\frac{da(t)}{dt} = a(t)div\mathbf{v}. \tag{5.60}$$

To get additional constraints, one can increase the order of moments. So, if we get six linearly independent equations, we can solve for the affine transformation parameters and combine the coefficients to recover the differential invariants. The error between the transformed and observed image contours helps to check the validity of the affine transformation. Note that certain contours in practice may lead to equations that are not independent or ill-conditioned. Under such circumstances, the normal components of image velocity are not sufficient to recover the true image velocity field globally. Waxman and Whon [172] termed this problem as the "aperture problem in the large." This was investigated in the article [20]. However, it is always possible to recover the divergence from a closed contour.

### Tracking Closed Contours

B-spline snakes are used to localize and track closed image contours. We can write the B-spline curve in the way,

$$\mathbf{x}(s) = \sum_{i=1} f_i(s)\mathbf{V}_i, \tag{5.61}$$

where $f_i$s are the spline basis functions and $\mathbf{V}_i$s are the control points of the curve and $s$ is a parameter, not necessarily arc length. The snakes are initialized as points in the center of the image and are forced to expand radially outwards until they are near the edge and the image forces stabilize the snake close to a high contrast closed contour. Subsequent image motion is automatically tracked by the snake. B-spline snakes have local control and continuity. The enclosed area is a function of control points and also applies to other moments.

From Green's theorem in the plane, the area enclosed by a curve with parametrization $x(s)$ and $y(s)$ is given by

$$a = \int_{s_o}^{s_N} x(s)y^{'}(s)ds. \tag{5.62}$$

Substituting the B-spine derivative in the above equation,

$$a(t) = \int_{s_o}^{s_N} \sum_i \sum_j (V_{x_i}, V_{y_j}) f_i f_j' ds$$
$$= \sum_i \sum_j (V_{x_i}, V_{y_j}) \int_{s_o}^{s_N} f_i f_j' ds. \tag{5.63}$$

The integrals can be computed in closed form. For a cubic B-spline, we need to use ten possible values due to symmetry. In the worst case, we need sixteen coefficient values. At each time instant, multiplication with the control point gives the area of the contour.

## 5.8 Recovery of Time to Contact and Surface Orientation

Cipolla and Blake [38] presented preliminary implementation of their theory. The examples are based on a camera mounted on a robot arm whose translations are deliberate while rotations around the camera center are performed to keep the target of interest in the center of its field of view. The camera intrinsic parameters (image center, scaling factors, and focal length) and orientation are unknown. The direction of translation is assumed known and expressed with bounds. Nelson and Aloimonos [127] demonstrated a robotics system that computed divergence using spatio-temporal techniques from images of highly textured visible surfaces, while Cipolla and Blake [38] used image contours for a real time implementation. The closed contour is localized automatically by initializing a closed loop B-spline snake in the center of the image. The snake explodes outwards and deforms under the influence of image forces that cause it to be attracted to high contrast edges. The robot manipulator then makes a deliberate motion towards the target. Tracking the area of the contour and computing its rate of change allows us to estimate the divergence. For motion along the visual ray, this provides sufficient information to estimate the time to contact. The manipulator, in fact, travels blindly after its sensing actions and at a uniform speed for the time before contact. In repeated trials, image divergences measured at distances of 0.5m to 1.0m were estimated accurately to the nearest half of a time unit. This corresponds to a positional accuracy of 20mm for a manipulator translational velocity of 40mm/s. The affine transformation approximation breaks down at close proximity to the target. This may lead to a degradation in the estimate of time to contact.

### 5.8.1 Braking and Object Manipulation

The experiment of Cipolla and Blake shows a sequence of images taken from a moving car approaching the windshield of a stationary car in front. In the first frame (time $t = 0$), the relative distance between the two cars is approximately 7m. The velocity of approach is uniform and approximately 1m/time unit. A B-spline snake is initialized in the center of the windshield and expands out until it localizes the closed contour of the edge of the windshield. The snake then automatically tracks the windshield over the sequence. For uniform translation along the optical axis, the relationship between area and time is given (from equations 5.48 and 5.60) as

$$\frac{d}{dt}(a(t)) = \left(\frac{2\mathbf{U}.\mathbf{Q}}{\lambda}\right) a(t). \tag{5.64}$$

Its solution is

$$a(t) = \frac{a(0)}{\left(1 - \frac{t}{t^c(0)}\right)^2}, \tag{5.65}$$

where $t^c(0)$ is the initial estimate of the time to contact as given by

$$t^c(0) = \frac{\lambda(0)}{\mathbf{U}.\mathbf{Q}}. \tag{5.66}$$

This is in close agreement with the data. For uniform motion, this should decrease linearly. For nonuniform motion, time to contact as a function of time is important for braking and landing. Lee [102] provided a braking condition for drivers that states

$$\frac{d}{dt}(t_c(t)) \geq -0.5. \tag{5.67}$$

This ensures that vehicles will decelerate uniformly and to avoid collision. Thus, the divergence of the image velocity field provides sufficient information to control over braking.

If the translational motion has a component parallel to the image plane, the image divergence is composed of two components. The first term determines time to contact, while the other term occurs due to image foreshortening when the surface has a non-zero slant. The two effects can be computed separately by measuring the deformation. The deformation also helps to recover the surface orientation. The only assumption of Cipolla and Blake [38] is of uniform motion and known direction of translation.

## 5.9 Concluding Remarks

B-spline has widespread applications in image processing and vision problems. The application of B-spline in machine vision problems discussed in this chapter shows its importance. Based on the original philosophy, different solutions have been suggested to render the snake more stable and to yield faster convergence results. An alternative approach to snakes, which also circumvents some of the problems, is to use a parametric B-spline representation of the curve, first introduced as B-snake [124], and improved in [62, 106, 170]. The basic concept of B-spline snakes has been extended in [30] to improve their efficiency, speed, and applicability in an interactive environment. We believe B-spline has the potential to become a mighty tool in the area of image processing and machine vision.

# 6

## Beta-Splines: A Flexible Model

### 6.1 Introduction

In general, a spline with greater flexibility is always desired because it enhances the strength for modeling a set of data points. A beta spline is a spline with such an ability. For its flexibility, it can be used in image processing as well as in vision problems in many different ways. Beta spline was developed by Barsky [15] and our discussion in this chapter is based on his thesis.

### 6.2 Beta-Spline Curve

A $\beta$-spline curve is a piecewise parametric cubic beta curve that is the weighted average of its control vertices. For every point of the curve, the weight $w$ is different and depends on two different shape parameters $\beta 1$, $\beta_2$, and position parameter, $t$ itself. Hence, we can represent the $i$th piece of a beta curve as

$$P_i(t) = \sum_{n=-2}^{n=1} w_n(\beta 1, \beta 2, t) V_{i+n}, \qquad 0 \le t < 1. \tag{6.1}$$

The weight, $w$, is a basis function of $\beta 1$, $\beta 2$ and can be computed for some values of the parameters $\beta 1$, $\beta 2$, and $t$. $V_{i+n}$ are the control points. Weight, $w$, is given by

$$w_n(\beta 1, \beta 2, t) = \sum_{m=0}^{m=3} c_{mn}(\beta 1, \beta 2) t^m \quad for \ n = -2, -1, 0, 1. \tag{6.2}$$

Consider two beta curve segments, say $P_i(t)$ and $P_{i+1}(t)$. Then from the position, first order and second order continuity we can write,

$$P_{i+1}(0) = P_i(1) \tag{6.3}$$

$$P'_{i+1}(0) = \beta_1 P'_i(1) \tag{6.4}$$

and

$$P''_{i+1}(0) = \beta_1^2 P''_i(1) + \beta_2 P'_i(1). \tag{6.5}$$

This leads to

$$\sum_{n=-2}^{n=1} w_n(\beta 1, \beta 2, 0) V_{i+1+n} = \sum_{n=-2}^{n=1} w_n(\beta 1, \beta 2, 1) V_{i+n} \tag{6.6}$$

$$\sum_{n=-2}^{n=1} w'_n(\beta 1, \beta 2, 0) V_{i+1+n} = \beta_1 \sum_{n=-2}^{n=1} w'_n(\beta 1, \beta 2, 1) V_{i+n} \tag{6.7}$$

$$\sum_{n=-2}^{n=1} w''_n(\beta 1, \beta 2, 0) V_{i+1+n} = \beta_1^2 \sum_{n=-2}^{n=1} w''_n(\beta 1, \beta 2, 1) V_{i+n}$$
$$+ \beta_2 \sum_{n=-2}^{n=1} w'_n(\beta 1, \beta 2, 1) V_{i+n}. \tag{6.8}$$

Equating coefficients of the vertices $V_{i+n}$, $n = -2, -1, 0, 2, 1$, we get,

$$0 = w_2(\beta 1, \beta 2, 1) \tag{6.9}$$

$$w_{n-1}(\beta 1, \beta 2, 0) = w_n(\beta 1, \beta 2, 1), \qquad r = -1, 0, 1 \tag{6.10}$$

$$w_1(\beta 1, \beta 2, 0) = 0 \tag{6.11}$$

$$0 = \beta 1 w'_2(\beta 1, \beta 2, 1) \tag{6.12}$$

$$w'_{n-1}(\beta_1, \beta_2, 0) = \beta_1 w'_n(\beta_1, \beta_2, 1), \; n = -1, 0, 1 \tag{6.13}$$

$$w'_1(\beta_1, \beta_2, 0) = 0 \tag{6.14}$$

$$0 = \beta_1^2 w''_2(\beta_1, \beta_2, 1) + \beta_2 w'_2(\beta_1, \beta_2, 1) \tag{6.15}$$

$$w''_{n-1}(\beta_1, \beta_2, 0) = \beta_1^2 w''_n(\beta_1, \beta_2, 1) + \beta 2 W'_n(\beta_1, \beta_1, 1), \; n = -1, 0, 1 \tag{6.16}$$

$$w''_1(\beta_1, \beta_2, 0) = 0. \tag{6.17}$$

We obtain the coefficient functions, $c_{mn}$, in equation(6.2) for $m = 0, 1, 2, 3$ and $n = -2, -1, 0, 1$ once we differentiate the basis functions and get their values at $t = 0$ and $t = 1$. These provide us a system of 15 linear equations in 16 unknowns. Hence, we need one more constraint to determine the coefficients uniquely. The adequate constraint is chosen to satisfy the convex hull property to normalize the basis functions at $t = 0$.

$$
\begin{aligned}
c_{3,-2} + c_{2,-2} + c_{1,-2} + c_{0,-2} &= 0 \\
c_{3,r} + c_{2,r} + c_{1,r} + c_{0,r} &= c_{0,r-1} \quad r = -1, 0, 1 \\
c_{0,1} &= 0 \\
\beta_1(c3, -2 + 2c2, -2 + c_{1,-2}) &= 0 \\
\beta_1(3c_{3,r} + 2c2, r + c_{1,r}) &= c_{1,r-1} \quad r = -1, 0, 1 \ (6.18) \\
c_{1,1} &= 0 \\
3(2\beta_1^2 + \beta_2)c_{3,-2} + 2(\beta_1^2 + \beta_2)c_{2,-2} + \beta_2 c_{1,-2} &= 0 \\
3(2\beta_1^2 + \beta_2)c_{3,r} + 2(\beta_1^2 + \beta_2)c_{2,r} + \beta_2 c_{1,r} &= 2c_{2,r-1} \quad r = -1, 0, 1 \\
c_{2,1} &= 0.
\end{aligned}
$$

The convex hull property to normalize the basis function at $t = 0$ is

$$c_{0,-2} + c_{0,-1} + c_{0,0} + c_{0,1} = 1. \tag{6.19}$$

Note that, $c_{0,1}$, $c_{1,1}$, and $c_{2,1}$ are zero. Hence we have effectively thirteen equations in thirteen unknowns. The unknowns are coefficient functions of $\beta_1$ and $\beta_2$. Barsky [15] used a computer algebra system "REDUCE" to determine the coefficients as

$$
\begin{aligned}
c_{0,-2} &= 2\beta_1^3/\delta \\
c_{1,-2} &= -6\beta_1^3/\delta \\
c_{2,-2} &= 6\beta_1^3/\delta \\
c_{3,-2} &= -2\beta_1^3/\delta \\
c_{0,-1} &= 4\beta_1^2 + 4\beta_1 + \beta_2/\delta \\
c_{1,-1} &= 6\beta_1(\beta_1^2 - 1)/\delta \\
c_{2,-1} &= 3(-2\beta_1^3 - 2\beta_1^2 - \beta_2)/\delta \\
c_{3,-1} &= 2(\beta_1^3 + \beta_1^2 + \beta_1 + \beta_2)/\delta \\
c_{0,0} &= 2/\delta \\
c_{1,0} &= 6\beta_1/\delta \\
c_{2,0} &= 3(2\beta_1^2 + \beta_2)/\delta \\
c_{3,0} &= -2(\beta_1^2 + \beta_1 + \beta_2 + 1)/\delta \\
c_{3,1} &= 2/\delta,
\end{aligned}
\tag{6.20}
$$

with $\delta = 2\beta_1^3 + 4\beta_1^2 + 4\beta_1 + \beta_2 + 2$.

$\beta_1$ and $\beta_2$ are the shape parameters because they are defined through the unit tangent vector and curvature vector. Hence, one can use these two parameters to control the shape of a curve at the time of design. Given the two pieces of curve segments, say $P_1(t)$ and $P_2(t)$, $\beta_1$ and $\beta_2$ are visualized through

$$P_2'(0) = \beta_1 P_1'(1) \tag{6.21}$$

and

$$P_2''(0) = \beta_1^2 P_1''(1) + \beta_2 P_1'(1). \tag{6.22}$$

We can observe that $\beta_1 = 1$ provides the continuity of the parametric first derivative vector and, $\beta_1 = 1$ and $\beta_2 = 0$ provides the continuity of the parametric first and second derivative vectors. For $\beta_1 > 0$ and $\beta_2 \geq 0$, they form a basis, i.e., they are linearly independent. With the coefficients so determined, one can compute the four $w_n$ values in equation (6.2). These values after simplification can be written as

$$w_{-2}(\beta 1, \beta 2, t) = 2\beta_1^3 (1-t)^3 / \delta \tag{6.23}$$

$$\begin{aligned} w_{-1}(\beta 1, \beta 2, t) = [2\beta_1^3 t[t^2 - 3t + 3] + 2\beta_1^2[t^3 - 3t^2 + 2] \\ + 2\beta_1[t^3 - 3t + 2] + \beta_2[2t^3 - 3t^2 + 1]]/\delta \end{aligned} \tag{6.24}$$

$$\begin{aligned} w_0(\beta 1, \beta 2, t) = [2\beta_1^2 t^2[-t + 3] + 2\beta_1 t[-t^2 + 3] \\ + \beta_2 t^2[-2t + 3] + 2[-t^3 + 1]]/\delta \end{aligned} \tag{6.25}$$

$$w_1(\beta 1, \beta 2, t) = 2t^3 / \delta. \tag{6.26}$$

## 6.3 Design Criteria for a Curve

In order to design a curve with two pieces of curve segments, say $P_1(t)$ and $P_2(t)$, we need to maintain position continuity, first order continuity, and curvature continuity. The $i$th curve segment in terms of $\beta_1$ and $\beta_2$ can be written as

$$\begin{aligned} P_i(t) = \ &(2\beta_1^3(1-t)^3/\delta)V_{i-2} \\ &+ ([2\beta_1^3 t[t^2 - 3t + 3] + 2\beta_1^2[t^3 - 3t^2 + 2] \\ &+ 2\beta_1[t^3 - 3t + 2] + \beta_2[2t^3 - 3t^2 + 1]]/\delta)V_{i-1} \\ &+ ([2\beta_1^3 t[t^2 - 3t + 3] + 2\beta_1^2[t^3 - 3t^2 + 2] \\ &+ 2\beta_1[t^3 - 3t + 2] + \beta_2[2t^3 - 3t^2 + 1]]/\delta)V_{i-0} \\ &+ ([2\beta_1^2 t^2[-t + 3] + 2\beta_1 t[-t^2 + 3] \\ &+ \beta_2 t^2[-2t + 3] + 2[-t^3 + 1]]/\delta)V_{i+1}. \end{aligned} \tag{6.27}$$

The first derivative of the curve $P_i'(t)$ can be computed through

$$w_{-2}'(\beta 1, \beta 2, t) = -6\beta_1^3(1-t^2)/\delta \tag{6.28}$$

$$w'_{-1}(\beta 1, \beta 2, t) = (6\beta_1^3[t^2 - 2t + 1] + \beta_1^2 t[t - 1] \\ + \beta_1[t^2 - 1] + \beta_2 t[t - 1])/\delta \tag{6.29}$$

$$w'_0(\beta 1, \beta 2, t) = 6(\beta_1^2 t(-t + 2) + \beta_1[-t^2 + 1] \\ + \beta_2 t[-t + 1] - t^2)/\delta \tag{6.30}$$

$$w'_1(\beta 1, \beta 2, t) = 6t^2/\delta. \tag{6.31}$$

Therefore,

$$P'_i(t) = (-6\beta_1^3(1 - t^2))V_{i-2}/\delta \\ + (6\beta_1^3[t^2 - 2t + 1] + \beta_1^2 t[t - 1] \\ + \beta_1[t^2 - 1] + \beta_2 t[t - 1])V_{i-1}/\delta \\ + 6(\beta_1^2 t(-t + 2) + \beta_1[-t^2 + 1] \\ + \beta_2 t[-t + 1] - t^2)V_0/\delta \\ + 6t^2 V_{i+1}/\delta. \tag{6.32}$$

The second derivative of the curve $P''_i(t)$ can be computed through

$$w''_{-2}(\beta 1, \beta 2, t) = 12\beta_1^3(1 - t)/\delta \tag{6.33}$$

$$w''_{-1}(\beta 1, \beta 2, t) = 6(2\beta_1^3[t - 1] + 2\beta_1^2[t - 1] \\ + 2\beta_1 t + \beta_2[2t - 1])/\delta \tag{6.34}$$

$$w''_0(\beta 1, \beta 2, t) = 6(2\beta_1^2(-t + 1) - 2\beta_1 t \\ + \beta_2[-2t + 1] - 2t)/\delta \tag{6.35}$$

$$w''_1(\beta 1, \beta 2, t) = 12t/\delta. \tag{6.36}$$

This yields,

$$P''_i(t) = (12\beta_1^3(1 - t))V_{i-2}/\delta \\ + 6(2\beta_1^3[t - 1] + 2\beta_1^2[t - 1] \\ + 2\beta_1 t + \beta_2[2t - 1])V_{i-1}/\delta \\ + 6(2\beta_1^2(-t + 1) - 2\beta_1 t \\ + \beta_2[-2t + 1] - 2t)V_0/\delta \\ + 12t V_{i+1}/\delta. \tag{6.37}$$

### 6.3.1 Shape Parameters

Barsky also examined the conditions for continuous shape parameters. Let $\beta_{1,i}(t)$ and $\beta_{2,i}(t)$ be the values of the shape parameters at the point $P_i(t)$, where $i = 1, 2, \cdots, m$. Hence, we can choose different values of shape parameters to exhibit the local behavior of the curve. Now, if we consider a complete curve consisting of many pieces, then at each joint between two such pieces, shape parameters should have unique values, i.e., at $P_{i+1}(0) = P_i$, $i = 1, 2, \cdots, m - 1$ we have,

$$\beta_{1,i+1}(0) = \beta_{1,i}(1),$$
$$\beta_{2,i+1}(0) = \beta_{2,i}(1), \quad i = 1, 2, \cdots, m - 1.$$

When an user specifies the values of $\beta_1$ and $\beta_2$, it can be taken as discrete parameter values. We represent the discrete values of $\beta_{1,i}$ and $\beta_{2,i}$ as $\alpha_{1,i}$ and $\alpha_{2,i}$ respectively. Therefore, we write, $\beta_{1,1}(0) = \alpha_{1,0}$ and $\beta_{2,1}(0) = \alpha_{2,0}$. Thus, between two pieces of curves we can write,

$$\beta_{1,i+1}(0) = \alpha_{1,i} = \beta_{1,i}(1),$$
$$\beta_{2,i+1}(0) = \alpha_{2,i} = \beta_{2,i}(1), \quad i = 1, 2, \cdots, m - 1.$$

Hence, $\alpha_{1,m} = \beta_{1,m}(1)$ and $\alpha_{2,m} = \beta_{2,m}(1)$. A solution for this is as follows:

$$\begin{aligned} \beta_{1,i}(t) &= (1 - t)\alpha_{1,i-1} + t\alpha_{1,i}, \\ \beta_{2,i}(t) &= (1 - t)\alpha_{2,i-1} + t\alpha_{2,i}, \quad i = 1, 2, \cdots, m - 1. \end{aligned} \quad (6.38)$$

In addition, $delta = 2\beta_1^3 + 4\beta_1^2 + 4\beta_1 + \beta_2 + 2$ becomes

$$\delta_i(t) = 2\beta_{1,i}^3(t) + 4\beta_{1,i}^2(t) + 4\beta_{1,i}(t) + \beta_{2,i}(t) + 2.$$

Finally, the discrete analogue to $\delta_i(t)$ is

$$\begin{aligned} \gamma_0 &= \delta_1(0), \\ \gamma_i &= \delta_i(1). \end{aligned}$$

### 6.3.2 End Conditions of Beta Spline Curves

Suppose we have $m+1$ control vertices, say $V_0, V_1, V_2, \cdots, V_m$. Then the control polygon defined by these vertices help to generate $m - 2$ pieces of a complete curve curve, namely, $P_2(t)$, $P_3(t)$, $\cdots$, $P_{m-1}(t)$. The $\beta$-spline curve starts at

$$P_2(0) = (2\alpha_{1,0}^3 V_0 + (\gamma_1 - 2\alpha_{1,0}^3 - 2)V_1 + 2V_2)/\gamma_1 \quad (6.39)$$

and ends at

$$P_{m-1}(1) = (2\alpha_{1,m}^3 V_{m-2} + (\gamma_{m-1} - 2\alpha_{1,m}^3 - 2)V_{m-1} + 2V_m)/\gamma_{m-1}. \quad (6.40)$$

In a real situation we should have the objective for the curve to start at $V_0$ and end at $V_m$. This is accomplished through the use of multiple vertices as well as by phantom vertices.

## Double Vertices

Double vertices mean a vertex is considered twice to generate a piece of curve. So, when $V_0$ and $V_m$ are considered twice, we get two more pieces of the complete curve, one at the beginning and the other at the terminal end. This means, instead of $P_2(t)$, $P_3(t)$, $\cdots$, $P_{m-1}(t)$, we get $P_1(t)$, $P_2(t)$, $P_3(t)$, $\cdots$, $P_{m-1}(t)$, $P_m(t)$. Additional pieces of the curve are then $P_1(t)$ and $P_m(t)$. These two pieces of the curve are given by

$$P_1(t) = (w_{-2}(t) + w_{-1}(t))V_0 + w_0(t)V_1 + w_1(t)V_2,$$
$$P_m(t) = w_{-2}(t)V_{m-2} + w_{-1}(t)V_{m-1} + (w_0(t) + w_1(t))V_m.$$

With these two additional pieces of curves, $\beta$-spline curve starts at

$$P_1(0) = (1 - \frac{2}{\gamma_0})V_0 + \frac{2}{\gamma_0}V_1,$$

and ends at

$$P_m(1) = 2\frac{\alpha_{1,m}^3}{\gamma_m}.V_{m-1} + (1 - 2\frac{\alpha_{1,m}^3}{\gamma_m})V_m.$$

The initial point of the curve is $\frac{2}{\gamma_0}$ along the vector from $V_0$ to $V_1$ and the terminal point is $(1 - 2\frac{\alpha_{1,m}^3}{\gamma_m})$ along the vector from $V_{m-1}$ to $V_m$. At both the end points, the curve is tangent to the control polygon.

The first derivative vector at the end points can be easily shown to be

$$P_1'(0) = 6\alpha_{1,0}(V_1 - V_0/\gamma_0),$$
$$P_m'(1) = 6\alpha_{1,m}(V_m - V_{m-1}/\gamma_m),$$

while the second derivative at each end point of the curve can be derived to be

$$P_1''(0) = 6(2\alpha_{1,0}^2 + \alpha_{2,0})(V_1 - V_0)/\gamma_0),$$
$$P_m''(1) = 6(2\alpha_{1,m} + \alpha_{2,m})(V_{m-1} - V_m)/\gamma_m).$$

From the above expressions for the first and second derivative vectors at each end point of the curve, we get after some algebraic manipulations

$$P_1''(0) = \{(2\alpha_{1,0}^2 + \alpha_{2,0})/\alpha_{1,0}\}P_1'(0),$$
$$P_m''(1) = \{-(2\alpha_{1,m} + \alpha_{2,m})/\alpha_{1,m}^2\}P_m'(1).$$

## Triple Vertices

For the use of double vertices, we get two extra pieces of curves at each end of the complete curve and these extra pieces of curves are $P_1(t)$ and $P_m(t)$. When we use triple vertices, we get one more piece of curve at each end, i.e., we get $P_0(t)$ and $P_{m+1}(t)$. These pieces of curves are given by

$$P_0(t) \quad = \{w_{-2}(t) + w_{-1}(t) + w_0(t)\}V_0 + w_1(t)V_1,$$
$$P_{m+1}(t) = w_{-2}(t)V_{m-1} + \{w_{-1}(t) + w_0(t) + w_1(t)\}V_m.$$

Upon substitution of these expressions, the basis functions become

$$P_0(t) \quad = \{1 - 2t^3/\delta_0(t)\}V_0 + \{2t^3/\delta_0(t)\}V_1,$$
$$P_{m+1}(t) = \{2(\beta_{1,m+1}(t)(1-t))^3/\delta_{m+1}(t)\}V_{m-1}$$
$$+\{1 - 2(\beta_{1,m+1}(t)(1-t))^3/\delta_{m+1}\}V_m.$$

As $t$ varies from 0 to 1, $P_0(t)$ traces a straight line segment starting at $V_0$ and ending at a point distant $2/\gamma_0$ along the vector $\mathbf{V_0 V_1}$. Similarly, $P_{m+1}(t)$ also traces a straight line segment from a point $-2\alpha_{1,m}^3/\gamma_m$ along the vector $\mathbf{V_{m-1} V_m}$ to the terminal point $V_m$. Use of triple vertices interpolates the end points.

**Phantom Vertices**

Phantom vertices are auxiliary vertices that are generally created for the purpose of additional pieces of curves. As these vertices are inaccessible to the users and are not displayed, they are named *phantom vertices*. Normally, they are defined in terms of the original control polygon vertices, and at each end point, the curve interpolates a specified point. This means $P_1(0) = P_0$ and $P_m(1) = P_m$.

From equation (6.1), solving for the phantom vertices we get,

$$V_1 \quad = (\gamma_0 P_0 - \{(\gamma_0 - 2\alpha_{1,0}^3 - 2)V_0 + 2V_1\})/2\alpha_{1,0}^3,$$
$$V_{m+1} = (\gamma_m P_m - \{(\gamma_m - 2\alpha_{1,m}^3 - 2)V_m + 2\alpha_{1,m}^3 V_{m-1}\})/2. \tag{6.41}$$

First derivatives are then

$$P_1'(0) \quad = 6\alpha_{1,0}(-\alpha_{1,0}^2 V_1 + (\alpha_{1,0}^2 - 1)V_0 + V_1)/\gamma_0,$$
$$P_m'(1) = 6(-\alpha_{1,m}^2 V_{m-1} + (\alpha_{1,m}^2 - 1)V_m + V_{m+1})/\gamma_m.$$

Substituting the expressions of phantom vertices in equation (6.41), the above expressions become

$$P_1'(0) \quad = 3(\{2(\alpha_{1,0}+1)V_1 + (\gamma_0 - 2\alpha_{1,0} - 2)V_0\}/\gamma_0 - P_0),$$
$$P_m'(1) = 3(\{(2\alpha_{1,m}^2(\alpha_{1,m}+1) - \gamma_m)V_m - 2\alpha_{1,m}^2(\alpha_{1,m}+1)V_{m-1}\}/\gamma_0 + P_m).$$

Similarly, the second derivative vector at each end point of the curve is

$$P_1''(0) = 6(\{(2\alpha_{1,0}^2 + \alpha_{2,0} - 2)V_1 - (\gamma_0 + 2\alpha_{1,0}^2 + \alpha_{2,0} - 2)V_0\}/\gamma_0$$
$$+P_0),$$
$$P_m''(1) = 6(\{(-2\alpha_{1,m}^3 + 2\alpha_{1,m} + \alpha_{2,m})V_{m-1} - (\gamma_m - 2\alpha_{1,m}^3 + 2\alpha_{1,m}$$
$$+\alpha_{2,m})V_m\}/\gamma_m + P_m). \tag{6.42}$$

The first and second derivative vectors at each end point of the curve are, in general, linearly independent. Thus, the curvature is non-zero at each end point of the curve.

**End Vertex Interpolation**

It is convenient as well as meritorious to start the curve at $V_0$ and end at $V_m$. It is a special case of the previous end conditions where $P_0 = V_0$ and $P_m = V_m$. From equation (6.41), phantom vertices can be written as

$$V_{-1} = \{(\alpha_{1,0}^3 + 1)V_0 - V_1\}/\alpha_{1,0}^3,$$
$$V_{m+1} = (\alpha_{1,m}^3 + 1)V_m - \alpha_{1,m}^3 V_{m-1}.$$

Values of the first derivative vectors at each end point are

$$P_1'(0) = 6(\alpha_{1,0} + 1)(V_1 - V_0)/\gamma_0,$$
$$P_m'(1) = 6\alpha_{1,m}^2(\alpha_{1,m} + 1)(V_m - V_{m-1})/\gamma_0.$$

This shows that the curve is tangent to the control polygon at each end point. Substitution into equation (6.42) gives

$$P_1''(0) = 6(2\alpha_{1,0}^2 + \alpha_{2,0} - 2)(V_1 - V_0)/\gamma_0,$$
$$P_m''(1) = 6(2\alpha_{1,m}^3 - 2\alpha_{1,m} - \alpha_{2,m})(V_m - V_{m-1})/\gamma_m.$$

Hence, at the initial point of the curve, the first and second derivative vectors are related as

$$P_1''(0) = \{(2\alpha_{1,0}^2 + \alpha_{2,0} - 2)/(\alpha_{1,0} + 1)\}P_1'(0),$$
$$P_m''(1) = \{(2\alpha_{1,m}^3 - 2\alpha_{1,m} - 2\alpha_{2,m})/\alpha_{1,m}^2(\alpha_{1,m} + 1)\}P_m'(1).$$

Assuming distinct vertices, the first and second derivatives are non-zero, and the first and second derivative vectors are linearly dependent at the initial and final points of the curve.

## 6.4 Beta-Spline Surface

A $\beta$ spline surface is a straightforward extension of the $\beta$ spline curve in two dimensions. Mathematically, it is the Cartesian cross product of two sets of orthogonal curves. The $(i, j)th$ $\beta$-spline surface patch is given by

$$S_{i,j}(u, v) = \sum_{n=-2}^{n=1} \sum_{m=0}^{m=3} c_{mn}(\beta 1, \beta 2) \, u^m \quad \times$$
$$\sum_{q=-2}^{q=1} \sum_{p=0}^{p=3} e_{pq}(\beta 1, \beta 2) \, v^p \, V_{i+n,j+q}. \tag{6.43}$$

Rearranging, we get

$$S_{i,j}(u,v) = \sum_{m=0}^{m=3} ( \sum_{n=-2}^{n=1} c_{mn}(\beta 1, \beta 2)) \, u^m \quad \times$$
$$\sum_{p=0}^{p=3} ( \sum_{q=-2}^{q=1} e_{pq}(\beta 1, \beta 2)) \, v^p \, V_{i+n,j+q}.$$

$$(6.44)$$

End conditions for a surface can be written exactly in the same way as for a curve.

## 6.5 Possible Applications in Vision

Since $\beta$-spline has two more shape parameters, it provides more flexibility and hence data can be approximated in a much better way. Normally, a $\beta$-spline surface interpolates the corner points but not all the other control points. Hence, a suitable interpolation technique can be envisaged and used to model the disparity data in stereo vision. The $\beta$ surface with minimum energy may produce a continuous smooth surface with suitable discontinuities controlled by shape parameters. A comparison between the Laplacian or biharmonic operator yielded surface and the $\beta$ surface, each based on disparity data, may be useful to judge the merit of the $\beta$ surface. It should be noted that both the Laplacian and biharmonic operator yield a good surface where the disparity is continuous but will provide a poor result when the disparity is discontinuous, e.g., over the region where one object occludes the other.

Another potential application of $\beta$-spline may be in feature extraction in pattern recognition. An object may be decomposed into many surface patches and each of them can be approximated well by the $\beta$-spline. The approximation parameters, which are essentially the approximated control points along with the values of two shape parameters, namely the $\beta_1$ and $\beta_2$ parameters, for each surface patch may act as its feature vector.

## 6.6 Concluding Remarks

$\beta$-spline has been examined from the standpoint of computer graphics and not from the viewpoint of other research areas. Very little work using $\beta$-spline has been done in image processing and machine vision. It may, therefore, be effective if the field is investigated thoroughly.

# Part III

Advanced Methodologies

# Discrete Splines and Vision

## 7.1 Introduction

This chapter presents a theoretical background of discrete splines: how it can be used in the area of subdivision so that refinement can be done for better representation and better visualization, and how to examine the feasibility of discrete smoothing splines to detect shapes of opaque physical objects from their shading. For this, we first look at the theory of discrete splines as developed by Cohen, Lyche, and Risenfeld [41] and use it for understanding the underlying structure of subdivision algorithms.

Next, we try to view knots of smoothing discrete splines as the discrete grid points defined in the greylevel image plane, and examine the feasibility of using such a spline to detect shapes of objects with the help of a reflectance map [77], defined in terms of image brightness values and surface gradients. The feasibility of using smoothing splines in the shape from shading problem has been discussed by David Lee [101].

## 7.2 Discrete Splines

Discrete splines were introduced by Mangasarian and Schumaker [118] as solutions to certain minimization problems involving differences instead of derivatives. Lyche [111, 112] studied approximation properties of discrete splines. Schumaker [148] provided discrete B-splines on a uniform partition, while de-Boor [55] provided the same on a nonuniform partition.

We have already discussed B-splines $B_{i,k}$ of order $k$ in a previous chapter. We now consider a piecewise polynomial $f(x)$ in terms of $B_{i,k}$, so that

$$f(x) = \sum_{i=1}^{n} B_{i,k}(x) P_i. \qquad (7.1)$$

The knots $\tau = \{\tau_1, \tau_2, \cdots \tau_{n+k}\}$ can be made uniform as well as multiple.

Let $\tau^a = \{\tau_1^a, \tau_2^a, \cdots \tau_l^a\}$ be the knots in addition to existing ones. If $m = n+l$ and $t = \{t_1, t_2, \cdots t_{m+k}\} = \tau \cup \tau^a$ is the new knot sequence in nondecreasing order, then $f(x)$ can be written as a linear combination of the B-splines, $N_{j,k}$ on $t$, with $j = 1, 2, \cdots m$, i.e.,

$$f(x) = \sum_{j=1}^{m} d_j N_{j,k}(x), \tag{7.2}$$

$d_j$s are unknown coefficients and need to be computed. There are several ways to compute $d_j$s. We cite a few of them.

(1) One can choose $m$ points, say, $\rho_1, \rho_2, \cdots, \rho_m$, and solve the following interpolation problem:

$$\sum_{j=1}^{m} d_j N_{j,k}(\rho_i) = f(\rho_i), \qquad i = 1, 2 \cdots, m. \tag{7.3}$$

This set of linear equations has a unique solution $d_1, d_2, \cdots d_m$ if $t_j < \rho_j < t_{j+k}, j = 1, 2, \cdots m$. The coefficient matrix is totally positive, banded, and can be inverted by Gaussian elimination without pivoting in $O(mk^3)$ operations [57].

(2) Another technique to compute $d_j$s is to use the quasi-interpolant of deBoor and Fix [56]. If

$$\lambda_i f = \frac{1}{(k-1)!} \sum_{r=0}^{k-1} (-1)^{k-1-r} \Psi_j^{(r)}(a_j) f^{(k-1-r)}(a_j), \tag{7.4}$$

where $a_j$ is any point on $(t_j, t_{j+k})$ and

$$\Psi_j(y) = \prod_{r=1}^{k-1} (y - t_{j+r}), \tag{7.5}$$

then

$$\lambda_j N_{i,k} = \delta_{i,j} = 1, \qquad i = j,$$
$$= 0, \qquad i \neq j.$$

Therefore, applying $\lambda_j$ on both sides of equation (7.2), we get

$$d_j = \lambda_j f, \qquad j = 1, 2, \cdots m. \tag{7.6}$$

Computation of $d_j$ gives advantages provided $f$ is given in its piecewise polynomial representation.

(3) One can also compute $d_j$ recursively. This method is similar to the subdivision scheme of Lane and Risenfeld [100] for the special case of Bézier curves (k-tuple knots) and for uniform knots.

Let us assume

$$d_j = \sum_{i=1}^{n} \alpha_{i,k}(j)P_i \tag{7.7}$$

for some $\alpha_{i,k}(j)$. Consider two different cases for understanding.
Case 1: $k = 1$ (step-functions)
In this case,

$$f(x) = \sum_{i=1}^{n} B_{i,1}(x)P_i, \tag{7.8}$$

where

$$\begin{aligned} B_{i,1} &= 1, \qquad \tau_i \le x < \tau_{i+1}, \\ &= 0, \qquad otherwise. \end{aligned}$$

If

$$f(x) = \sum_{j=1}^{m} N_{j,1}(x)d_j, \tag{7.9}$$

where

$$\begin{aligned} N_{j,1} &= 1, \qquad t_j \le x < t_{i+1}, \\ &= 0, \qquad otherwise, \end{aligned} \tag{7.10}$$

then

$$d_j = P_i, \qquad \tau_i \le t_j < \tau_{i+1}.$$

Therefore, in equation (7.7) we must have,

$$\begin{aligned} \alpha_{i,1}(j) &= 1, \qquad \tau_i \le t_j < \tau_{i+1}, \\ &= 0, \qquad otherwise. \end{aligned}$$

Hence, one can easily note that $\alpha_{i,1}(j) = B_{i,1}(t_j)$
Case 2: $k = 2$ (piecewise linear functions)
For this case, we can consider

$$f(x) = \sum_{i=1}^{n} B_{i,2}(x)P_i, \tag{7.11}$$

where

$$\begin{aligned} B_{i,2}(x) &= (x - \tau_i)/(\tau_{i+1} - \tau_i), \qquad \tau_i \le x < \tau_{i+1}, \\ &= (\tau_{i+2} - x)/(\tau_{i+2} - \tau_{i+1}), \qquad \tau_{i+1} \le x < \tau_{i+2}, \\ &= 0, \qquad\qquad\qquad\qquad\qquad otherwise. \end{aligned}$$

Now suppose

$$f(x) = \sum_{j=1}^{m} N_{j,2}(x)d_j, \tag{7.12}$$

where

$$\begin{aligned} N_{j,2}(x) &= (x - t_j)/(t_{j+1} - t_j), \qquad t_j \le x < t_{i+1}, \\ &= (t_{j+2} - x)/(t_{j+2} - t_{j+1}), \qquad t_{j+1} \le x < t_{i+2}, \\ &= 0, \qquad\qquad\qquad\qquad\qquad otherwise. \end{aligned}$$

If $\nu$ and $j$ are such that

$$\tau_\nu \le t_{j+1} < \tau_{\nu+1},$$

then

$$
\begin{aligned}
f(t_{j+1}) &= d_j \\
&= \{(\tau_{\nu+1} - t_{j+1})P_{\nu-1} + (t_{j+1} - \tau_\nu)P_\nu\}/(\tau_{\nu+1} - \tau_\nu).
\end{aligned}
\tag{7.13}
$$

Now, equation (7.7) is valid with,

$$
\begin{aligned}
\alpha_{i,2}(j) &= (t_{j+1} - \tau_i)/(\tau_{i+1} - \tau_i), & \tau_i \le t_{j+1} < \tau_{i+1}, \\
&= (t_{i+2} - t_{j+1})/(\tau_{i+2} - \tau_{i+1}), & \tau_{i+1} \le t_{j+1} < \tau_{i+2}, \\
&= 0, & otherwise.
\end{aligned}
$$

Hence, we note that $\alpha_{i,2}(j) = B_{i,2}(t_{j+1})$. Here, we observe that the numbers $\alpha_{i,2}(j)$ are related to the B-spline $B_{i,k}$ for $k = 1, 2$. $\alpha_{i,k}(j)$ is a discrete spline.

## 7.2.1 Relation Between $\alpha_{i,k}$ and $B_{i,k}$, $k > 2$

We have assumed $N_{i,k}$ as B-splines on a partition $\{t_j\}$ and $B_{i,k}$ as B-splines on a coarser subpartition $\{\tau_i\}$. Let us now consider the following theorem.
**Theorem 1**:
For all $x$, we have,

$$B_{i,k}(x) = \sum_{j=1}^m \alpha_{i,k}(j)N_{j,k}(x) \qquad i = 1, 2, \cdots m, \tag{7.14}$$

where

$$\alpha_{i,j}(j) = (\tau_{i+k} - \tau_i)[\tau_i, \cdots \tau_{i+k}]\phi_{j,k}, \tag{7.15}$$

$$\phi_{j,k}(y) = (y - a_j)_+^0 \Psi_{j,k}(y), \tag{7.16}$$

with $\Psi_{j,k}(y)$ given by equation (7.5). Here,

$$
\begin{aligned}
(y - a_j)_+^0 &= 1 & y > a_j \\
&= 0 & otherwise,
\end{aligned}
$$

$a_j$ can be chosen anywhere in $[t_j, t_{j+k})$, and $[\tau_i, \cdots \tau_{i+k}]\phi_{j,k}$ denotes a divided difference. We have the following remarks:
(1) $\alpha_{i,k}(j)$ is called a discrete spline.
(2) The numbers $\alpha_{i,k}(j)$ in equation (7.7) are the discrete B-splines given by equation (7.15).
From equation (7.1) and equation (7.14), we have,

$$f(x) = \sum_{i=1}^{n} B_{i,k}(x) P_i$$

$$= \sum_{i=1}^{n} \sum_{j=1}^{m} P_i \alpha_{i,k}(j) N_{j,k}(x)$$

$$= \sum_{j=1}^{m} [\sum_{i=1}^{n} P_i \alpha_{i,k}(j)] N_{j,k}(x)$$

where $\alpha_{i,k}(j)$ is given by equation (7.15). Comparing this with equation (7.7), we get the following statement:

(3) For $k = 1$, from equation (7.15),

$$\alpha_{i,1}(j) = (\tau_{i+1} - a_j)_+^0 - (\tau_i - a_j)_+^0. \tag{7.17}$$

It agrees with $\alpha_{i,1}(j)$ given by case 1, for any $a_j \in [t_j, t_{j+1})$. Similarly, for $k = 2$ we get,

$$\alpha_{i,2}(j) = [\tau_{i+1}, \tau_{i+2}]\phi_{j,2} - [\tau_i, \tau_{i+1}]\phi_{j,2}$$

with

$$\phi_{j,2}(y) = (y - a_j)_+^0 (y - t_{j+1}).$$

This agrees with $\alpha_{i,2}(j)$ for the case 2, described above, for any $a_j \nu[t_j.t_{j+2})$.

Now to prove Theorem 1, we present two lemmas. The first lemma is due to Marsden [120].

**Lemma 1**:

For any $y \in \Re$ and any $x \in [t_k, t_{m+1})$, we have

$$(y - x)^{k-1} = \sum_{j=1}^{m} \Psi_{j,k}(y) N_{j,k}(x), \tag{7.18}$$

where $\Psi_{j,k}$ is given by equation (7.5).

*Proof* (deBoor [53]):

For $k = 1$ we get from the lemma 1, $1 = \sum_{j=1}^{m} N_{j,1}(x)$, which follows from equation (7.10). For $k \geq 2$, one can use the recurrence relation of deBoor [53], Cox [47]

$$N_{j,k}(x) = (x - t_j)Q_{j,k-1}(x) + (t_{j+k} - x)Q_{j+1,k-1}(x), \tag{7.19}$$

where

$$\begin{aligned} Q_{j,k}(x) &= N_{j,k}(x)/(t_{j+k} - t_j), & t_{j+k} > t_j, \\ &= 0, & otherwise. \end{aligned} \tag{7.20}$$

Letting $\zeta_k = (y - x)^{k-1}$ in equation (7.18), we get

$$\zeta_k = \sum_{j=1}^{m} \Psi_{j,k}(y)[(x - t_j)Q_{j,k-1}(x) + (t_{j+k} - x)Q_{j+1,k-1}(x)].$$

Since $x \in [t_k, t_{m+1})$, we have $Q_{1,k-1}(x) = Q_{m+1,k-1}(x) = 0$. Hence, $\zeta_k$ can be written as

$$\zeta_k = \sum_{j=2}^{m} \gamma_{j,k}(x, y)Q_{j,k-1}(x), \tag{7.21}$$

where

$$\gamma_{j,k}(x, y) = \Psi_{j,k}(y)(x - t_j) + \Psi_{j-1,k}(y)(t_{j+k-1} - x).$$

But it can be shown in a straightforward way that

$$\gamma_{j,k}(x, y) = (y - x)(t_{j+k-1} - t_j)\Psi_{j,k-1}(y).$$

Therefore, $\zeta_k$ can be written as

$$\zeta_k = (y - x) \sum_{j=2}^{m} \Psi_{j,k-1}(y)(t_{j+k-1} - t_j)Q_{j,k-1}(x).$$

Since, $(t_{j+k-1} - t_j)Q_{j,k-1}(x) = N_{j,k-1}(x)$ and $N_{1,k-1}(x) = 0$, we get $\zeta_k = (y - x)\zeta_{k-1}$ (from equation (7.18)). But then $\zeta_k = (y - x)^{k-1}\zeta_1$. since $\zeta_1 = 1$, equation (7.18), follows.

**Lemma 2**:

Let $\phi_j$ and $a_j$ be as in Theorem 1. For any $y \in t$ and any $x \in [t_k, t_{m+1})$,

$$(y - x)_+^{k-1} = \sum_{j=1}^{m} \phi_{j,k}(y)N_{j,k}(x). \tag{7.22}$$

*Proof:*

Let us fix $x$ and $\mu$ be such that $t_\mu \le x < t_{\mu+1}$. Since $N_{j,k}(x) = 0$ for $x \notin [t_j, t_{j+k})$, we have to show that

$$(y - x)_+^{k-1} = \sigma_k \overset{\text{def}}{=} \sum_{j=\mu-k+1}^{\mu} \phi_{j,k}(y)N_{j,k}(x). \tag{7.23}$$

Assume $y = t_\mu$. Since, $\phi_{j,k}(t_\mu)$ contains a factor $t_\mu - t_\mu$ for $j = \mu-k+1, \cdots, \mu-1$, we have $\sigma_k = \phi_{\mu,k}(t_\mu)N_{\mu,k}(x)$. But $\phi_{\mu,k}(t_\mu) = 0$ since $a_\mu \in [t_\mu, t_{\mu+k})$. Hence, $\sigma_k = 0 = (t_\mu - x)_+^{k-1}$ and equation (7.23) follows in this case. Similarly, if $y = t_{\mu-1}$, then $\sigma_k = \phi_{\mu-1,k}(t_{\mu-1})N_{\mu-1,k}(x) + \phi_{\mu,k}(t_{\mu-1})N_{\mu,k}(x) = 0 = (t_{\mu-1} - x)_+^{k-1}$. Continuing in this way, we see that equation (7.23) holds for $y = t_s$ and $s \le \mu$. Next let us assume $y = t_{\mu+1}$. Then $\sigma_k = \phi_{\mu-k+1,k}(t_{\mu+1})N_{\mu-k+1,k}(x)$. But $\phi_{\mu-k+1,k}(t_{\mu+1}) = \Psi_{\mu-k+1,k}(t_{\mu+1})$ and equation (7.23) follows from equation (7.18). Similarly, equation (7.23) follows from equation (7.18) for $y = t_s$ and $s \ge t_{\mu+1}$.

We shall now turn to the proof of Theorem 1.

Proof of Theorem 1:

Suppose $a_j \notin \{t_{j+1}, \cdots, t_{j+k-1}\}$. We can apply the divided difference equation (7.22) $[\tau_i, \cdots, \tau_{i+k}]$ on both sides of equation (7.22). Multiplying also by $\tau_{i+k} - \tau_i$, equation (7.14) follows. Since the right-hand side of equation (7.22) is constant as a function of $a_j \in [t_j, t_{j+k})$, $\alpha_{i,k}(j)$ is also independent of $a_j$. One can then let $a_j \in \{t_{j+1, \cdots, t_{j+k-1}}\}$ and take limits from either left or right.

We next describe a recurrence relation in Theorem 2 for $\alpha_{i,k}(j)$. One can see its proof in the article by Cohen et al. [41].

**Theorem 2:**

Suppose $\tau_{i+k} > \tau_i$ and that $\alpha_{i,k}(j)$ is given by equation (7.15). Then

$$\begin{aligned} \alpha_{i,1}(j) &= 1, & \tau_i \leq t_j < \tau_{i+j}, \\ &= 0, & otherwise. \end{aligned} \tag{7.24}$$

Moreover for $k \geq 2$ and for all $i, j$,

$$\alpha_{i,k}(j) = (t_{j+k-1} - \tau_i)\beta_{i,k-1}(j) + (\tau_{i+k} - t_{j+k-1})\beta_{i+1,k-1}(j), \tag{7.25}$$

where

$$\begin{aligned} \beta_{i,k}(j) &= \alpha_{i,k}(j)/(\tau_{i+k} - \tau_i), & \tau_{i+k} > \tau_i, \\ &= 0, & otherwise. \end{aligned} \tag{7.26}$$

The discrete splines $\alpha_{i,k}(j)$ is thus seen to have properties similar to those for $B_{i,k}$.

### 7.2.2 Some Properties of $\alpha_{i,k}(j)$

If $\alpha_{i,k}(j)$ are as in Theorem 2, then we can consider some of its properties in the following corollary.

Corollary 1:

(1) $\alpha_{i,k}(j) = 0$ for $i \notin \{\mu - k + 1, \cdots, \mu\}$ with $1 \leq j \leq m$ and $\mu$ be such that $\tau_\mu \leq t_j < \tau_{\mu+1}$;

(2) $\alpha_{i,k}(j) \geq 0, \forall (i, j)$;

(3) $\sum_{i=1}^{n} \alpha_{i,k}(j) = 1, \tau_k \leq t_j < \tau_{n+1}$.

Property (1) says that for each $j$, there are at most $k$ discrete B-splines $\alpha_{\mu-k+1,k}(j), \cdots, \alpha_{\mu,k}(j)$ with a (possible) nonzero value.

One can now compute $d_j$ in equation (7.7) when $P_i$s are known. Equation (7.7) can be written as

$$d(j) = \sum_{i=1}^{n} \alpha_{i,k} P_i. \tag{7.27}$$

$\alpha_{i,k}(j)$ is a discrete B-spline and $d(j)$ is a linear combination of $\alpha_{i,k}(j)$ and so it is a discrete B-spline. Discrete splines have local support, as can be seen from the corollary 1. Similarity between the recurrence relations for $\alpha_{i,k}(j)$ in equation (7.25) and $B_{i,k}$ in equation (7.3) hence makes the computation of $d(j)$ very similar to the computation of $f(x)$ for some $x$ with $f(x)$ as given below.

$$f(x) = \sum_{i=1}^{n} B_{i,k}(x)P_i. \tag{7.28}$$

### 7.2.3 Algorithms

We shall now consider two different algorithms to compute discrete B-splines. We have already seen the discrete B-spline as

$$d(j) = \sum_{i=1}^{n} \alpha_{i,k}(j)P_i.$$

When $\tau_\mu \le t_j < \tau_{\mu+1}$,

$$d(j) = \sum_{i=\mu-k+1}^{\mu} \alpha_{i,k}(j)P_i. \tag{7.29}$$

To compute the spline, we need to compute $\alpha_{i,k}(j)$.

Algorithm 1:

For integers $k \ge 2$ and $j, \mu$ let $\tau_{\mu+2-k}, \cdots, \tau_{\mu+k-1}$ and $t_{j+1}, \cdots, t_{j+k-1}$ be given such that

$$\tau_{\mu+2-k} \le \cdots \le \tau_\mu < \tau_{\mu+1} \le \cdots \le \tau_{\mu+k-1} \tag{7.30}$$

and

$$\tau_\mu \le t_j < \tau_{\mu+1}. \tag{7.31}$$

The algorithm 1, computes $\alpha_{ir} = \alpha_{i,r}(j)$ as given by equation (7.15) or equation (7.25), $r = 1, 2, \cdots k$; $i = \mu + 1 - r, \cdots, \mu$. The discrete B-splines here are of order $\le k$ that can be nonzero for the given $j$. Steps in algorithm 1 are described as follows.

Step 1: $\alpha(\mu, 1) = 1; \mu2 = \mu;$

Step 2: for $r = 1, 2, \cdots k - 1$ do

        begin

           $\beta_1 = 0; tj = t(j + r);$

           for $i = \mu_2, \mu_2 + 1, \cdots, \mu$ do

           begin

               $d1 = tj - \tau(i); d2 = \tau(i + r) - tj;$

               $\beta = \alpha(i, r)/(d1 + d2);$

               $\alpha(i - 1, r + 1) = d2 * \beta + \beta_1;$

               $\beta_1 = d1 * \beta;$

        end

$$\alpha(\mu, r+1) = \beta_1;$$
$$\mu 2 = \mu 2 - 1;$$
end

One can also use an alternative algorithm to compute $d(j)$ as given by equation (7.29). Now, before we describe the algorithmic steps, we first consider the underlying background of it. By equation (7.25),

$$d(j) = \sum_{i=\mu-k+1}^{\mu} \alpha_{i,k(j)} P_i$$
$$= \sum_{i=\mu-k+1}^{\mu} [(t_{j+k-1} - \tau_i)\beta_{i,k-1}(j) + (\tau_{i+k} - t_{j+k-1})\beta_{i+1,k-1}(j)] P_i.$$

Since $\beta_{\mu-k+1,k-1(j)=\beta_{\mu+1,k-1}(j)} = 0$ by (1) in the corollary, we get,

$$d(j) = \sum_{i=\mu-k+2}^{\mu} \alpha_{i,k-1}(j) P_{i,j}^{[2]},$$

where

$$P_{i,j}^{[2]} = [(t_{j+k-1} - \tau_i)P_i + (\tau_{i+k-1} - t_{j+k-1})P_{i-1}]/(\tau_{i+k-1} - \tau_i).$$

In general, for $r = 1, 2, \cdots, k$,

$$d(j) = \sum_{i=\mu-k+r}^{\mu} \alpha_{i,k-r+1}(j) P_{i,j}^{[r]},$$

with

$$P_{i,j}^{[1]} = P_i$$

and

$$P_{i,j}^{[r+1]} = [(t_{j+k-r} - \tau_i)P_{i,j}^{[r]} + (\tau_{i+k-r} - t_{j+k-r})P_{i-1,j}^{[r]}]/(\tau_{i+k-r} - \tau_i).$$

Therefore, when $r = k$, we have

$$d(j) = \alpha_{\mu,1}(j) P_{\mu,j}^{[k]}$$
$$= P_{\mu,j}^{[k]}.$$

With this, we write down Algorithm 2 to compute $d(j)$.
Algorithm 2:
Step 1: $\mu 2 = \mu - k + 1$;
Step 2: for $i = \mu_2, \mu_2 + 1, \cdots, \mu$ do
    begin
    $P_i^{[1]} = P_i$;
Step 3: for $r = 1, 2, \cdots, k - 1$ do

```
        begin
            μ2 = μ2 − 1; kr = k − r; tj = t(j + kr);
            for i = μ, μ − 1, · · · , μ2
            begin
```
$$d1 = tj − \tau(i); \quad d2 = \tau(i + kr) − tj;$$
$$P_i^{[r+1]} = (P_i^{[r]} * d1 + P_{i-1}^{[r]} * d2)/(d1 + d2)$$
```
            end
        end
    end
```

Step 4: $d(j) = P_\mu^{[k]}$

Since $\tau_\mu < \tau_{\mu+1}$, we must always have $d1 + d2 > 0$. Also, $k, j, \mu, \tau_i$ and $t_j$ are exactly the same as in Algorithm 1.


## 7.3 Subdivision of Control Polygon

Subdivision of a control polygon helps to refine a curve or a surface. Subdivision basically is to introduce new control points. The refinement or modification, so achieved, enhances the curve or surface accuracy in visualization. This section examines the Oslo algorithm to insert new control points. We use algorithm 2 for this purpose.

**Input**:

Total number of vertices in the original polygon = N.

Vertices of the original polygon in planar or spatial coordinates,
$P = (P(0), P(1), · · · , P(N))$. Order of the B-spline curve = K.

Knot vector in the original polygon is $Tau = (Tau(0), Tau(1), · · · , Tau(N + K))$.

Refinement knot vector $T = (T(0), T(1), · · · , T(N))$ for a particular application, $Q \geq N + K$.

**Output**:

Vertices $D = (D(0), D(1), · · · , D(Q − K)) = D$ of the subdivided polygon for the same curve.

Pseudo code for the algorithm is as follows.

```
procedure loop (K,N,Q,P,Tau,T,D)
begin
        for j=0 to (Q-K)do
        begin
            find (K+N,Tau,T,j,Mu);
            subdiv (P,K,Tau,T,K,Mu,j,D(j));
        end
end
procedure find (KN,Tau,T,j,Mu);
/* this routine finds the unique Mu */
/* so that Tau(MU)≤ T(j) < Tau(MU+1) */
```

```
begin
    for i=0 to (KN-1)do
    if(T(j) ≥ Tau(i))then MU=i;
end
```

recursive procedure subdiv(P,K,Tau,T,RP1,I,J,PP);
/* PP is output and equals $D_{ij}^{[RP1]}$ */

```
begin
    r=RP1-1;
    if (r > 0) then begin
                        PP2=0;
                        PP1=0;
                        P1=T(J+K-r)-Tau(I);
                        P2=Tau(I+K-r)-T(J+K-r);
                        if (P1 <> 0) subdiv(P,K,Tau,T,r,I,J,PP1);
                        if (P2 <> 0) subdiv(P,K,Tau,T,r,I-1,J,PP2);
                        PP=(P1*PP1+P2*PP2)/(P1+p2);
                   end
              else PP=P(I);
end
```

An iterative form for subdiv can also be found in [41].

## 7.4 Smoothing Discrete Splines and Vision

To recover the shape of a 3d surface from the reflectance map is an important problem in shape from shading. Reflectance map, developed by Horn [77], relates image brightness to surface orientation. Reflectance map, therefore, is a powerful concept behind the recovery of the shape of a physical surface from its image brightness values and is a major starting point. Ikeuchi and Horn [81] initiated numerical shape from shading. David Lee [101] followed the model of Ikeuchi and Horn [81] and constructed a smoothing spline as a solution using regularization. He reduces the problem to solving a large system of non-linear equations for a discrete spline. For the difficulty of the direct method, he provided an iterative method. The algorithm converges for a range of the regularization parameter and the discrete smoothing spline is unique for that range. It has been seen that even provably convergent iterative schemes are difficult to devise [81, 78].

## 7.5 Occluding Boundaries and Shape from Shading

Occluding boundary is important and informative in the shape from shading problem because for all points on such a boundary one can compute surface orientations directly from image brightness values. Suppose the image domain $D$ of an object is connected and compact. Let $\partial D$ be the boundary and $D^i$

the interior of $D$, respectively. The silhouette for an object in the image plane provides the outline of projection. If the object has a smooth surface, then the silhouette provides occluding boundaries, where the surface orientation is known. Though it has a problem, even then surface orientations can be made known depending on the nature of the reflectance map, e.g., if the reflectance map is a strictly monotonic function of gradients along $x$ and $y$ axes. David Lee, however, considered the surface orientations known on the boundary $\partial D$ of the image domain that contains the occluding boundary.

### 7.5.1 Image Irradiance Equation

For a Lambertian surface illuminated by a single distant point source, the reflectance map is

$$R(p,q) = \frac{1 + pp_s + qq_s}{\sqrt{1 + p^2 + q^2}\sqrt{1 + p_s^2 + q_s^2}}. \tag{7.32}$$

$R(p,q)$ is the function of surface gradient $(p,q)$ and the gradient $(p_s, q_s)$ specifies the direction of the source. The reflectance map tells the relation of image brightness on surface orientation. In the image plane at a particular point $(x,y)$, we record the image irradiance $I(x,y)$. It is proportional to the image radiance at the corresponding point on the surface. $R(p,q)$ is known as the image radiance. Hence, by normalizing, we get the image irradiance equation as

$$R(p,q) = I(x,y). \tag{7.33}$$

If we take $f(x,y)$ and $g(x,y)$ as two different functions for $p$ and $q$, then the reflectance map can also be written as

$$R(f(x,y), g(x,y)) = I(x,y). \tag{7.34}$$

In the present case, $(x,y) \in D$. The function $R(f,g)$ can be determined theoretically or experimentally if distribution of light sources, viewing geometry, and intrinsic reflecting properties of the materials composing the surface are known [80]. One easily note that in stereographic projection, the Northern Hemisphere is projected into a plane, namely the $fg$ plane, tangent to the Gaussian sphere at the North Pole with the South Pole as the center of projection. As it is a bijection of the Northern Hemisphere onto a disc $S$ of radius 2 in the $fg$-plane, points in $S$ provide surface orientations of visible parts of the object's surface. Points on the circumference of $S$ are, therefore, the orientations of the points on the occluding boundaries. Therefore, for any point $(x,y)$ on the occluding boundary, we must have,

$$f^2(x,y) + g^2(x,y) = 4. \tag{7.35}$$

One can assume for interior points $(x,y) \in D^i$, $I(x,y) > 0$ and, for occluding boundary points, $(x,y) \in \partial D$, $I(x,y) = 0$.

We cannot determine surface orientations uniquely from the image irradiance equation, even with supplementary boundary information. The problem is ill-posed and regularization is used [162, 81, 21].

### 7.5.2 Method Based on Regularization

To find a smoothing spline $(f^*(x,y), g^*(x,y))$, Ikeuchi and Horn used regularization [81] that minimizes the error

$$E(f,g) = \int \int_D ((f_x^2(x,y) + f_y^2(x,y) + g_x^2(x,y) + g_y^2(x,y)) \qquad (7.36)$$
$$+ \; \lambda(R(f(x,y), g(x,y)) - I(x,y))^2) dx dy.$$

The first term, the squared gradient of the surface orientations, in the integrand is the departure from smoothness and the second term is the error in the image irradiance equation. $\lambda$ is the penalty parameter. When the brightness measurements are accurate, $\lambda$ is chosen large.

Three critical issues in regularization method are as follows:
(1) The existence of the solution.
(2) The uniqueness of the solution.
(3) The well-conditioning of the problem.
Of these three issues, existence of smoothing splines is ensured but the uniqueness and well-conditioning cannot be guaranteed. Smoothing splines without boundary conditions, in general, are not unique.

**Theorem 1:**
Without any boundary conditions, the smoothing splines are in general not unique, and the problem of computing a smoothing spline is ill-conditioned. Ikeuchi and Horn [81] mentioned a number of boundary conditions, e.g., occluding boundaries, self-shadow boundaries, specular points, and singular points.

### 7.5.3 Discrete Smoothing Splines

Any image domain $D$ can be embedded into a rectangular region $\bar{D}$ where all four sides can always be thought to intersect $\partial D$ through proper shrinking of $\bar{D}$.

Suppose we discretize $\bar{D}$ with mesh size $h$. Further assume the region $D$ is divided into $m + 2$ rows and that the $i - th$ row contains $n_i + 2$ grid points, for $i = 0, 1, \cdots, m = 1$. The total number of interior grid points in $D^i$ is

$$N = \sum_{i=1}^{m} n_i.$$

Let

$$n = \max_i \{n_i\}.$$

One can assume that $m \leq n$ and $h = \frac{1}{m}$. Now if we designate the surface orientation at the grid point $(i, j)$ by $(f_{ij}, g_{ij})$ and the image brightness by $I_{ij}$, then $(f_{ij}, g_{ij})$ are known if $(i, j \in \partial D)$. Consider a vector $\mathbf{x}$ of surface orientations at an interior grid point $D^i$ as

$$\mathbf{x} = (\cdots, f_{ij}, \cdots, \quad , \cdots, g_{ij}, \cdots)^T.$$

Then $\mathbf{x}$ is defined on a compact set $S^N$, where $S$ is disc of radius 2 in the $fg$-plane and $N$ is the number of interior grid points in $D^i$. A corresponding smoothing spline or $DSS$ minimizes the following error between all $\mathbf{x}$:

$$e(\mathbf{x}) = \sum_{i,j} (\frac{1}{h^2}((f_{i+1,j} - f_{i,j})^2 + (f_{i,j+1} - f_{i,j})^2 \tag{7.37}$$
$$+ (g_{i+1,j} - g_{i,j})^2 + (g_{i,j+1} - g_{i,j})^2 + \lambda(R(f_{i,j}, g_{i,j}) - I_{i,j})^2).$$

The term $(i, j)$ is included in the sum if and only if $\{(i, j), (i+1, j), (i, j+1)\} \in D$. The minimization is subject to the condition $\{f_{ij}, g_{ij}\} \in \partial D$, so that $f_{ij}$ and $g_{ij}$ are known.

### 7.5.4 Necessary Condition and the System of Equations

One can find the necessary condition for a $DSS$ and hence the system of equations by computing the partial derivatives of $e(\mathbf{x})$ in equation (7.37) with respect to $f_{ij}$ and $g_{ij}$ for all $(i, j)$ in $D^i$. Equating these derivative to zero, one gets in a generalized form the necessary condition,

$$\mathbf{Mx} = -\lambda h^2 \mathbf{b}(\mathbf{x}) + \mathbf{r}. \tag{7.38}$$

Here, $\mathbf{M} = diag(A, A)$ where $A$ is the $N \times N$ Laplacian Matrix of $D^i$.

$$\mathbf{b}(\mathbf{x}) = (\cdots, (R(f_{ij}, g_{ij}) - I_{ij})\frac{\partial R(f_{ij}, g_{ij})}{\partial f_{ij}}, \cdots,$$
$$\cdots, (R(f_{ij}, g_{ij}) - I_{ij})\frac{\partial R(f_{ij}, g_{ij})}{\partial g_{ij}}, \cdots)^T$$

and $\mathbf{r} = (\cdots, r_{ij}, \cdots)^T$. Now, $r_{ij} = 0$ when all the four neighbors of $(i, j)th$ pixel are within the region $D^i$, otherwise $r_{ij} \neq 0$ and its value depends on the number of pixels lying outside the region. Obviously, there can be a number of situations; for example, suppose the grid points at $(i - 1, j)$ and $(i, j - 1)$ are the boundary points and $f_{i-1,j}$, $f_{i,j-1}$, $g_{i-1,j}$, and $g_{i,j-1}$ are known. This provides $r_{ij} = f_{i-1,j} + f_{i,j-1}$. For details see the article by David Lee [101]. The remaining cases can be treated similarly. Equation (7.38) is equivalent to

$$\mathbf{x} = (\mathbf{I} - \mathbf{M})\mathbf{x} - \lambda \mathbf{h}^2 \mathbf{b}(\mathbf{x}) + \mathbf{r}, \tag{7.39}$$

where $\mathbf{I}$ is the identity matrix of size $2N$. An algorithmic approach to solve equation (7.39) is described below [81].

**Algorithm 1**:

$\mathbf{x}^{(0)} = 0$;

$\mathbf{x}^{(k)} = (\mathbf{I} - \mathbf{M})\mathbf{x}^{(k-1)} - \lambda h^2 \mathbf{b}(\mathbf{x}^{(k-1)}) + \mathbf{r}$, for $k = 1, 2, \cdots$

The following three points here are worth paying attention to:

(1) Existence and uniqueness of the solution of equation (7.38) were not addressed.

(2) Convergence of Algorithm 1 was not shown.

(3) Necessary condition did not have dependence on the interior points. The constraint $f_{ij} + g_{ij} < 4$ for interior points is not taken into account.

Lee showed that for a range of $\lambda$, equation (7.38) has a unique solution that provides a unique $DSS$. His proposed algorithm converges to this unique solution.

### 7.5.5 Some Important Points About $DSS$

(1) A $DSS$ minimizes the error expression $e(\mathbf{x})$ of equation (7.37) between all $\mathbf{x}$ in the compact set $S^N$.

(2) If $R(f, g)$ is continuous, then $e(\mathbf{x})$ is a continuous functional of $\mathbf{x}$ and its infimum is in $S^N$. This means $DSS$ exists.

(3) A $DSS$ $\mathbf{x}$ is regular, if for all $(i, j)$ in $D^i$, $f_{ij}^2 + g_{ij}^2 < 4$.

(4) A regular $DSS$ minimizes expression (7.37) and is an interior point in $S^N$, so it satisfies equation (7.38).

(5) One can show that add $DSS$s are regular.

**Theorem 2**:

If the function $R$ in the image irradiance equation (7.34) is continuous, then discrete smoothing splines exist and are regular.

From Theorem 2, one can tell that a regular $DSS$ $\mathbf{x}^*$ exists that minimizes error $e(\mathbf{x})$ between all $\mathbf{x}$ and also satisfies equation (7.38). Hence we can write,

$$\mathbf{M}\mathbf{x}^* = -\lambda h^2 \mathbf{b}(\mathbf{x}^*) + \mathbf{r}.$$

Matrix $M$ is symmetric and positive definite, and so it has an inverse $M^{-1}$. This leads to:

$$\mathbf{x}^* = -\lambda h^2 M^{-1}(\mathbf{x}^*) + M^{-1}\mathbf{r}. \tag{7.40}$$

## 7.6 A Provably Convergent Iterative Algorithm

To provide the algorithm, Lee rewrote equation (7.38) as

$$\mathbf{x} = -\lambda h^2 M^{-1}\mathbf{b}(\mathbf{x}) + M^{-1}\mathbf{r}, \tag{7.41}$$

and based on this the algorithm is as follows.

**Algorithm 2**

$\mathbf{x}^{(0)} = 0$;

$\mathbf{x}^{(k)} = -\lambda h^2 M^{-1}\mathbf{b}(\mathbf{x}^{(k-1)}) + M^{-1}\mathbf{r}, \quad k = 1, 2, \cdots$

### 7.6.1 Convergence

To discuss convergence, Lee assumed $(R(f,g) - I_{ij})\frac{\partial R(f,g)}{\partial f}$ and $(R(f,g) - I_{ij})\frac{\partial R(f,g)}{\partial g}$ are Lipschitz functions for all $(i,j)$. This means for $(f,g),(f',g') \in S$,

$$|(R(f,g) - I_{ij})\frac{\partial R(f,g)}{\partial f} - (R(f',g') - I_{ij})\frac{\partial R(f',g')}{\partial f}|$$
$$\leq L_{ij}^{(1)}\sqrt{(f-f')^2 + (g-g')^2},$$

and

$$|(R(f,g) - I_{ij})\frac{\partial R(f,g)}{\partial g} - (R(f',g') - I_{ij})\frac{\partial R(f',g')}{\partial g}|$$
$$\leq L_{ij}^{(2)}\sqrt{(f-f')^2 + (g-g')^2},$$

where $L_{ij}$s are Lipschitz constants. Then for $\mathbf{x}, \mathbf{x}' \in S^N$,

$$\|\mathbf{b}(\mathbf{x}) - \mathbf{b}(\mathbf{x}')\|_2 \leq \nu\|\mathbf{x} - \mathbf{x}'\|_2, \tag{7.42}$$

where

$$\nu = \sqrt{\max_{ij}\{(L_{ij}^{(1)})^2 + (L_{ij}^{(2)})^2\}}.$$

Note that $\nu$ is also a Lipschitz constant and $\|.\|_2$ is the $L_2$-norm.

Some of the interesting results in connection to $DSS$ are as follows:

(1) **Theorem 3**:

If $\mathbf{x}^*$ is a discrete smoothing spline, then for the range

$$\lambda \in [0, \frac{4s(n,m)}{h^2\nu}), \quad s(n,m) = sin^2\frac{\pi}{2(m+1)} + sin^2\frac{\pi}{2(n+1)}$$

$\mathbf{x}^{(k)}$ in Algorithm 2 converges to $\mathbf{x}^*$. $\lambda$ is the penalty parameter in expression (7.37). $h$ is the mesh size of discretization, $m$ is the number of rows in $D^i$, $n$ is the maximum number of grid points in a single row, and $\nu$ is Lipschitz constant determined by the function $R(f,g)$ and $I(x,y)$.

(2) **Theorem 4**:

For

$$\lambda \in [0, \frac{4s(n,m)}{h^2\nu}),$$

Algorithm 2 converges to the unique regular discrete smoothing spline, which is also the unique solution of equation (7.38). Algorithm 2 can be modified in a number of ways to make it more efficient for regular and irregular regions. Interested readers may have look at the article of David Lee [101]. Some of the drawbacks of Algorithm 2 are:

• It does not consider the integrability constraint, which plays an important part in surface description.

• Implementation of Algorithm 2 is not straightforward for irregular regions. This is for the computation of $M^{-1}$, the matrix $M$ being equal to $diag(A,A)$, where $A$ is the Laplacian matrix of $D^i$, $M^{-1} = diag(A^{-1}, A^{-1})$. As $A^{-1}$ is irregular, there is no method for multiplying $A^{-1}$ efficiently by any vector.

• We cannot say anything about the optimality of $\lambda$. Interested readers can consult the book [79].

## 7.7 Concluding Remarks

This chapter provides a theoretical background for discrete splines, which can be used effectively in designing a high quality surface. Resolution of a surface can be increased with the addition of knots in steps. This is the process of repeated refinement. The impact of discrete smoothing spline in computer vision shows that it is only possible to have a range of the regularization parameter for which an iterative algorithm can be devised to explore the shape of a physical surface from its image brightness values.

As splines are a powerful tool, their capability in different aspects should be re-investigated thoroughly. This tool is equally useful both in analysis and synthesis.

# Spline Wavelets: Construction, Implication, and Uses

## 8.1 Introduction

At the beginning of the eighties while doing the seismic data analysis, J. Morlet introduced wavelets as a tool for signal analysis. His success led A. Grossman to make a detailed study of the wavelet transform [69]. Later on, Y. Meyer pointed out that there was a connection between signal analysis methods and existing powerful techniques in the mathematical study of singular integral operators. Ingrid Daubechies, together with Grossman and Meyer [50], provided first the construction of a special type of frames. Later on in 1988, Daubechies [48] provided a major breakthrough with her construction of the families of orthonormal wavelets with compact support. The remarkable papers of Mallat [114, 115] and Daubechies [48] came out in 1988 and 1989. The subject, along with its applications, then grew out in many diverse fields during the last two decades.

To have an idea about various developments on wavelets, readers can go first through an introduction to continuous wavelet transform in [156, 49]. Wavelet bases of Meyer, Battle [18] and Lemarié [103] can be easily realized using orthonormal multirate filter banks. But the filters involved are not rational and the corresponding wavelets cannot be computed exactly. Hence they are limited from the signal processing viewpoint. Daubechies' compactly supported wavelets [48] are based on finite impulse response (FIR) filter banks. Orthogonal filter banks and their relation to wavelet bases have been studied in [164, 165, 166]. Details about wavelets and various applications can be found in books [49, 166, 116, 14]. Other books can also be consulted.

Different, well-known wavelets have been widely used in many problems. Some are more efficient and more capable compared to others. Excepting these remarkable wavelets, another class of wavelets that has gained attention, interest, and importance (due to their simplicity in construction) is the class of spline wavelets. These wavelets are found to secure a good place in signal processing, as they have merit in implementations. They are also relatively easy to understand and simple in their construction. The easiest of them uses cardinal B-spline functions. We shall, therefore, discuss cardinal splines first in this chapter. Readers can consult Schoenberg and Chui [147, 37] for an extensive study on cardinal splines and their uses.

In this chapter, we shall restrict ourselves to spline wavelets and their properties but to understand them well, we shall also discuss the related essentials.

## 8.2 Cardinal Splines

Cardinal splines are polynomial spline functions with equally spaced knots. Because of the simple knot structure, these splines can be used easily with computational advantages. One of the major advantages of cardinal splines over others is that cardinal splines have essentially only one B-spline of a given order. All others of the same order are (scaled) translates of this one. Further simplicity and convenience can be achieved if we consider that knots are integers. Let us assume $n$ is an integer, $n \geq 0$ and $S_n = \{f(x)\}$, Class of polynomial functions of order at most n, with $f(x) \in C^{n-2}(\mathbb{R})$ and $f(x) \in \pi_{n-1}$. $\pi_n$ is the collection of all algebraic polynomials of degree not exceeding $n$ and $f(x)$ are $n-2$ times differentiable. Elements of $S_n$ are called cardinal spline functions of degree $n$. Therefore, if we restrict our attention to any interval $[j, j+1)$ where j is an integer, then the function in $[j, j+1)$ is

$$f \in \pi_{n-1}, \quad j \in \mathbb{Z}.$$

We can now connect two polynomial pieces of functions in adjacent intervals. Consider two intervals $[j, j+1)$ and $[j-1, j)$. Let the polynomials in these two intervals be $p_{n,j}^{(l)}$ and $p_{n,j-1}^{(l)}$ from the collection of $\pi_{n-1}$ and $j = -N, \cdots, N-1$. Considering the continuity of the two polynomials at the point $x = j$, one can write

$$p_{n,j}^{(l)}(j) - p_{n,j-1}^{(l)}(j) = 0, \quad l = 0, 1, \cdots, n-2, \quad n \geq 2.$$

Now the order of the polynomials is $n$. Hence the degree of each of the polynomials is $n-1$. After $(n-1)$th differentiation each of them is a constant that is different at the knot sequence $\mathbb{Z}$, as we approach it from the right and left sides of $j$. This means we can write this difference as

$$
\begin{aligned}
c_j &= p_{n,j}^{(n-1)}(j+) - p_{n,j-1}^{(n-1)}(j-) \\
&= \lim_{\epsilon \to 0} \{f^{(n-1)}(j+\epsilon) - f^{(n-1)}(j-\epsilon)\}.
\end{aligned}
\tag{8.1}
$$

$c_j$ is the jump of $f^{(n-1)}$ and can be used to link between the polynomial pieces in two adjacent intervals. $\frac{c_j}{(n-1)!}$ can be taken as the leading coefficient of the difference polynomial between the two adjacent intervals. Note that other coefficients are zero. Hence

$$p_{n,j}(x) = p_{n,j-1}(x) + \frac{c_j}{(n-1)!}(x-j)^{n-1}. \tag{8.2}$$

Then considering for all $x \in [-N, N]$, one can write $f(x)$ as

$$f(x) = f_{[-N, -N+1)}(x) + \sum_{j=-N+1}^{N-1} \frac{c_j}{(n-1)!}(x - j)_+^{n-1}, \qquad (8.3)$$

where we use the following notation,

$$\begin{aligned} x_+ &= max(0, x), \\ x_+^{n-1} &= (x_+)^{n-1}, \qquad n \geq 2. \end{aligned} \qquad (8.4)$$

The collection of $n + 2N - 1$ functions

$$\{x^0, x^1, \cdots, x^{n-1}, (x + N - 1)_+^{n-1}, \cdots, x - N + 1)_+^{n-1}\} \qquad (8.5)$$

is a basis of $S_{n,N}$. We can replace the monomials $1, x, \cdots, x^{n-1}$ by truncated powers:

$$(x + N + n - 1)_+^{n-1}, \cdots, (x + N)_+^{n-1}.$$

With this, we now can generate the entire set of truncated powers by integer translates of a single function, $x_+^{n-1}$ as,

$$\{(x - r)_+^{n-1}, \quad r = -N - n + 1, \cdots, N - 1\}. \qquad (8.6)$$

This is also a basis of $S_{n,N}$.

Now for different values of $N$, different spaces $S_{n,N}$ can be visualized; each of them is of finite dimension when $N$ is finite. Making $N$ infinitely large and considering the union of all such spaces, we can make the space $S_n$ of infinite dimension and the basis in equation (8.6) will, therefore, be a different basis of the infinite dimensional space $S_n$ (due to the different bases for the values of $N$). This basis can be written as

$$B_1 = \{(x - r)_+^{n-1}, \quad r \in \mathbb{Z}. \qquad (8.7)$$

To find cardinal splines in $L^2(\mathbb{R})$, one can consider backward differences with recursion as

$$\begin{aligned} (\triangle f)(x) &= f(x) - f(x - 1) \\ (\triangle^k f)(x) &= (\triangle^{k-1}(\triangle f)), \qquad k = 2, 3, \cdots \end{aligned} \qquad (8.8)$$

For $n$th order polynomial, the $n$th order difference is zero, i.e.,

$$\triangle^n f = 0, \qquad f \in \pi_{n-1}.$$

Let us now define a linear combination of the basis functions given in equation (8.7) as

$$M_n(x) = \frac{1}{(n-1)!}\triangle^n x_+^{n-1}, \qquad n \geq 2 \qquad (8.9)$$

where $M_1 = N_1$, the characteristic function of $[0, 1)$, i.e.,

$$N_1(x) = 1, \quad 0 \leq x < 1,$$
$$= 0, \quad otherwise. \tag{8.10}$$

Now,

$$(\Delta^2 f)(x) = (\Delta(\Delta f))(x),$$
$$= (\Delta(f(x) - f(x - 1))),$$
$$= (\Delta f)(x) - (\Delta f)(x - 1),$$
$$= (f(x) - f(x - 1)) - (f(x - 1) - f(x - 2)),$$
$$= \sum_{k=0}^{2}(-1)^k \binom{2}{k}(x - k)_+,$$

where, $f(x) = (x - 0)_+^n - 1$, $f(x - 1) = (x - 1)_+^n - 1$ and $f(x - 2) = (x - 2)_+^n - 1$ for $n = 2$. Proceeding this way, one can easily show that

$$M_n(x) = \frac{1}{(n-1)!} \sum_{r=0}^{n}(-1)^r \binom{n}{r}(x - r)_+^{n-1}. \tag{8.11}$$

Obviously, $M_n(x) = 0$ for $x \geq n$. Also, $M_n(x) = 0$ for $x < 0$ (since, $x_+ = max(0, x)$). This helps to establish

$$supp \, M_n = [0, n].$$

With this, we observe that:
(1) The collection $B = \{M_n(x - r), \, r \in \mathbb{Z}\}$ reduces to $B_2 = \{M_n(x - r), \, r = -N - n + 1, \cdots, N - 1\}$.
(2) $M_n(x - r) = 0$ for $r > N - 1$ and $r < -N - m + 1$.
(3) $\{M_n(x - r)\}$ is a linearly independent set.
Hence, $B_2$ is a basis of $S_{n,N}$. We can take the union of $S_{n,N}$ over $N = 1, 2, 3, \cdots$ and we come to $B$. This helps to write a spline series as

$$f(x) = \sum_{r=-\infty}^{\infty} a_r M_n(x - r). \tag{8.12}$$

We shall now describe the importance of the space $L^2(\mathbb{R})$ and the basis set from the engineering point of view. $L^2(\mathbb{R})$ space is important in signal processing. This is the space of all functions $f(t)$, which can be used to represent a signal. The energy of the signal can be taken as the integral of the square of the modulus of the function. Since, this integral is finite, it corroborates the fact of finite energy of a signal in practice. $\mathbb{R}$ indicates the time instant $t$ of occurrence of the signal (also the independent variable of integration) is a number on the whole real line.

Now if we start with the vector space of signals $S$, then if any $f(t) \in S$ can be expressed as $f(t) = \sum_k a_k \phi_k(t)$, then the set of functions $\phi_k(t)$ is called an expansion set for the space $S$. If the representation is unique, then the set is a basis. One could also start with the expansion set or basis set and define the

space $S$ as the set of all functions that can be expressed by $f(t) = \sum_k a_k \phi_k(t)$.
This is called the span of the basis set. In many cases, the signal spaces are taken as the closure of the space, spanned by the basis set. This closure tells us the space contains not only all signals that can be expressed by a linear combination of the basis functions, but also the signals that are the limit of these infinite expansions.

### 8.2.1 Cardinal B-Spline Basis and Riesz Basis

Since in wavelets we consider functions in $L^2(\mathbb{R})$ and our objective in this chapter is to study spline wavelets, we consider cardinal splines that are both in $S_n$ and and $L^2(\mathbb{R})$, i.e., in $S_n \cap L^2(\mathbb{R})$. We now suppose that $V_0^n$ is its closure. This means $V_0^n$ is the smallest closed subspace of $L^2(\mathbb{R})$ that contains $S_n \cap L^2(\mathbb{R})$. Since $M_n$ has compact support, one can visualize $B \subset V_0^n$.

For simplicity we have considered cardinal splines with sequence of integer knots $\mathbb{Z}$. Now we consider the space $S_n^j$ of cardinal spline functions with knot sequences $2^{-j}\mathbb{Z}$, $j \in \mathbb{Z}$. Since a spline function with knot sequence $2^{-j_1}\mathbb{Z}$ is also a spline with knot sequence $2^{-j_2}\mathbb{Z}$, whenever $j_1 < j_2$, we can write a nested sequence

$$\cdots \subset S_n^{-1} \subset S_n^0 \subset S_n^1 \subset \cdots$$

of cardinal spline spaces, with $S_n^0 = S_n$. If we let $V_j^n$ to denote the $L^2(\mathbb{R})$ closure of $S_n^j \cap L^2(\mathbb{R})$, then the nested sequence

$$\cdots \subset V_{-1}^n \subset V_0^n \subset V_1^n \subset \cdots$$

of closed spline subspaces of $L^2(\mathbb{R})$. Thus, the nested sequence of subspaces satisfies

$$\overline{\bigcup_{j \in \mathbb{Z}} V_j^n} = L^2(\mathbb{R}),$$
$$\bigcap_{j \in \mathbb{Z}} V_j^n = \{0\}, \tag{8.13}$$

where the overhead bar indicates the closure.

We now write the $n$th order cardinal B-spline basis through the convolution of

$$N_n(x) = (N_{n-1} * N_1)(x)$$
$$= \int_0^1 N_{n-1}(x-t)dt. \qquad m \geq 2 \tag{8.14}$$

$N - 1$ is the characteristic function of the interval $[0, 1)$. Setting $M_n = N_n$ for $n \geq 2$, we can tell $N_n$ is an $n$th cardinal spline function in $V_0^n \subset S_n$. The cardinal B-spline basis

$$B = \{N_n(x - r)\}, \quad r \in \mathbb{Z} \tag{8.15}$$

is a Riesz basis of $V_0^n$. Now a basis is a Riesz basis, if it satisfies the Riesz condition. If we have a function $\phi \in L(\mathbb{R})$ and two constants $A$ and $B$ with $0 < A \leq B < \infty$, then we say that $\{\phi(. - r), \quad r \in \mathbb{Z})\}$ satisfies the Riesz condition if

$$A\|\{c_r\}\|^2 \leq \| \sum_{r=-\infty}^{\infty} c_r \phi(. - r) \|^2 \leq B\|\{c_r\}\|^2, \quad \{c_r\} \in l^2,$$

and the Fourier transform $\widehat{\phi}$ of $\phi$ satisfies

$$A \leq \sum_{r=-\infty}^{\infty} |\widehat{\phi}(x + 2\pi r)|^2 \leq B, \quad a.e.$$

In order to find the condition for the cardinal B-spline, we should detect the lower and upper bounds $A$ and $B$. From equation (8.14),

$$\begin{aligned}
N_n(x) &= N_{n-1}(x) * N_1(x) \\
&= N_{n-2}(x) * N_1(x) * N_1(x) \\
&= N_1(x) * N_1(x) * N_1(x) * \cdots * N_1(x),
\end{aligned}$$

and hence taking the Fourier transform, we get

$$\widehat{N}_n(\omega) = (\widehat{N}_1)^n(\omega).$$

Since,

$$\begin{aligned}
\widehat{N}_1(\omega) &= \int_0^1 e^{-i\omega x} dx \\
&= \frac{1 - e^{-i\omega}}{i\omega}.
\end{aligned} \tag{8.16}$$

Therefore.

$$|\widehat{N}_n(\omega)|^2 = \left| \frac{1 - e^{-i\omega}}{i\omega} \right|^{2n}.$$

Now,

$$\begin{aligned}
\frac{1 - e^{-i\omega}}{i\omega} &= \frac{e^{-i\omega/2}(e^{i\omega/2} - e^{-i\omega/2})}{i\omega}, \\
&= e^{-i\omega/2} \frac{2}{\omega} \sin(\omega/2), \\
&= e^{-i\omega/2} \frac{\sin(\omega/2)}{(\omega/2)}.
\end{aligned}$$

Therefore, considering $2\pi$ periodicity with replacement of $\omega$ by $2x$ and summing over $r$, the expression for $|\widehat{N}_n(\omega)|^2$ becomes

$$\begin{aligned}
\sum_{r=-\infty}^{\infty} |\widehat{N}_n(2x + 2\pi r)|^2 &= e^{-4inx/2} 2^{2n} \sum_{r=-\infty}^{\infty} \frac{\sin^{2n}(x + \pi r)}{(2x + 2\pi r)^{2n}}, \\
&= e^{-2inx}(\sin^{2n} x) \sum_{r=-\infty}^{\infty} \frac{1}{(x + \pi r)^{2n}}, \\
&= (\sin^{2n} x) \sum_{r=-\infty}^{\infty} \frac{1}{(x + \pi r)^{2n}},
\end{aligned} \tag{8.17}$$

since, $e^{-i2nx} = (\cos 2nx - i \sin 2nx) = 1$.

Now,

$$\cot x = \lim_{l \to \infty} \sum_{r=-l}^{l} \frac{1}{(x + \pi r)},$$

and hence

$$\sum_{r=-\infty}^{\infty} \frac{1}{(x + \pi r)^{2n}} = -\frac{1}{(2n-1)!} \frac{d^{2n-1}}{dx^{2n-1}} \cot x.$$

This provides

$$\sum_{r=-\infty}^{\infty} |\widehat{N}_n(2x + 2\pi r)|^2 = -\frac{\sin^{2n} x}{(2n-1)!} \frac{d^{2n-1}}{dx^{2n-1}} \cot x. \tag{8.18}$$

Equation (8.18) helps to compute optimal Riesz bounds. For smaller values, the computation of spline order is straightforward, while for larger values, algebraic exercise to some extent is needed.

There could be other approaches. One such approach establishes [37]

$$\sum_{r=-\infty}^{\infty} |\widehat{N}_n(\omega + 2\pi r)|^2 = \sum_{r=-n+1}^{n-1} N_{2n}(n+r) e^{-ir\omega},$$

and using the properties of cardinal B-splines, one can show

$$\sum_{r=-\infty}^{\infty} |\widehat{N}_n(\omega + 2\pi r)|^2 \leq 1.$$

The Riesz basis bound $B = 1$. To get the greatest lower bound, one can consider "Euler-Frobenius polynomials:"

$$E_{2n-1}(z) = (2n-1)! \, z^{n-1} \sum_{r=-n+1}^{n-1} N_{2n}(n+r) z^r$$

of order $2n - 1$. Since its degree is $2n - 2$, it has $2n - 2$ roots. All these $2n - 2$ roots, say, $\lambda_1, \lambda_2, \cdots, \lambda_{2n-2}$ are negative, simple, real, and are found to hold the relation

$$0 > \lambda_1 > \lambda_2 > \cdots > \lambda_{2n-2},$$

and

$$\lambda_1 \lambda_{2n-2} = \cdots = \lambda_{n-1} \lambda_n = 1.$$

This provides,

$$A_n = \frac{1}{(2n-1!)} \prod_{r=1}^{n-1} \frac{(1+\lambda_r)^2}{|\lambda_r|} > 0.$$

Also using the properties of Euler-Frobenius polynomial, one can show

$$\sum_{r=-\infty}^{\infty} |\widehat{N}_n(\omega + 2\pi r)|^2 = \frac{1}{(2n-1!)} \prod_{r=1}^{n-1} \frac{1 - 2\lambda_r \cos\omega + \lambda_r^2}{|\lambda_r|},$$

since $\lambda_r$s are negative and $-1 \leq \cos\omega \leq 1$ we have,

$$A_n \leq \sum_{r=-\infty}^{\infty} |\widehat{N}_n(\omega + 2\pi r)|^2 \leq 1.$$

Hence, for any integer $n \geq 2$ the cardinal B-spline basis $B = \{N_n(x-r)\}$, $r \in \mathbb{Z}$ is a Riesz basis of $V_0^n$ with bounds $A = A_n$ and $B = 1$.

Example: Compute the optimal Riesz bounds for the first and second order cardinal B-splines, $N_1$ and $N_2$. From equation (8.18), we have

$$\sum_{r=-\infty}^{\infty} |\widehat{N}_1(2x + 2\pi r)|^2 = -\frac{\sin^2 x}{1!} \frac{d}{dx} \cot x,$$

$$= -\sin^2 x(-cosec^2 x),$$
$$= 1,$$

or,

$$\sum_{r=-\infty}^{\infty} |\widehat{N}_1(\omega + 2\pi r)|^2 = 1,$$

and,

$$\sum_{r=-\infty}^{\infty} |\widehat{N}_2(2x + 2\pi r)|^2 = -\frac{\sin^4 x}{3!} \frac{d^3}{dx^3} \cot x,$$

$$= -\frac{\sin^4 x}{6}\{-2(cosec^4 x + 2cosec^x \cot^x)\},$$
$$= \frac{2}{6}(1 + 2\cos^2 x),$$
$$= \frac{1}{3}(1 + 2\cos^2 x),$$

or,

$$\sum_{r=-\infty}^{\infty} |\widehat{N}_2(\omega + 2\pi r)|^2 = \frac{1}{3} + \frac{2}{3}\cos^2\left(\frac{\omega}{2}\right).$$

Hence, $\{N_1(.-r)\}$ is orthonormal and

$$\frac{1}{3} \leq \sum_{r=-\infty}^{\infty} |\widehat{N}_2(\omega + 2\pi r)|^2 \leq 1.$$

## 8.2.2 Scaling and Cardinal B-Spline Functions

Since the cardinal B-spline basis $B$ is a Riesz basis of $V_0^n$, one can conclude that

$$\{2^{j/2} N_n(2^j x - r), \quad r \in \mathbb{Z}\} \tag{8.19}$$

is also a Riesz basis of $V_j^n$ with the same bounds as of $B$ for any $j \in \mathbb{Z}$. We shall now check if the cardinal B-spline can act as a scaling function. Also, if we would like to view the image in terms of signal space, then we should write the functions in terms of a time variable $t$ rather than of $x$. A scaling function $\phi$ is a function that generates a multiresolution analysis (MRA). We shall see an $n$th order cardinal B-splines $N_n$ satisfies all the conditions of an MRA, and since a wavelet system can be defined in terms of a scaling function, cardinal B-splines can be successfully used in wavelet systems. This helps to construct different spline wavelets efficiently that can be used effectively.

Consider a scaling function $\phi$. The set of scaling functions based on integer translates of the mother scaling function is

$$\phi_r(t) = \phi(t - r), \quad r \in \mathbb{Z}, \ \phi \in L^2(\mathbb{R}).$$

The subspace of $L^2(\mathbb{R})$ spanned by these functions is given by

$$V_0 = \overline{span_r\{\phi_r(t)\}}.$$

Hence, any function $f(t) \in V_0$ can be written as

$$f(t) = \sum_r a_r \phi_r(t).$$

Now instead of the mother scaling function, if we look at the scaling functions at different resolutions, i.e., instead of $t$ in the mother scaling function, if we consider $2^j t$, then

$$\phi_{j,r}(t) = 2^{j/2} \phi(2^j t - r).$$

This helps us to write $f(t) \in V_j$ as

$$f(t) = \sum_r a_r \phi(2^j t + r).$$

Obviously,

$$V_j = \overline{span_r\{\phi_r(2^j t)\}}$$
$$= \overline{span_r\{\phi_{j,r}(t)\}}.$$

To visualize the effect of $j$ in the scaling function $\phi$, we can think of approximation of a graylevel image by the scaling function. As an image is a two-dimensional function, we can approximate row-wise and column-wise or vice-versa. It is evident that as $j = 1, 2, \cdots$, $\phi_{j,r}(t)$ becomes narrower and narrower and hence it represents finer and finer details. On the other hand, if $j = -1, -2, -\cdots$, $\phi_{j,r}(t)$ becomes wider and wider and hence it represents coarser and coarser information. For narrower $\phi_{j,r}$, the span is larger while for wider $\phi_{j,r}$, span is smaller. Thus, $V_j s$ represent the approximation spaces and as $j$ increases, the size of these approximation spaces increases.

Below we will explain the concepts of an MRA but before that, we will examine what is meant by wavelets.

## 8.3 Wavelets

A wavelet $\psi(t)$ is a function in the $L^2(I\!R)$ space over the real line $I\!R$ that it satisfies the following conditions.

- The admissibility condition $C_\psi$ must remain finite, i.e.,

$$C_\psi = \int_{-\infty}^{+\infty} \frac{\mid \widehat{\psi}(\omega) \mid^2}{\mid \omega \mid} \, d\omega \ < \infty, \qquad (8.20)$$

  where $\widehat{\psi}(\omega)$ is the Fourier transform of $\psi(t)$. $\widehat{\psi}(\omega) = \int_{-\infty}^{+\infty} \psi(t)e^{-i\omega t} \, dt$.
  $\mid \widehat{\psi}(\omega) \mid^2$ is the total power contained in $\psi(t)$ and $C_\psi$ is, therefore, the total power per every frequency component present in $\psi(t)$.

- Its Fourier transform must be zero when the frequency is zero. This means when $\omega = 0$,

$$\widehat{\psi}(\omega) = \widehat{\psi}(0) \ = \ 0.$$

As a result, we obtain $\int_{-\infty}^{+\infty} \psi(t) dt \ = \ 0$. $\int \psi(t) dt$ is the area under the curve $\psi(t)$. Since it is zero, $\psi(t)$ must change its sign, i.e., $\psi(t)$ must be oscillatory in nature or will have a wavelike behavior.

Since the sum of the power per every frequency component is finite, we must have $\frac{\mid \widehat{\psi}(\omega) \mid^2}{\mid \omega \mid} \to 0$ when $\omega \to 0$. Now, $\omega \to 0$ implies $\frac{1}{\mid \omega \mid} \to \infty$. Therefore, to have

$$\frac{\mid \widehat{\psi}(\omega) \mid^2}{\mid \omega \mid} \to 0,$$

we must have $\mid \widehat{\psi}(\omega) \mid^2 \to 0$ with a faster rate. Such a basic wavelet is called a mother wavelet.

The mother wavelet represents a family of functions with two parameters: one of them is for position and the other one is for frequency. In other words, the family of functions is

$$\psi_{a,b}(t) = \frac{1}{\sqrt{|a|}} \psi(\frac{t-b}{a}),$$

where $a \neq 0$ and $b \in I\!R$.

### 8.3.1 Continuous Wavelet Transform

Let us consider the family of functions

$$\psi_{a,b}(t) = \frac{1}{\sqrt{|a|}} \psi(\frac{t-b}{a}), \qquad (8.21)$$

that one can obtain by shifting and scaling a mother wavelet, $\psi(t)$. Here $a$ and $b$ are the scale and shift parameters ($a \neq o$). From the admissibility condition, we can say that $\widehat{\psi}(\omega)$ will always have sufficient decay. Because the Fourier transform is zero at the origin and the spectrum decays at high frequencies, the wavelet has a bandpass behavior. Normalizing the wavelet to unit energy, we get

$$
\begin{aligned}
\parallel \psi(t) \parallel^2 &= \int_{-\infty}^{+\infty} |\psi(t)|^2 dt, \\
&= \frac{1}{2\pi} \int_{-\infty}^{+\infty} |\widehat{\psi}(t)|^2 d\omega, \\
&= 1.
\end{aligned}
\tag{8.22}
$$

The continuous wavelet transform of a function $ft) \in L^2(\mathbb{R})$ is then defined as

$$
\begin{aligned}
T_{cw}(f(a,b)) &= \int_{-\infty}^{+\infty} \psi_{a,b} f(t) dt \\
&= < \psi_{a,b}(t), f(t) > .
\end{aligned}
\tag{8.23}
$$

The inverse of $T_{cw}(f(a,b))$ can be written as

$$
f(t) = \frac{1}{C_\psi} \int_{-\infty}^{+\infty} \int_{-\infty}^{+\infty} T_{cw}(f(a,b)) \psi_{a,b}(t) \frac{da\, db}{a^2}.
\tag{8.24}
$$

Thus, any $f(t) \in L^2(\mathbb{R})$ can be written as a superposition of shifted and dilated wavelets.

### 8.3.2 Properties of Continuous Wavelet Transform

- Linearity: Since the linearity is satisfied by the inner product, we can write

$$
T_{cw}(f_1(a,b)) + T_{cw}((f_2(a,b)) = T_{cw}((f_1(a,b) + f_2(a,b)).
$$

- Shift: If $f(t)$ has a continuous wavelet transform $T_{cw}(f(a,b))$, then the continuous wavelet transform of $f(t-k)$ is given by $T_{cw}(f(a,b-k))$. Note that the wavelet transform of $f(t)$ is

$$
\int_{-\infty}^{+\infty} \psi_{a,b} f(t) dt = T_{cw}(f(a,b)).
$$

Therefore, the wavelet transform of $f(t-k)$ is

$$
\begin{aligned}
\int_{-\infty}^{+\infty} \psi_{a,b} f(t-k) dt &= \frac{1}{\sqrt{|a|}} \psi(\frac{t-b}{a}) f(t-k)\, dt, \\
&= \frac{1}{\sqrt{|a|}} \int_{-\infty}^{+\infty} \psi(\frac{T+k-b}{a}) f(T)\, dT, \\
&= T_{cw}(f(a,b-k)).
\end{aligned}
$$

- Scale: If $f(t)$ has a continuous wavelet transform $T_{cw}(f(a,b))$, then the continuous wavelet transform of the scaled function $\frac{1}{\sqrt{s}}f(\frac{t}{s}, \frac{b}{s})$ is $T_{cw}(f(\frac{a}{s}, \frac{b}{s}))$. The continuous wavelet transform of $\frac{1}{\sqrt{s}}f(\frac{t}{s}, \frac{b}{s})$

$$\frac{1}{\sqrt{|a|}\,s}\int_{-\infty}^{+\infty}\psi(\frac{t-b}{a})f(\frac{t}{s})\,dt = \sqrt{\frac{s}{|a|}}\int_{-\infty}^{+\infty}\psi(\frac{sT-b}{a})f(T)\,dT,$$
$$= \sqrt{\frac{s}{|a|}}\int_{-\infty}^{+\infty}\psi(\frac{T-\frac{b}{s}}{\frac{a}{s}})f(T)\,dT,$$
$$= T_{cw}(f(\frac{a}{s}, \frac{b}{s})),$$

  where we let $\frac{t}{s} = T$. Thus, when the function is scaled, its $T_{cw}$ is also scaled.
- Energy of conservation: Continuous wavelet transform has an energy conservation property similar to that of Fourier transform.
- Localization: The continuous wavelet transform has sharp time localization at high frequencies and this distinguishes the wavelet transform from the traditional Fourier or Fourier-like transform.
- Time localization: To check the time localization of a particular wavelet, one can examine the wavelet transform of a Dirac pulse using the wavelet in question. For a given scale factor, the transform is equal to the scaled wavelet reversed in time and centered at the location of the Dirac.

## 8.4 A Glimpse of Continuous Wavelets

Continuous wavelets can be viewed in two different forms, isotropic and anisotropic wavelets, depending on how they can be applied in real life problems. For point-wise analysis, i.e., when no oriented features are present or relevant in the signal, we may choose an analyzing wavelet $\psi$, which is invariant under rotation. A typical example of an isotropic wavelet is the Mexican hat wavelet. But when directional features are in the signal or when one is interested in directional filtering, anisotropic wavelets are of much use. Typical directional or anisotropic wavelets are Morelet wavelet or the Cauchy wavelets. Whether isotropic or anisotropic, these are all the basic wavelets.

### 8.4.1 Basic Wavelets

Below, we describe two important basic wavelets.

### Gaussian Wavelet

A Gaussian wavelet is simply the derivative of Gaussian function. The Gaussian function is

$$g_\sigma(t) = \frac{1}{\sqrt{2\pi}\,\sigma}\, e^{-\frac{t^2}{2\sigma^2}},$$

$$= \frac{1}{2\sqrt{\pi\alpha}}\, e^{-\frac{t^2}{4\alpha}}, \qquad letting \quad \sigma^2 = 2\alpha.$$

The Gaussian wavelet is, therefore,

$$\psi(t) = -\frac{t}{4\alpha\sqrt{\pi\alpha}}\, e^{-\frac{t^2}{4\alpha}}.$$

Its Fourier transform is

$$\widehat{\psi}(\omega) = \int_{-\infty}^{\infty} \psi_\alpha(t)\, e^{-i\omega t}\, dt,$$

$$= i\omega\, e^{-\alpha\omega^2}.$$

## Morlet Wavelet

The Morlet wavelet uses a windowed complex exponential. This was proposed in [69] for signal analysis and is given by

$$\psi(t) = \frac{1}{\sqrt{2\pi}}\, e^{-i\omega_o t}\, e^{-t^2/2}.$$

Its Fourier transform is

$$\widehat{\psi}(\omega) = e^{-(\omega-\omega_o)^2/2},$$

where $\omega_o$ is the center frequency and the factor $1/\sqrt{2\pi}$ guarantees $\parallel \psi(t) \parallel = 1$. The center frequency $\omega_o$ is normally so chosen that the second maximum of the real part of $\psi(t)$, $t > 0$ is half of the first one at $t = 0$. This provides $\omega_0 = \pi\sqrt{\frac{2}{ln2}} = 5.336$. One can notice that Morlet wavelet is not admissible since $\widehat{\psi}(0) \neq 0$. But it does not present any problem in practice since its value is very small, roughly, $\widehat{\psi}(0) \approx 7.10^{-7}$.

An important topic in wavelet theory is the discretization of the continuous wavelet transform, $T_{cw}(f(a,b))$. We would like to have the wavelet $\psi$ such that $f$ can be recovered from $T_{cw}(f(a,b))$ values on a certain grid in the $(a,b)$ plane, i.e., from the values

$$T_{cw}(f(2^{-j}, 2^{-j}k)), \qquad j, k \in \mathbb{Z}.$$

Note that $\psi$ should have a property that the wavelets

$$2^{j/2}\, \psi\, (2^j\, x\, -\, k), \qquad j, k \in \mathbb{Z}$$

constitute an orthonormal basis of $L^2(\mathbb{R})$. The Mexican hat or Marr wavelet does not have this property. Such a function $\psi$ is called the mother wavelet. Often prior to the construction of the mother wavelet $\psi$, one constructs a function $\phi$ such that the functions $\{\phi(t - k)\}$, $k \in \mathbb{Z}$ constitute an orthonormal system. $\phi$ is, sometimes, called the father wavelet. This orthonormal system then can be supplemented to a full orthonormal basis of $L^2(\mathbb{R})$ with the functions

$$2^{j/2}\, \psi\, (2^j\, t\, -\, k), \qquad j \in Z_+, \; k \in \mathbb{Z}.$$

## 8.5 Multiresolution Analysis and Wavelet Bases

The concept of multiresolution analysis was first published in 1989 by Mallat [115] and Meyer in 1990 [125]. Here the main objective is to find a function $\psi$ such that $\{\psi_{j,r}\}$ is an orthonormal basis of $L^2(\mathbb{R})$. In $\{\psi_{j,r}\}$, we have two parameters: one is the translation parameter and the other is the dilation parameter designated respectively by $r$ and $j$. Now, considering the Fourier transform, we can write

$$| \widehat{\psi}_{j,r}(\omega) | = 2^{-j/2} | \widehat{\psi}(\frac{\omega}{2^j}) | .$$

Therefore, for fixed $j$, we get a fixed bandwidth in the signal.

**Definition (MRA)**: A multiresolution analysis consists of a sequence of embedded closed subspaces

$$\cdots V_2 \subset V_1 \subset V_0 \subset V_1 \subset V_2 \cdots \tag{8.25}$$

such that we have
(1) Upward completeness:

$$\overline{\bigcup}_{j \in Z} V_j = L^2(\mathbb{R}) \tag{8.26}$$

(2) Downward completeness:

$$\bigcap_{j \in Z} V_j = \{0\} \tag{8.27}$$

(3) Scale invariance:

$$f(t) \in V_j \Longleftrightarrow f(2^j\, t) \in V_{j+1} \tag{8.28}$$

(4) Shift invariance:

$$f(t) \in V_0 \Longrightarrow f(t - r) \in V_0 \ \forall r \in \mathbb{Z} \tag{8.29}$$

(5) Existence of a basis: There exists $\phi \in V_0$, such that

$$\{\phi(t - r) \,| r \in \mathbb{Z}\} \tag{8.30}$$

is an orthonaormal basis for $V_0$. Because of the embedding spaces of functions (equation(8.25)) and the scaling property (equation(8.28)), one can verify that the scaling function $\phi(t)$ satisfies a two-scale equation. Since $V_0$ is included in $V_1$, $\phi(t)$, which belongs to $V_0$, belongs to $V_1$ as well. As such, $\phi(t)$ can be written as a linear combination of the weighted sum of shifted $\phi(2t)$. Thus $\phi(t)$ can be expressed as

$$\phi(t) = \sqrt{2} \sum_{k=-\infty}^{\infty} h[k]\phi(2t - k) \ \ k \in \mathbb{Z}. \tag{8.31}$$

$h[k]$ are called the scaling function coefficients or the scaling filter coefficients.
With the above normalization, $\| h[k] \| = 1$ and $h[k] = \sqrt{2} < \phi(2t - k), \phi(t) >$. Taking the Fourier transform of both sides, we get

$$
\begin{aligned}
\widehat{\phi}(\omega) &= \int \phi(t) \, e^{-i\omega t} dt, \\
&= \int \sqrt{2} \sum_{k=-\infty}^{\infty} h[k]\phi(2t - k)e^{-i\omega t}, \\
&= \sqrt{2} \sum_{k=-\infty}^{\infty} h[k] \int \phi(t_1) \, e^{-i\omega(t_1/2+k/2)} \frac{1}{2} dt_1, \\
&= \sqrt{2} \sum_{k=-\infty}^{\infty} h[k] \frac{1}{2} \int \phi(t_1) \, e^{-i\omega/2 t_1} e^{-i\omega/2 k} dt_1, \\
&= \frac{1}{\sqrt{2}} \sum_{k=-\infty}^{\infty} h[k]e^{-i(\omega/2)k} \int \phi(t_1)e^{-i(\omega/2)t_1} \, dt_1, \\
&= \frac{1}{\sqrt{2}}\widehat{h}(\omega/2)\widehat{\phi}(\omega/2),
\end{aligned}
\tag{8.32}
$$

where $\widehat{h}(\omega/2) = \sum_{k \in Z} h[k]e^{-i\omega/2k}$. An important property of $\widehat{h}(e^{i\omega})$ is the following:

$$
|\widehat{h}e^{i\omega})|^2 + |\widehat{h}(e^{i(\omega+\pi)})|^2 = 2.
\tag{8.33}
$$

We have already seen that the scaling function $\phi$ can approximate a function $f(t)$ in different subspaces and these subspaces can be obtained by increasing the index $j$, i.e., increasing the size of the subspaces spanned by the scaling functions. However, this procedure is not efficient and hence, we take help of wavelet functions at different scales, i.e., at different wavelet subspaces. The wavelets $\psi_{j,r}(t)$ generated from the mother wavelet $\psi(t)$ span the difference between the spaces that are spanned by the different scales of the scaling functions. Scaling functions and wavelets are assumed to be orthogonal for a number of reasons from the standpoint of computation. $W_j$ is defined as the orthogonal complement of $V_j$ in $V_{j+1}$, so that all elements of $V_j$ are orthogonal to all elements of $W_j$. For this, we need the following inner product condition to hold true.

$$
\begin{aligned}
< \phi_{j,k}(t), \psi_{j,l}(t) > &= \int \phi_{j,k}(t)\psi_{j,l}(t)dt, \\
&= 0, \quad j, k, l \in \mathbb{Z}.
\end{aligned}
$$

The wavelet spanned subspace at $j = 0$ is $V_1 = V_0 \oplus W_0$. Similarly, $V_2 = V_1 \oplus W_1 = V_0 \oplus W_0 \oplus W_1$. Proceeding this way, we finally get

$$
\cdots \oplus W_2 \oplus W_1 \oplus W_0 \oplus W_1 \oplus W_2 \oplus \cdots = L^2.
$$

The scaling subspace $V_0$ can be viewed as

$$
W_{-\infty} \oplus \cdots \oplus W_1 = V_0.
$$

In practice, we choose those wavelet subspaces that are sufficient to represent the coarse information. As $W_0 \subset V_1$, the wavelets can be expressed as

$$\psi(t) = \sqrt{2} \sum_{k=-\infty}^{\infty} h_1[k]\phi(2t - k) \quad k \in \mathbb{Z}, \tag{8.34}$$

where $h_1[k]$ are the wavelet function coefficients and are given by

$$h_1[k] = (-1)^k h[1 - k].$$

The function $\psi$ in equation (8.34) provides a set of functions

$$\psi_{j,r}(t) = 2^{j/2}\psi(2^j t - r).$$

Here, $2^j$ is the scaling of $t$. Any function $f(t)$ can then be approximated by

$$f(t) = \sum_r c_j(r)2^{j/2}\phi(2^j t - r) + \sum_r d_j(r)2^{j/2}\psi(2^j t - r),$$

where

$$c_j(r) = <f(t), \phi_{j,r(t)}>,$$
$$= \int f(t)2^{j/2}\phi(2^j t - r)dt.$$

Now if we scale and translate the time variable, we can write from equation (8.31)

$$\phi(2^j t - r) = \sum_k h[k]\sqrt{2}\phi(2^{j+1}t - 2r - k),$$
$$= \sum_l h(l - 2r)\sqrt{2}\phi(2^{j+1}t - l),$$

after substituting $l = 2r + k$. With this, $c_j(r)$ becomes

$$c_j(r) = \sum_l h(l - 2r) \int f(t)2^{(j+1)/2}\phi(2^{j+1}t - l),$$
$$= \sum_l h(l - 2r)c_{j+1}(l).$$

Similarly, $d_j(r)$ can be written as

$$d_j(r) = \sum_l h_1(l - 2r)c_{j+1}(l).$$

For infinite $k$, $h[k]$ and $h_1[k]$ are coefficients of IIR filter, while when $k$ is finite, they form the coefficients of FIR filter. When the filter length, N (say) is even, $h$ and $h_1$ are connected by

$$h_1[k] = (-1)^k h[N - 1 - k].$$

## 8.6 Spline Approximations

Polynomial spline approximations do smooth approximations with fast asymptotic decay. One can construct a Riesz basis of polynomial splines with box splines. In this section, we present a slightly different approach to find the filter coefficients. The method is simple and straightforward. A box spline, $\alpha_n$, of order $n$, is computed by convolving the box window $1_{[0,1]}$ with itself $n$ times. Hence, considering the previous equation

$$\widehat{N}_n(\omega) = (\frac{\sin \omega/2}{\omega/2})^n e^{-i\beta\omega/2}.$$

When $n$ is odd, $\beta = 1$ and $\alpha$ is centered at $t = 1/2$, while when $n$ is even, $\beta = 0$, then $\alpha(t)$ is symmetric about $t = 0$. For $n \geq 1$, $\alpha(t - r)$, $r \in \mathbb{Z}$ is a Riesz basis of $V_0$.

Now, let us consider the following theorem.

**Theorem.** Let $\{V_j\}$, $j \in \mathbb{Z}$ be a multiresolution approximation and $\phi$ be scaling function whose Fourier transform is

$$\widehat{\phi}(\omega) = \frac{\widehat{N}_n(\omega)}{(\sum\limits_{r=-\infty}^{\infty} |\widehat{N}_n(\omega + 2\pi r)|^2)^{1/2}}. \tag{8.35}$$

If

$$\phi_{j,k} = 2^{j/2}\phi(2^j t - k),$$

then the family $\phi_{j,k}$, $j, k \in \mathbb{Z}$ is an orthonormal basis of $V_j$ for all $j \in \mathbb{Z}$.

Proof.

In order to construct an orthonormal basis, we need a function $\phi \in V_0$ that can be expanded in basis of $N_n(t - k)$, i.e., we must have

$$\phi(t) = \sum_{-\infty}^{\infty} a[k]N_n(t - k).$$

Taking Fourier transform we get,

$$\widehat{\phi}(\omega) = \widehat{a}(\omega)\widehat{N}_n(\omega).$$

$\widehat{a}(\omega)$ is a $2\pi$ periodic Fourier series of finite energy. For computation of $\widehat{a}(\omega)$, we take help of orthogonality of $\{\phi(t - k)\}$. Assuming $\bar{\phi}(t) = \phi^*(-t)$, we can write

$$< \phi(t - k), \phi(t - p) > = \int_{-\infty}^{\infty} \phi(t - k)\phi^*(t - p)dt,$$
$$= \phi * \bar{\phi}^*(p - k).$$

Hence, $\{\phi(t - k)\}$ is orthonormal if and only if $\phi * \bar{\phi}(k) = \delta[k]$. Computing Fourier transform, we get

$$\sum_{r=-\infty}^{\infty} |\widehat{\phi}(\omega + 2\pi r)|^2 = 1. \tag{8.36}$$

This is because $\phi * \bar{\phi}(t)$ is $|\widehat{\phi}(\omega)|^2$ and sampling a function periodizes its Fourier transform. Equation (8.36) is true if we choose

$$\widehat{a}(\omega) = \frac{1}{(\sum_{r=-\infty}^{\infty} |\widehat{N}_n(\omega + 2\pi r)|^2)^{1/2}}.$$

Using the above result we can write,

$$\begin{aligned}
\widehat{\phi}(\omega) &= \frac{2^n \sin^n \omega/2 e^{-i\beta\omega/2}}{\omega^n (\sum_{r=-\infty}^{\infty} |\widehat{N}_n(\omega + 2\pi r)|^2)^{1/2}}, \\
&= \frac{2^n \sin^n \omega/2 e^{-i\beta\omega/2}}{\omega^n 2^n \sin^n \omega/2 (\sum_{r=-\infty}^{\infty} \frac{1}{(\omega + 2\pi r)^{2n}})^{1/2}}, \tag{8.37} \\
&= \frac{e^{-i\beta\omega/2}}{\omega^n \sqrt{S_{2n}}},
\end{aligned}$$

where

$$\begin{aligned}
S_{2n} &= \sum_{r=-\infty}^{\infty} \frac{1}{(\omega + 2\pi r)^{2n}}, \\
&= -\frac{1}{2^{2n}} \frac{1}{(2n-1)!} \frac{d^{2n-1}}{dx^{2n-1}} \cot x. \tag{8.38}
\end{aligned}$$

Example 1: Linear splines
For linear splines, the order of the polynomial is $n = 2$. Also when $n$ is even, $\beta = 0$ and $\beta = 1$ when $n$ is odd. Hence, from equation (8.38),

$$S_4(\omega) = \frac{1}{48} \frac{1 + 2\cos^2 x}{\sin^4 x}.$$

Therefore,

$$\sqrt{S_4(\omega)} = \frac{1}{4\sqrt{3}} \frac{\sqrt{1 + 2\cos^2 x}}{\sin^2 x},$$

and so,

$$\widehat{\phi}(\omega) = \frac{1}{\omega^2} \frac{4\sqrt{3} \sin^2 x}{\sqrt{1 + 2\cos^2 x}}.$$

Example 2: Cubic splines
For cubic spline, $n = 4$. Hence, from equation (8.38),

$$
\begin{aligned}
S_8 &= \frac{-1}{2^8}\frac{1}{7!}\frac{d^7}{dx^7}\cot x, \\
&= \frac{-1}{2^8}\frac{1}{105.48}\frac{-16}{\sin^8 x}[4\cos^6 x + 10\cos^4 x + 26.4\cos^4 x + 26.3\cos^2 x \\
&\quad + 17.6\cos^2 x + 17], \\
&= \frac{1}{2^8}\frac{1}{105.48}\frac{16}{\sin^8 x}[4(1 - 3\sin^2 x + 3\sin^4 x - \sin^6 x) \\
&\quad + 3.38\cos^4 x + 3.60\cos^2 x + 7], \\
&= \frac{1}{2^8}\frac{1}{105\sin^8 x}[(5 + 30\cos^2 x + 30\sin^2 x \cos^x) \\
&\quad + (70\cos^4 x + 2\sin^4 x \cos^2 x + \tfrac{2}{3}\sin^6 x)].
\end{aligned}
$$

## 8.6.1 Battle-Lemarié Wavelets

Battle and Lemarié wavelets are polynomial splines. These wavelets can be computed from multiresolution approximation. To get these wavelets in a general form, one can consider splines of order $n$ for which $\widehat{h}(\omega)$ and first $n-1$ derivatives are zero at $\omega = \pi$. The wavelet $\psi$ has $n$ vanishing moments. Being a polynomial of order $n$, it has degree $n-1$ and hence it is $n-2$ times continuously differentiable. Also, when the degree of the polynomial is odd, $\psi$ is symmetric about $\frac{1}{2}$ and when the degree is even, $\psi$ is antisymmetric about $\frac{1}{2}$.

From equation (8.34),

$$
\begin{aligned}
\widehat{\psi}(\omega) &= \int \psi(t)\, e^{-i\omega t} dt, \\
&= \int \sqrt{2}\sum_{k=-\infty}^{\infty} h_1[k]\phi(2t - k)e^{-i\omega t}, \\
&= \sqrt{2}\sum_{k=-\infty}^{\infty} h_1[k]\int \phi(t_1)\, e^{-i\omega(t_1/2 + k/2)}\frac{1}{2}dt_1, \\
&= \sqrt{2}\sum_{k=-\infty}^{\infty} h_1[k]\frac{1}{2}\int \phi(t_1)\, e^{-i\omega/2 t_1}e^{-i\omega/2k}dt_1, \\
&= \frac{1}{\sqrt{2}}\sum_{k=-\infty}^{\infty} h_1[k]e^{-i(\omega/2)k}\int \phi(t_1)e^{-i(\omega/2)t_1}\, dt_1, \\
&= \frac{1}{\sqrt{2}}\widehat{h}_1(\omega/2)\widehat{\phi}(\omega/2),
\end{aligned}
\tag{8.39}
$$

where, $\widehat{h}_1(\omega) = \sum_{k\in Z} h[k]e^{-i\omega k}$, and for any scale $2^j$, $\{\psi_{j,r}\}$, $j, r \in \mathbb{Z}$ is an orthonormal basis of $L^2(\mathbb{R})$. $\widehat{h}_1(\omega)$ is connected to $\widehat{h}(\omega)$ through

$$
\widehat{h}_1(\omega) = e^{-i\omega}\widehat{h}^*(\omega + \pi).
$$

Mallat and Meyer [116] proved that $\{\psi_{j,r}\}$, $r \in \mathbb{Z}$ is an orthonormal basis of $W_j$ if and only if

$$
|\widehat{h}_1(\omega)|^2 + |\widehat{h}_1(\omega + \pi)|^2 = 2
$$

and

$$\widehat{h}_1(\omega)\widehat{h}^*(\omega) + \widehat{h}_1(\omega + \pi)\widehat{h}^*(\omega + \pi) = 0.$$

Thus, we have

$$\widehat{\psi}(\omega) = \tfrac{1}{\sqrt{2}}\widehat{h}_1(\omega/2)\widehat{\phi}(\omega/2),$$
$$= \tfrac{1}{\sqrt{2}}e^{-i\omega/2}\widehat{h}^*(\omega/2 + \pi)\widehat{\phi}(\omega/2).$$

Now from $\widehat{h}(\omega)$-$\widehat{\phi}(\omega)$ relation, we can write (from equation (8.32))

$$\widehat{\phi}(\omega) = \frac{1}{\sqrt{2}}\widehat{h}(\omega/2)\widehat{\phi}(\omega/2).$$

Therefore,

$$\widehat{\phi}(2\omega) = \frac{1}{\sqrt{2}}\widehat{h}(\omega)\widehat{\phi}(\omega)$$

or,

$$\widehat{h}(\omega) = \sqrt{2}\frac{\widehat{\phi}(2\omega)}{\widehat{\phi}(\omega)},$$
$$= \sqrt{2}\frac{e^{-i\beta\omega}}{(2\omega)^n\sqrt{S_{2n}(2\omega)}} \cdot \frac{\omega^n\sqrt{S_{2n}(\omega)}}{e^{-i\beta\omega/2}}, \tag{8.40}$$
$$= e^{-i\beta\omega/2}\sqrt{\frac{S_{2n}(\omega)}{2^{2n-1}S_{2n}(2\omega)}}.$$

With this, we are in a position to compute Battle and Lemarié wavelets in a straightforward way. The generalized form of the Fourier transform of these wavelet functions from equation (8.39) can be written as

$$\widehat{\psi}(\omega) = \tfrac{1}{\sqrt{2}}\widehat{h}_1(\omega/2)\widehat{\phi}(\omega/2),$$
$$= \tfrac{1}{\sqrt{2}}e^{-i\omega/2}\widehat{h}^*(\omega/2 + \pi)\widehat{\phi}(\omega/2),$$
$$= \tfrac{1}{\sqrt{2}}e^{-i\omega/2}\sqrt{\frac{S_{2n}(\omega/2+\pi)}{2^{2n-1}S_{2n}(2(\omega/2+\pi))}} \cdot \frac{1}{(\omega/2)^n\sqrt{S_{2n}(\omega/2)}}, \tag{8.41}$$
$$= \frac{e^{-i\omega/2}}{\omega^n}\sqrt{\frac{S_{2n}(\omega/2+\pi)}{S_{2n}(\omega)S_{2n}(\omega/2)}}.$$

One can compute the spline of any degree following the procedure for computation adopted for linear and cubic splines for $n = 2$ and $n = 4$. The conjugate mirror filters for $n = 2$ and $n = 4$ are given by respective $\widehat{h}(\omega)$, and their impulse response $h(k)$ is listed in Table 8.1.

## 8.7 Biorthogonal Spline Wavelets

We have already seen the underlying concept of splines in orthogonal wavelet systems. Use of splines in biorthogonal systems is equally simple, straightforward, and efficient. The main advantages of biorthogonal systems over orthogonal systems are more flexibility and greater ease of design. As far as the filter design is concerned, orthogonal wavelet and scaling filters must have equal length. This restriction, however, is not present in biorthogonal systems.

**Table 8.1.** Conjugate mirror filter h[k] for linear and cubic splines [116].

| n | k | h[k] | n | k | h[k] |
|---|---|---|---|---|---|
|   | 0 | 0.817645956 |   | 7,-7 | -0.017982291 |
|   | 1,-1 | 0.397294430 |   | 8,-8 | 0.008685294 |
|   | 2,-2 | -0.069101020 |   | 9,9 | 0.008201477 |
| 2 | 3,-3 | -0.051945337 | 4 | 10,-10 | -0.004353840 |
|   | 4,-4 | 0.016974805 |   | 11,-11 | -0.003882426 |
|   | 5,-5 | 0.009990599 |   | 12,-12 | 0.002186714 |
|   | 6,-6 | -0.003883261 |   | 13,-13 | 0.001882120 |
|   | 7,-7 | -0.002201945 |   | 14,-14 | -0.001103748 |
|   | 8,-8 | 0.000923371 |   | 15,-15 | -0.000927187 |
|   | 9,-9 | 0.000511636 |   | 16,-16 | 0.000559952 |
|   | 10,-10 | -0.000224296 | 17,-17 | 0.000462093 |   |
|   | 11,-11 | -0.000122686 |   | 18,-18 | -0.000285414 |
|   | 0 | 0.766130398 | 4 | 19,-19 | -0.000232304 |
|   | 1,-1 | 0.433923147 |   | 20,-10 | 0.000146098 |
|   | 2,-2 | -0.050201753 |   |   |   |
| 4 | 3,-3 | -0.110036987 |   |   |   |
|   | 4,-4 | 0.032080869 |   |   |   |
|   | 5,-5 | 0.042068328 |   |   |   |
|   | 6,-6 | -0.017176331 |   |   |   |

In a biorthogonal system, two pairs of filters are normally used. One pair is called the analysis filter and the other pair is called the synthesis filter. Hence, if $\tilde{h}, \tilde{g}$ are the analysis filters and $h$ and $g$ are the synthesis filters, then they should be connected to each other suitably. According to Cohen, Daubechies, and Feauveau [40], they are connected by

$$\tilde{g}[k] = (-1)^k h(1 - k),$$
$$g[k] = (-1)^k \tilde{h}[1 - k],$$

i.e., they are cross related by time reversal and flipping signs of every other member. When $\tilde{h}[k] = h[k]$, $g[k]$ reduces to $g[k] = (-1)^k h[1 - k]$. This tells us about scaling and wavelet coefficients for orthogonal wavelets, wherein $g[k] = (-1)^k h[1 - k]$. From the perfect reconstruction condition, we can write

$$\sum_k \tilde{h}[k]h[k + 2r] = \delta(r). \tag{8.42}$$

Thus, $\tilde{h}$ is orthogonal to $h$. Hence, if we assume $\tilde{h}[k]$ is not zero for $\tilde{N}_1 \leq r \leq \tilde{N}_2$ and $h[k]$ is not zero for $N_1 \leq r \leq N_2$, then

$$N_2 - \tilde{N}_1 = 2l + 1,$$
$$\tilde{N}_2 - N_1 = 2\tilde{l} + 1, \quad l, \tilde{l} \in \mathbb{Z}.$$

$h[k]$ and $\tilde{h}[k]$ are called the coefficients of the scaling and dual scaling functions. Similarly, $g[k]$ and $\tilde{g}[k]$ are called the coefficients of the wavelet and dual wavelet functions. Hence the scaling and wavelet functions and their respective dual are given by

$$\phi(t) = \sum_k h[k]\sqrt{2}\phi(2t - k), \tag{8.43}$$

$$\tilde{\phi}(t) = \sum_k \tilde{h}[k]\sqrt{2}\tilde{\phi}(2t - k), \tag{8.44}$$

with

$$\sum_k h[k] = \sum_k \tilde{h}[k],$$
$$= \sqrt{2}.$$

And,

$$\psi(t) = \sum_k g[k]\sqrt{2}\phi(2t - k),$$
$$= \sum_k (-1)^k \tilde{h}[1 - k]\sqrt{2}\phi(2t - k). \tag{8.45}$$

Its dual is

$$\tilde{\psi}(t) = \sum_k \tilde{g}[k]\sqrt{2}\tilde{\phi}(2t - k),$$
$$= \sum_k (-1)^k h[1 - k]\sqrt{2}\tilde{\phi}(2t - k). \tag{8.46}$$

We list below the filter coefficients for some members of the Cohen-Daubechies-Feauveau (CDF) family of biorthogonal spline wavelets. It is easy to observe from Table 8.2 that they are symmetric.

**Table 8.2.** Coefficients for some members of Cohen-Daubechies-Feauveau family of biorthogonal spline wavelets [14].

| $h/\sqrt{2}$ | $\tilde{h}/\sqrt{2}$ |
|---|---|
| 1/2,1/2 | -1/16,1/16,1/2,1/16,-1/16 |
| 1/4,1/2,1/4 | -1/8,1/4,3/4,1/4,-1/8 |
| 1/8,3/8,3/8,1/8 | $-5/512, 15/512, 19/512, -97/512, -13/256, 175, 256, \cdots$ |

## 8.8 Concluding Remarks

Spline wavelets have been discussed in a simple way so that one can get some idea about them without any difficulty. A brief background for wavelets may be helpful to students. Continuous wavelet transform, along with some continuous wavelet functions, have been examined. Multiresolution analysis for wavelets can be used to design spline wavelets using splines of various degrees. One of the areas involving B-spline wavelet transform and multiresolution is the Chinese character processing, which can be found in [158]. The work is based on three stages, namely pre-processing, wavelet transform, and objective processing. Initially, a Chinese character is represented by its contours. Each contour with its coordinates is interpolated by a cubic B-spline function. The coefficient sequences, called the control points of the B-spline interpolation curves, are then linked with the coordinate points of the contour curves. Multiresolution analysis is then used to describe the interpolated curves. The book [158] describes several algorithms using both the global and local approaches for objective processing of curves.

# 9

## Snakes and Active Contours

## 9.1 Introduction

### 9.1.1 Splines and Energy Minimization Techniques

If we examine the origin and historical usage of splines, there is a clear link between smooth curves and energy minimization. Splines were originally thin, wooden strips used in both traditional ship and aircraft building techniques to help create the curved hulls needed to allow the ship or aircraft to travel speedily through the water or air. The splines were used for the process of lofting, which is required to expand the small scale plan from a boat designer into the full-size plans required for construction. The rescaling was done by transferring a series of measurements called offsets on to the large lofting floor of the lofthouse and then interpolating these offset points by bending splines into smooth interpolative curves. The wooden splines were bent into shape with the aid of a small number of weights, called ducks, and clamps that kept the wood in position as shown in Figure 9.1. The ducks provided positional constraints and the clamps could provide both positional and tangential (i.e., derivative) constraints. Wooden splines have a natural tendency to assume a smooth shape to minimize overall bending energy while satisfying the imposed constraints.

This energy minimization approach to producing smooth curves is fundamentally different from the approach taken with Bernstein-Bézier and B-splines. In the former approach, the smoothness derives naturally from the minimization of energy—as in the case of the wooden spline. By contrast, the latter approach ensures smoothness by representing a shape as a sum of smooth mathematical functions. So it could be persuasively argued that energy minimization methods are more faithful to the historical concept of splines than the modern concept of mathematical splines developed by Bézier et al.

Indeed Kass, Witken, and Terzopoulos [88, 89] referred to snakes as a form of spline in their groundbreaking paper presented at the very first ICCV

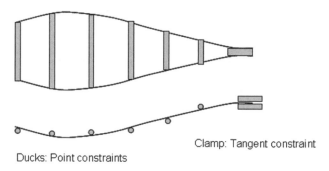

Clamp: Tangent constraint

Ducks: Point constraints

**Fig. 9.1.** Wooden splines for boat building.

held in London in 1987. They introduced the concept of snakes by stating that, "A snake is an energy minimizing spline guided by external contraint forces and influenced by image forces that pull it towards lines and edges." Unlike Bernstein-Bézier splines, the splines of Kass et al. could determine their own control points directly from the image under analysis by using constraints based on image intensity and gradient. This was an exciting time in computer vision research and represented a major break from image analysis via the sequential linking of low level features such as edges and intensities.

Kass, Witken, and Terzopoulos were working for Schlumberger Palo-Alto Research and were interested in using snakes to speed up the manual labeling of seismic data as required for oil exploration. These seismic images are complicated and their interpretation requires the input of interpretation experts. Indeed, sometimes there would be little agreement between the experts. In the words of Kass et al. [88]:

> Different seismic interpreters can derive significantly different perceptual organizations from the same seismic sections depending on their knowledge and training. Because a single "correct" interpretation cannot always be defined, we suggest low-level mechanisms which seek appropriate local minima instead of searching for global minima.

Thus the authors saw snakes as an interactive "power assist" for manual labeling by a human expert rather than as a fully automatic image interpreter algorithm in its own right. The human expert would adjust the snake by hand until it was close to the desired solution, and the snake energy minimization would do the rest.

In the case of seismic sections, the effort of manually labeling the images is relatively low compared to the huge expense and effort of collection. However, in the case of, say, computer analysis of closed circuit television feeds for building security, the process of image analysis must be completely automatic and reliable to be effective. Fortunately, in many image labeling tasks, interpretation is much more straightforward than for seismic sections. Indeed, in many cases, virtually all people would agree on the same interpretation.

For example, when presented with a photograph of an unobstructed person, almost everyone would agree on the same partitioning of such an image into person and background. Yet, this important and seemingly trivial task of image labeling is extraordinarily difficult to achieve automatically. It turns out that snakes and general energy minimization techniques are some of the most promising methods for automated analysis—though all methods have their weaknesses.

## 9.2 Classical Snakes

An active contour or *snake* as proposed by Kass et al. [88] is a closed or open curve defined within a 2D image domain that is able to evolve or deform to conform to features, such as edges and lines, in the image under analysis. The evolution of the snake is formulated as an iterative energy minimization process in which the snake is deformed to reach a locally minimum energy configuration.

The total energy associated with the snake is defined as the sum of an *internal energy term*, an *external energy term*, and an *external force term*. The internal energy influences the shape and smoothness of the snake and depends only on the properties of the snake itself, independent of the underlying image (*cf* the bending strain in a wooded spline). The external energy is what causes the snake to align itself with image features and is derived from the underlying image. The force term allows the user to manually force the snake to move in particular directions to aid in finding the best solution.

In general, curves cannot be described by one-dimensional functions as they may double back on themselves, so we parametcrize the snakes along their length as follows:

$$\nu(s) = (x(s), y(s)), s \in [0, 1]. \tag{9.1}$$

Thus as $s$ varies from 0 to 1 inclusive, we traverse the entirety of the snake. In practice, we discretize this parameterization and evaluate the energy of the snake at, say, $N$ sample points, often called control points, along the contour. These points actually define the snake so they must be spaced somewhat closer than would be the case for the control points of a Bernstein-Bézier spline—generally they are spaced just a few pixels apart so that small image features are not missed.

Thus we have initially a set of $N$ points such that

$$\nu_n = \nu(s)|_{s=k/N}, k \in [0..N - 1]. \tag{9.2}$$

In other words, we place the $N$ control points successively along the length of the snake at locations $(x_n, y_n) = \nu_n = \nu(s)$ evaluated at monotonically increasing values of $s$ by assumption. Normally, we try to space the points evenly along the snake initially. However, even if we don't, the membrane term (see Section 9.3) of the snake internal energy will quickly even out the points during the evolution phase. Figure 9.3 shows the evolution of a closed snake when applied to the cell segmentation problem.

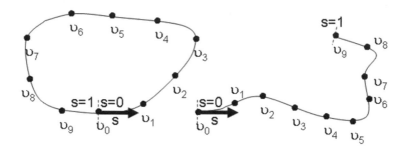

**Fig. 9.2.** Parameterized and discretized closed and open snakes.

## 9.3 Energy Functional

The initial position of the snake is usually specified by the user based on *a priori* knowledge of the image under analysis. Often the initial snake may be drawn with a mouse or drawing tablet for convenience. Once initialized, the evolution of the snake can be considered as the process of minimizing the following energy functional[1]:

$$E_{snake} = \int_0^1 E_{int}(\nu(s)) + E_{image}(\nu(s)) + E_{forces}(\nu(s)) \qquad (9.3)$$

where $E_{int}$ is the internal energy term, $E_{image}$ is the image energy term, and $E_{forces}$ is the external forces constraints term. In Kass et al. [88], the internal energy of the snake is defined as follows:

$$E_{int}(\nu(s)) = \alpha(s) \underbrace{\left| \frac{\partial}{\partial s} \nu(s) \right|^2}_{\text{membrane term}} + \beta(s) \underbrace{\left| \frac{\partial^2}{\partial s^2} \nu(s) \right|^2 / 2}_{\text{thin-plate term}} . \qquad (9.4)$$

The spline energy is defined by a first-order term controlled by $\alpha(s)$ and a second-order term controlled by $\beta(s)$. The first-order term provides behavior similar to the elasticity exhibited by a membrane[2] and the second-order term provides behavior similar to the stiffness exhibited by a thin metal plate. The

---

[1] A functional is a function of a function.

[2] Equation (9.4) is a membrane equation known from mechanics combined with a stiffness-term.

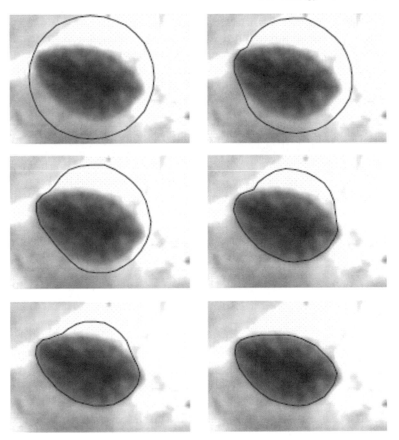

**Fig. 9.3.** Application of a Kass et al. closed snake for screening for cervical cancer using Pap smear images. Here we wish to segment the cell nucleus from the cytoplasm (from [11]).

behavior of snakes is easier to understand if we examine the discrete form of the internal energy as follows [3]:

$$E_{int}(\nu_i) = \underbrace{\alpha_i |\nu_i - \nu_{i-1}|^2}_{\text{membrane term}} + \underbrace{\beta_i |\nu_{i+1} - 2\nu_i + \nu_{i-1}|^2}_{\text{thin-plate term}}. \qquad (9.5)$$

Now the membrane term

$$|\nu_i - \nu_{i-1}|^2 = \sqrt{(x_i - x_{i-1})^2 + (y_i - y_{i-1})^2}$$

just represents the square of the distance between successive control points. Since $E_{int}$ is the sum of the squared distances between the control points, this energy is minimized when the distances are all equal and the control points are collinear. In the case of an open snake, this low energy configuration will be satisfied by a straight line with uniformly spaced control points. Note that if there are no external forces imposed, the sum of the membrane terms in the snake energy is minimized by contracting all control points into a single point; just like a soap bubble that becomes a tiny droplet when the air escapes. The membrane term is often considered to be providing *elasticity*—it makes the snake shrink during evolution somewhat like a stretched elastic band.

The membrane term also penalizes curvature indirectly because curvature increases the snake energy by increasing the distance between the control points—a straight line is always the shortest distance between two points in a Euclidean space. Note that in the case of a closed snake, there must always be some curvature to allow the snake to connect back on to itself.

The second-order or thin-plate term in (9.5) penalizes changes in curvature and makes the snake behave like a thin metal plate.[3] The thin-plate term only penalizes *changes* in the distance between the control points. This becomes obvious if we rewrite the argument of the modulus in the thin-plate term of (9.5),

$$\nu_{i+1} - 2\nu_i + \nu_{i-1},$$

in the form

$$(\nu_{i+1} - \nu_i) - (\nu_i - \nu_{i-1}).$$

So unlike the membrane term, minimization of the thin-plate term does not provide the elastic behavior that collapses the snake to a single point under evolution. Rather it provides *stiffness* as exhibited by, say, a thin metal plate that ensures that both the control points and the curvature are uniformly distributed. This term makes the snake form smooth curves during evolution just like the traditional wooden spline for lofting in shipbuilding. Thus during evolution, a closed snake with no external constraints will tend to become circular due to the stiffness provided by the thin-plate term before it finally collapses to a single point due to the elasticity provided by the membrane term.

The image energy is formulated so that its value is minimal at the location of the desired image features. Kass et al. [88] considered a weighted set of features based on lines, edges, and terminations (*i.e.*, the end points of lines) as follows:

$$E_{image} = w_{line}E_{line}(\nu_s) + w_{edge}E_{edge}(\nu_s) + w_{term}E_{term}(\nu_s). \tag{9.6}$$

In this chapter and henceforth, we will only consider edge energy, so a suitable image energy term is:

$$E_{image} = E_{edge}(\nu(s)) = -|\nabla I(x, y)|^2 \tag{9.7}$$

where $\nabla I(x, y)$ is the gradient of the image intensity.

---

[3] *cf* a thin-plate spline, is the surface with minimum mean square second derivative energy that interpolates a given collection of points.

Finally the force term can be expressed by the following term [89]:

$$E_{force} = -k(x_1 - x_2)^2. \tag{9.8}$$

This force energy $E_{force}$ represents the energy of a spring connected between a point $x_1$ on the contour and some point $x_2$ in the image plane. In practice, there could be multiple force terms—one for each spring added. These forces may be used by a human expert to direct and guide the evolution of the snake.

## Special Cases and Variations on a Theme

By adjusting the values of the $\alpha$ and $\beta$ terms in the internal energy of (9.5), snakes of varying elasticity and stiffness can be produced. If $\beta_i$ is set to zero at control point $\nu_i$, we allow the snake to become second-order discontinuous (flexible) at $\nu_i$ and develop a corner. This is analogous to folding a piece of corrugated cardboard to make a cardboard box—the fold then behaves like a flexible hinge between the stiff cardboard sides. This property allows snakes to better conform to corners of objects such as car licenseplates and allows for the possibility of embedding shape grammars into snakes.

In some applications, the contractive behavior of the membrane term is inconvenient, as it may pull the snake away from the best solution. In such cases, setting $\alpha$ to a low value or zero yields the so-called *thin-plate splines*, which behave much more like wooden splines and are best compared to Bernstein-Bézier and B-splines.

Due to the contractive nature of the membrane term, snakes must always be initialized outside the region of interest, so they can contract down onto the image features like a contracting elastic band. In some situations, this behavior may be inconvenient. For this reason, Cohen [43] proposed both inflationary and deflationary forces normal to the surface of closed snakes to force them to either grow or shrink as illustrated in Figure 9.4; he used the term *balloons* to refer to these modified closed snakes. Balloons can be initialized either within or outside image objects of interest. Figure 9.5 shows the application of a balloon to the cell image segmentation problem.

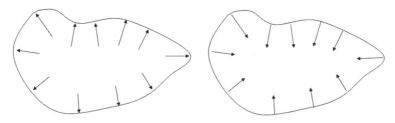

**Fig. 9.4.** Balloons with inflationary and deflationary forces.

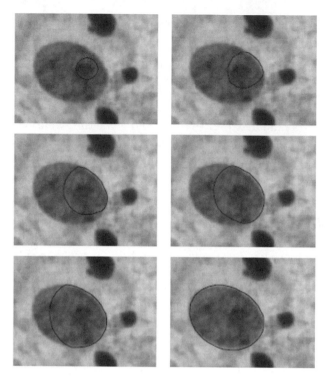

**Fig. 9.5.** Balloon applied to the cell image segmentation problem (from [11]).

## 9.4 Minimizing the Snake Energy Using the Calculus of Variations

As minimizing the snake energy is an optimization problem we can use techniques from calculus of variations. In particular, we will use Lagrangian multipliers.

Following the development of Amini, Weymouth, and Jain [3], we let $E_{ext} = E_{image} + E_{forces}$ where $E_{ext}$ is the external energy. Substituting (9.4) into (9.3), we have

$$E_{snake} = \int_0^1 \alpha(s) \left| \frac{\partial}{\partial s} \nu(s) \right|^2 + \beta(s) \left| \frac{\partial^2}{\partial s^2} \nu(s) \right|^2 + E_{ext}(\nu(s)) \, ds. \qquad (9.9)$$

For simplicity, we represent the integrand by $F(s, \nu_s, \nu_{ss})$, then the Euler-Lagrange necessary condition for minimization is derived by

$$F_\nu = \frac{\partial}{\partial s} F_{\nu_s} + \frac{\partial^2}{\partial s^2} F_{\nu_{ss}} = 0. \qquad (9.10)$$

Substituting the terms in the above equation, we obtain a pair of independent Euler-Lagrange equations,

$$-\alpha x_{ss} + \beta x_{ssss} + \frac{\partial E_{ext}}{\partial x} = 0$$

and

$$-\alpha y_{ss} + \beta y_{ssss} + \frac{\partial E_{ext}}{\partial y} = 0.$$

This is best to solve numerically. The Euler-Lagrange equations with

$$f_x(i) = \partial E_{ext}/\partial x_i$$

and

$$f_y(i) = \partial E_{ext}/\partial y_i$$

are discretized, yielding

$$\alpha_i(\nu_i - \nu_{i-1}) - \alpha_{i+1}(\nu_{i+1} - \nu_i) + \beta_{i-1}(\nu_{i-2} - 2\nu_{i-1} + \nu_i)$$
$$- 2\beta_i(\nu_{i-1} - 2\nu_i + \nu_{i+1}) + \beta_{i-1}(\nu_i - 2\nu_{i+1} + \nu_{i+2})$$
$$+ (f_x(i), f_y(i)) = 0.$$

Writing the equation in matrix forms, one for $x$ and another for $y$, yields

$$Ax + f_x(x, y) = 0$$

and

$$Ay + f_y(x, y) = 0.$$

We can now solve for position vectors iteratively by,

$$x_t = (A + \gamma I)^{-1}(\gamma x_{t-1} - f_x(x_{t-1}, y_{t-1}))$$

and

$$y_t = (A + \gamma I)^{-1}(\gamma y_{t-1} - f_y(x_{t-1}, y_{t-1})).$$

Amini, Weymouth, and Jain identified several problems with the above calculus of variations approach as originally proposed by Kass, Witten, and Terzopoulos in 1987. In particular, they raised the following objections:

1. There is a significant risk that the above procedure does not converge.
2. Optimality cannot be guaranteed as the Euler-Lagrange equations are a necessary but not a sufficient condition for optimality in a local sense.
3. Constraints are required to be differentiable, which cannot be guaranteed in general.
4. The requirement for differentiability of the images will lead to instability unless the image is smoothed leading to poor localization of features.
5. If a snake is not subject to appropriate external forces, it will contract to a line or a point.
6. If a snake is not placed close to image features, it will not get attracted.

For these reasons, they proposed the dynamic programming approach to minimizing the energy [3]. This method has now been adopted as the standard algorithm by most researchers and will be used henceforth in this chapter.

## 9.5 Minimizing the Snake Energy Using Dynamic Programming

One of the most popular methods today is the dynamic programming approach as implemented by the Viterbi algorithm [167] as proposed by Amini, Weymouth, and Jain [3] and extended by Geiger et al. [66]. The approach of dynamic programming is to solve the optimization problem by studying a collection, or family, of problems where the particular problem in question is a member. This concept is known as *embedding*.

The Viterbi method is closely related to Dijkstra's algortithm [59], which solves for the shortest path in a network between two points by finding the shortest paths to all points. The major difference is that the Viterbi algorithm calculates the shortest path on a *trellis*, whereas Dijkstra's algorithm finds the shortest path in a network. Returning to the snake minimization problem at hand, instead of attempting to find the local minimum directly, the Viterbi algorithm efficiently evaluates a very large set of alternative solutions in the neighborhood of the current best solution and then picks the minimum. The process is repeated until convergence is attained.

The dynamic programming formulation of snakes requires the snake to be discretized to a finite set of points in the image pixel domain as before. To limit the number of possible solutions examined, the position of each control point on the snake on the next iteration is constrained to a finite set of positions, $x_i \in X_i$, where each set $X_i$ contains $m$ positions. With the snake discretized and the domain of possible solutions constrained in this manner, the set of all possibilities for the next configuration of the snake can be visualized as a trellis as illustrated in Figure 9.6.

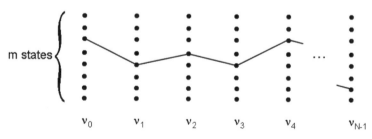

**Fig. 9.6.** Snake configuration space visualized as a trellis.

It is possible, but not at all practical, to exhaustively enumerate all possible configurations to determine the snake with minimum energy. This would require $O(m^N)$ evaluations of the energy function, where $m$ is the number of candidate positions and $N$ is the number of control points forming the snake. This is prohibitively expensive for even small values of $m$ and $N$. For example, if $m = N = 30$, this task would require $30^{30} = 2 \times 10^{44}$ evaluations. Assuming each energy evaluation takes just 1 microsecond, the exhaustive minimization would require almost $7 \times 10^{30}$ years—much, much longer than the age of the universe. Yet with the Viterbi algorithm we can calculate the exact same minimal value in just $O(Nm)$ time, which is equivalent to just 900 evaluations, or barely one millisecond!

The Viterbi algorithm is therefore deservedly referred to as a *fast* algorithm. Along with the more famous family of Fast Fourier Transform algorithms, it is one of the classic fast algorithms of digital signal processing [28]. The inventor of the algorithm, Andrew Viterbi, was a co-founder of Qualcomm, a wireless telecommunications research and development company based in San Diego, California. The algorithm still finds wide application in communications including the widely-used V32 and V90 telephone modem standards. It is instrumental in decoding highly efficient trellis and convolutional codes for high-speed data communication. The algorithm also finds application in pattern recognition, where it forms the basis of the forward and backward algorithms for learning and recognition via hidden Markov models for speech and gesture recognition [138].

Returning to the problem at hand, the Viterbi algorithm is used to efficiently calculate the optimal configuration of the snake, which minimizes total energy. This is possible because of the decoupled form of the discrete internal energy function of (9.5). We observe that the internal energy of each control point is only dependent on the points immediately preceding and following it. So the total energy of the snake can be written in the form:

$$E_{snake} = E_1(\nu_0, \nu_1, \nu_3) + E_2(\nu_1, \nu_2, \nu_3) + \ldots + E_{N-2}(\nu_{N-3}, \nu_{N-2}, \nu_{N-1}).$$
$$(9.11)$$

## Dynamic Programming and the Principle of Optimality

Dynamic programming in general can be applied to any problem that observes the *Principle of Optimality*. Bellman [19], the inventor of dynamic programming, states:

> An optimal policy has the property that, whatever the initial state and optimal first decision may be, the remaining decisions constitute an optimal policy with regard to the state resulting from the first decision.

If a problem observes the Principle of Optimality it means that optimal solutions of subproblems can be used to find the optimal solutions to the overall problem.

In the case of the shortest (or equivalently minimum energy) path problem in a network as addressed by Dijkstra's algorithm [59], this means that all subpaths A to B, say, of the shortest path from A to Z, must themselves be shortest paths. In order to explain this seemingly obvious but very powerful principle better, let's consider the the shortest path between the cities of Brisbane and Sydney. We assume that the shortest path between these cities passes through the city of, say, Armidale. Immediately we can say that the shortest path between Brisbane and Armidale is just that section of the Brisbane-Sydney shortest path that lies between Brisbane and Armidale. Why? Well, if there existed a path between Brisbane and Armidale that was shorter than the one already found, then that original path from Brisbane to Sydney via Armidale could not have been the shortest path between those cities—so we have proof by contradiction. Hence all subpaths of a shortest path must themselves be shortest paths between their respective endpoints. Reversing the argument, we see that new shortest paths can be found by recursively extending known shortest paths.

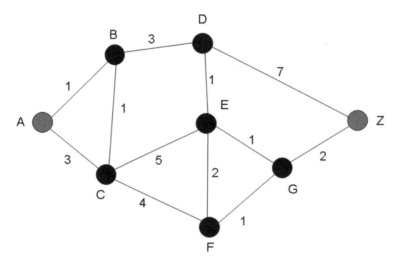

**Fig. 9.7.** Shortest path in a graph or network problem.

## Dijkstra's Algorithm for the Shortest Path on a Network

The above insight leads directly to Dijkstra's algorithm for the single-source shortest path problem for a directed graph with nonnegative edge weights. Let us determine the shortest path from node A to Z, say, in the network of Figure 9.7. We know initially that the shortest path to A is the null path of cost 0. From the Principle of Optimality we know our solution can be obtained by extending known shortest paths, in this case the null path. So we follow all paths leading out of A to reach the following nodes with their associated path costs:

$$(\text{known}) \ A0 \mid B1, C3 \ (\text{trial}).$$

Here we have partitioned our nodes into *known*, where we now know the shortest path to the node, and *trial* where we are yet to determine the shortest path. Now AB of cost 1 must be the shortest path from A to B as any alternative path must go via AC, which has cost 3 already. It will always be the case that the trial node with minimum path cost found so far will be the end node of a new shortest path. Now we know that the shortest path AZ can be constructed by extending shortest paths, so now we follow all paths leading out of B, except those leading back to known nodes, and then add B to the known nodes list, which yields the following nodes and costs:

$$(\text{known}) \ A0, B1 \mid C2, D4. \ (\text{trial}).$$

In this case, we have found an alternate route to C via B with cost 2, which is lower than the cost found so far. So we have updated the cost to C with the new value. We now know that there is no shorter path to C other than the one we have found since any alternate path would have to go via D, which has cost 4. This process is repeated until we reach reach node Z. The complete sequence is given in Table 9.1. All that remains to complete the algorithm is to maintain a list of backward pointers for each node, which will allow us to backtrack along the shortest paths to the starting node. The steps of the algorithm including the backward pointers are shown in Table 9.2 and the pseudo-code is given in Figure 9.8.

**Table 9.1.** Evolution of Dijkstra's algorithm on the network of Figure 9.7. Shortest path costs to known nodes are shown in bold. The cost of the shortest path from A to Z is 8.

| A | B | C | D | E | F | G | Z |
|---|---|---|---|---|---|---|---|
| 0 | $\infty$ | $\infty$ | $\infty$ | $\infty$ | $\infty$ | $\infty$ | $\infty$ |
| 0 | 1 | 3 | $\infty$ | $\infty$ | $\infty$ | $\infty$ | $\infty$ |
| 0 | 1 | 2 | 4 | $\infty$ | $\infty$ | $\infty$ | $\infty$ |
| 0 | 1 | 2 | 4 | 7 | 6 | $\infty$ | $\infty$ |
| 0 | 1 | 2 | 4 | 5 | 6 | 6 | 11 |
| 0 | 1 | 2 | 4 | 5 | 6 | 6 | 11 |
| 0 | 1 | 2 | 4 | 5 | 6 | 6 | 8 |
| 0 | 1 | 2 | 4 | 5 | 6 | 6 | 8 |

It is useful to visualize the evolution of Dijkstra's algorithm as an expanding wavefront. At each stage of the algorithm, the minimum distance node is found and paths leading out of this node are followed yielding another shortest path. Dijkstra's algorithm is closely related to the Fast Marching Algorithm introduced by Sethian [149, 150], which is used in both Level Sets and Geodesic Active Contours.

**Table 9.2.** Stages of Dijkstra's algorithm on the network of Figure 9.7 including the backward pointers. Shortest path costs to known nodes are shown in bold. The shortest path to Z is the path ABDEGZ of cost 8.

| A | B | C | D | E | F | G | Z |
|---|---|---|---|---|---|---|---|
| **0** | $\infty$ | $\infty$ | $\infty$ | $\infty$ | $\infty$ | $\infty$ | $\infty$ |
| $\emptyset$ | $\emptyset$ | $\emptyset$ | $\emptyset$ | $\emptyset$ | $\emptyset$ | $\emptyset$ | $\emptyset$ |

| A | B | C | D | E | F | G | Z |
|---|---|---|---|---|---|---|---|
| **0** | 1 | 3 | $\infty$ | $\infty$ | $\infty$ | $\infty$ | $\infty$ |
| $\emptyset$ | A | A | $\emptyset$ | $\emptyset$ | $\emptyset$ | $\emptyset$ | $\emptyset$ |

| A | B | C | D | E | F | G | Z |
|---|---|---|---|---|---|---|---|
| **0** | **1** | 2 | 4 | $\infty$ | $\infty$ | $\infty$ | $\infty$ |
| $\emptyset$ | A | B | B | $\emptyset$ | $\emptyset$ | $\emptyset$ | $\emptyset$ |

| A | B | C | D | E | F | G | Z |
|---|---|---|---|---|---|---|---|
| **0** | **1** | **2** | 4 | 7 | 6 | $\infty$ | $\infty$ |
| $\emptyset$ | A | B | B | C | C | $\emptyset$ | $\emptyset$ |

| A | B | C | D | E | F | G | Z |
|---|---|---|---|---|---|---|---|
| **0** | **1** | **2** | **4** | 5 | 6 | $\infty$ | 11 |
| $\emptyset$ | A | B | B | D | C | $\emptyset$ | D |

| A | B | C | D | E | F | G | Z |
|---|---|---|---|---|---|---|---|
| **0** | **1** | **2** | **4** | **5** | 6 | 6 | 11 |
| $\emptyset$ | A | B | B | D | C | E | D |

| A | B | C | D | E | F | G | Z |
|---|---|---|---|---|---|---|---|
| **0** | **1** | **2** | **4** | **5** | **6** | 6 | 11 |
| $\emptyset$ | A | B | B | D | C | E | D |

| A | B | C | D | E | F | G | Z |
|---|---|---|---|---|---|---|---|
| **0** | **1** | **2** | **4** | **5** | **6** | **6** | 8 |
| $\emptyset$ | A | B | B | D | C | E | G |

| A | B | C | D | E | F | G | Z |
|---|---|---|---|---|---|---|---|
| **0** | **1** | **2** | **4** | **5** | **6** | **6** | **8** |
| $\emptyset$ | A | B | B | D | C | E | G |

```
function Dijkstra(G, w, s)              // G = graph
                                        // w = costs
                                        // s = start node
for each vertex v in V[G]               // Initializations
      d[v] := infinity
      previous[v] := undefined
d[s] := 0
S := empty set                          // S = known nodes
Q := V[G]                               // Q = trial nodes
while Q is not an empty set             // The algorithm
      u := Extract_Min(Q)
      S := S union {u}
      for each edge (u,v) outgoing from u
            if d[u] + w(u,v) < d[v]
                  d[v] := d[u] + w(u,v)
                  previous[v] := u
```

**Fig. 9.8.** Pseudocode for Dijkstra's Algorithm for finding the shortest path on a graph or network.

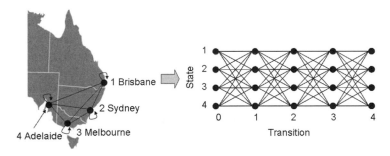

**Fig. 9.9.** Air transportation network converted to a trellis.

**Viterbi Algorithm for the Shortest Path on a Trellis**

The Viterbi algorithm finds the shortest path on a trellis rather than on a network. A trellis can be derived from a network by associating a state with each node of the network and then representing the set of states vertically as a column. This column of states is then replicated horizontally to indicate increasing increments of time or equivalently transitions or "hops" between states. Connecting lines are used to show the allowable state transitions and possible paths. Note that self-transitions are often permissible on a trellis and may incur non-zero cost.

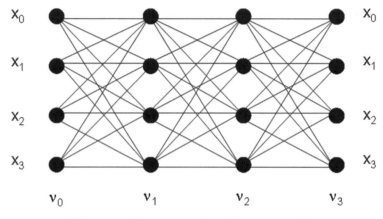

**Fig. 9.10.** Shortest path problem in a trellis.

Figure 9.9 shows the paths available through an air transportation network between a set of cities represented by a trellis. Each flight from city to city would be just one leg of an overall itinerary (*cf* path) and a self-transition could be a flight returning to the city of departure. In the above example, we show direct flights between all cities, but that is not always the case in a general air transportation network. If there were no direct flights between two particular cities, a common problem is finding the cheapest itinerary requiring just $N$ stopovers. This is a problem that can be rapidly solved using the Viterbi algorithm as follows.

Consider the trellis illustrated in Figure 9.10 with $M = 4$ states and length $N = 4$ hops. We examine paths from the starting node[4] $\nu_0$ in state $x_i \in [x_0..x_{M-1}]$ reaching a terminating node $\nu_{N-1}$ in state $x_j \in [x_0..x_{M-1}]$ on the right. Let the distance measure $d(i, j, k)$ denote the cost of transitioning from state $x_i$ in node $\nu_k$ to state $x_j$ in node $\nu_{k+1}$.

---

[4] Here we use the word "node" to refer to a junction in the trellis that corresponds to a particular state at a particular hop count.

Now the cost of a path on the trellis is simply the sum of the costs along the path. For example, the cost of traveling from $\nu_0$ to $\nu_3$ along the illustrated path in Figure 9.11 is given by

$$\text{Total Cost} = d(2,1,0) + d(1,2,1) + d(2,3,2).$$

Now we wish to determine the shortest path between two nodes on the trellis. The possible number of paths in a fully-connected[5] trellis equals $M^N$ which can be an enormous number—exhaustive evaluation of all possible paths is out of the question. The trick that makes the Viterbi algorithm so incredibly fast is again due to the Principle of Optimality. This tells us that if we maintain the shortest path to each of the $M$ states as we progress through the trellis, we can find the overall shortest path by recursively extending these $M$ paths. Thus the computational load is linear with respect to the length of the trellis, $O(MN)$, rather than exponential, $O(M^N)$. As for Dijkstra's algorithm, we maintain a list of backward pointers so that we can eventually recover the shortest paths.

The pseudocode for the complete Viterbi algorithm is shown in Figure 9.12. The algorithm progresses along the trellis one hop at a time maintaining a record of the shortest path to each destination node from the starting node. After a hop, the algorithm extends the shortest paths to the previous set of destination nodes in all directions to find the shortest paths to each of the current set of destination nodes, and then it hops again. However, unlike Dijkstra's algorithm, which can extend known paths in any direction, the Viterbi algorithm marches through the trellis column by column updating the paths. If it was useful to visualize the evolution of Dijkstra's algorithm as an expanding wavefront, perhaps the Viterbi algorithm is more akin to an electromagnetic wave traveling down a waveguide.

Note that in the Viterbi algorithm pseudocode of Figure 9.12, we have chosen to initialize the algorithm with the distance to the starting node set to 0 and the distance to all other nodes set to infinity (*i.e.*, unreachable) to force all paths to start at the starting node. Nevertheless, there are situations where we may not know the best starting node or we may have a choice of several starting nodes. In these cases, we could initialize the distances to all possible starting nodes to 0 and the Viterbi algorithm would then calculate the shortest path to the best choice from the set of starting nodes. If we follow the backward pointers back from the destination node, we can determine which of the stating nodes was actually chosen for the particular shortest path at hand.

Following the same reasoning, when the Viterbi algorithm is used with discrete hidden Markov models (HMMs) [138] for, say, speech recognition, it is common practice to assign a particular probability to each of the starting states based on *a priori* knowledge. Indeed, when used with HMMs, the costs of transitioning between the states are actually state transition probabilities

---

[5] For example, where a state can transition to any other state.

representing the likelihood of transitioning from one state to the next. In this application, the multiplication of these very small numbers leads to a risk of arithmetic underflow in the calculation of the Viterbi algorithm, which is overcome by using the logarithm of probability and other scaling techniques.

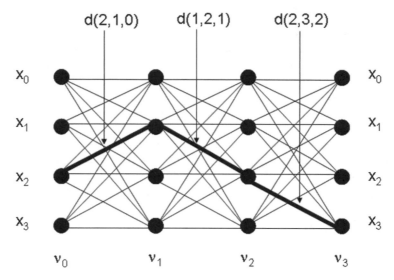

**Fig. 9.11.** Example path in a trellis.

```
function Viterbi(T, w, s)                    // T = trellis
                                             // w = costs
                                             // s = start state
      for each state x in X[T]               // Initializations
            d[x] := infinity
            previous[x,0] := undefined       // Index on state,hop
      d[s] := 0
      for each hop h in H[T]                 // H[T] is hops
            for each state v in X[T]         // Destination states
                  dist[v] := infinity        // Flag v as trial
            for each state u in X[T]         // Source states
                  for each edge (u,v) outgoing from u
                        if d[u] + w(u,v) < dist[v]
                              d[v] := d[u] + w(u,v) // Flag v as known
                              previous[v,h] := u
```

**Fig. 9.12.** Pseudocode for Viterbi algorithm for finding the shortest path on a trellis.

## Dynamic Programming for Open Snakes

Returning now to the calculation of evolving snakes, the usage of the Viterbi algorithm is quite straightforward. For each control point, we determine a set of candidate points for the next evolution of the snake spread along a short distance in a direction perpendicular to the snake as illustrated in Figure 9.13. Then the problem of minimizing snake energy becomes the problem of finding the minimum cost path on this (distorted) trellis. We can allow the starting node to remain fixed, or by using the initialization trick above, we can allow both ends of the snake to move freely to a new minimal energy configuration. This algorithm can be applied iteratively to allow the snake to evolve over a larger area.

A problem that can be encountered is that the control points of the snake may bunch up and become uneven after several iterations. Thus it becomes necessary to reinterpolate the control points from time to time. Another problem common to all snake techniques is the risk of the snake crossing itself or forming loops that may be undesirable for the purposes of image segmentation. While many researchers have tackled this problem [82, 128, 123], most solutions are somewhat inelegant and add significant complexity to the approach.

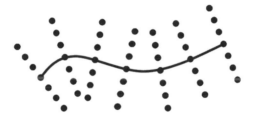

**Fig. 9.13.** An open snake converted to a trellis.

## Dynamic Programming for Closed Snakes

Closed snake energy minimization presents a challenge because the efficient application of dynamic programming is not entirely straightforward. Geiger et al. [66] address this problem in the context of dynamic programming for energy minimization. Their approach is to unwrap the circular domain to form a linear trellis as shown in Figure 9.14. To ensure that the solution is indeed a closed contour, they examine shortest paths where the start and finish nodes have the same index and select the global minimum contour. Thus if $m$ candidate points are to be examined, this method would require the Viterbi algorithm to be run $m$ times for each possible starting node instead of just

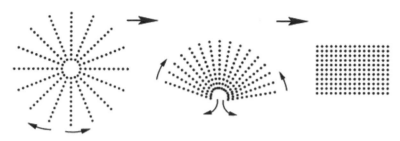

**Fig. 9.14.** A closed snake search space converted to a trellis.

once. So with a value of, say, $m = 30$, the optimal closed snake evolution would run 30 times slower than the open snake evolution.

As this would be unacceptably slow, Geiger et al. suggest a heuristic speed-up that requires only two passes of the algorithm. The Viterbi algorithm is run once using an arbitrary start point—in practice, it is best to choose the candidate point with highest image gradient that is likely to be on the optimal contour. Then for the second run the contour is reordered so as to start and terminate from the second point of the trellis. The argument for this procedure would be that the second point is more likely to be on the optimal contour that the arbitrary first point since the snake energy minimization process will have "pulled" it toward the optimal contour. Now assuming our trellis has $N$ control points, if the second point is more likely to be on the optimal contour than the first, why not unwrap the trellis at the $N/2^{th}$ point on the other side of the circular search space?

This idea leads us to the mid-point heuristic. The mid-point heuristic can be stated as, *the optimal positions of the mid-points of a snake are generally independent of the positions of the end-points.* This led Gunn and Nixon [71] to propose a similar two-pass technique to use dynamic programming to solve the closed snake problem using two open snakes. The closed snake is converted to an open snake problem by unwrapping about an arbitrary cut point as before. First an open snake minimization is performed using no smoothness or continuity constraints on the endpoints. The two points at the mid-point of this contour are then taken as the start and end points for the closed contour. The Viterbi algorithm is run again with the start and end points fixed. Thus we only require two runs of the Viterbi algorithm instead of the $m$ runs required for the optimal method.

Although these heuristics work well in practice, there is a theoretical possibility that they may fail to find the true optimal contour. We address this issue in Section 10.2 and describe a fast and optimal minimization method using branch and bound techniques.

## 9.6 Problems and Pitfalls

Traditional snakes minimize energy within a local search space only. This leads to difficulties in many applications because the snakes become stuck on local minima rather than on finding global solutions that may be preferable for fully automated image segmentation. As a result of the gradient descent nature of the traditional snake, the answer obtained is very dependent on initialization and stopping criteria, and these criteria, may be very difficult to determine in general.

An example of this difficulty with a traditional closed snake or balloon on the cell image segmentation problem is shown in Figure 9.15, where the contour is stuck in a local minimum. If we increase the deflationary force, we may be able to contract the contour down on to the nuclear membrane. Unfortunately, we may also run the very real risk of the contour being pushed right inside the membrane—especially if the image gradient on the nuclear membrane is less than on the surrounding artifacts.

Gunn and Nixon [72] attempt to address this issue by using a dual active contour model. Their idea is to initialize balloons both inside and outside the object of interest. The inner balloon would then expand and the outer balloon would contract. If the two balloons did not meet, the inflationary and deflationary forces would be increased until the balloons were forced together. This approach has the advantage of clear initialization and stopping criteria, but does not necessarily yield the optimal minimal energy solution in general. The dual active contour process is illustrated in Figure 9.16 on the cell image problem.

## 9.7 Connected Snakes for Advanced Segmentation

Snakes can be used to segment quite complicated images with a little guidance from a human expert. Usually only one snake is evolved, but some situations call for a far more complex segmentation where many snakes must be evolved simultaneously. Figure 9.17 shows a set of connected objects and an initial hand-drawn rough segmentation. Our goal is to use snakes to refine the rough object segmentation into an acceptable segmentation with good boundary delineation. This approach was developed by Walford [168] to fuse spatial LIDAR information with image data for the automatic analysis of rock wall faces in a mine.

We treat each section of the boundary between the joins as an open-ended snake as illustrated in Figure 9.18. Now our problem is to find the minimum energy configuration of snakes by evolving all snakes simultaneously. At first glance, this appears to be a very challenging problem. Nevertheless, a good solution can be found if we decouple the problem by taking advantage of the mid-point heuristic as described in Section 9.5.

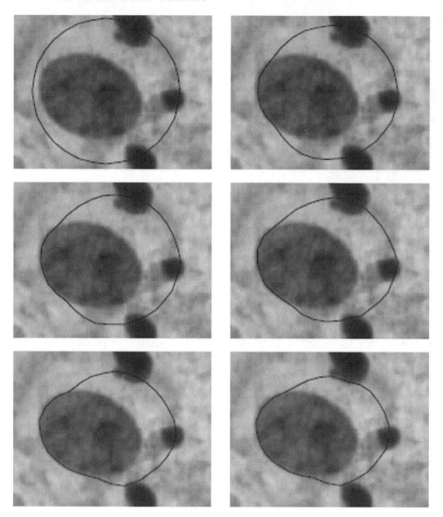

**Fig. 9.15.** Closed snake being prematurely stopped by a local minimum when applied to cell image segmentation problem (from [11]).

Each snake in the network is evolved within its search space as an open-ended snake, without regard to its connectivity to other snakes in the network to estimate the optimal position of its mid-points. Next, each snake is split in two at the mid-points to create two new half-snakes. We fix the location of the mid-point end of each half-snake and perform a forward pass of the Viterbi algorithm. This yields the minimum energy of each half-snake for all $m$ possible positions of its joint-end. All half-snakes that are connected by a joint have the same $m$ possible positions for their joint-end so we can then determine the common joint-end position that minimizes the total energy of

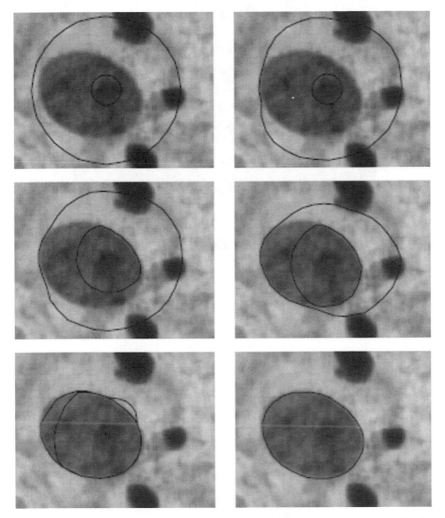

**Fig. 9.16.** The Gunn and Nixon dual active contour approach to handle local minimum problem applied to cell image segmentation problem (from [11]).

all half-snakes that meet at that joint. Once we know the common joint-end position, we can follow the backward pointers of the Viterbi algorithm to determine the position of all remaining points on the half-snake. The refined half-snakes are then reconnected to form the final result as shown in Figure 9.19.

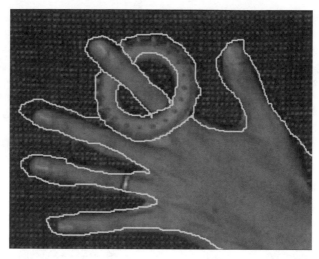

**Fig. 9.17.** Hand drawn segmentation of a connected object (from [168]).

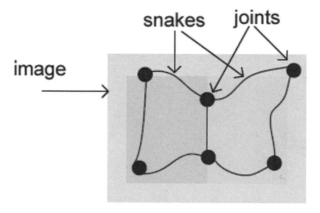

**Fig. 9.18.** Viewing segmentation boundaries as a network of connected snakes (from [168]).

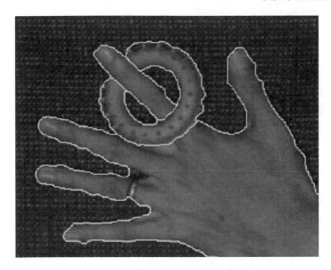

**Fig. 9.19.** Refined segmentation of the connected object using a connected snake network (from [168]).

## 9.8 Conclusions

Snakes use energy minimization techniques to form smooth curves. However, snakes are mainly used for image segmentation and interpretation rather than mathematical interpolation per se. Rather than interpolating between known control points as is the case with Bernstein-Bézier splines, snakes find their own control points using image features such as edges, lines, and line terminations in an image under analysis. The formulation of internal snake energy has a membrane term that provides a form of elasticity similar to an elastic band, and a thin-plate term that provides a form of stiffness like a traditional wooden spline.

Traditionally, a local gradient descent method is used to determine the minimum energy contour. This leads to the well-known pitfalls in the application of conventional snakes due to the inability to find satisfactory answers to the following problems.

- How do we initialize the snake to find the best solution?
- When do we stop the snake evolving?
- How do we avoid unsatisfactory local minima?

Gunn and Nixon [71] argue that, "A weakness of the evolutionary, or local minimum, approach is the sensitivity to initialization and difficulty in determining suitable parameters. This can be exaggerated by noise." They then advocate techniques based on global energy minimization rather than local minimization.

Techniques to find optimal global minimum energy solutions may be preferable for fully automated image segmentation applications because they will usually lead to a unique answer for a given search space. Moreover, there is no need to specify initialization and starting criteria for the search. Note that the global minimum is not always the best solution for a given segmentation problem but, in our experience, it can work surprisingly well if the search space is well chosen.

Henceforth we will concentrate on methods for finding globally optimal solutions to the energy minimization problem and then apply this to the optimal image segmentation problem. In the next chapter, we will relate the development of this theme over a number of years through case studies from several research projects.

# 10

# Globally Optimal Energy Minimization Techniques

## 10.1 Introduction and Timeline

In 1992, we began a research project to automatically segment cell images from Pap smear slides for the detection of cancer of the cervix. We investigated simple low-level techniques based on edge detection, grayscale thresholding, and grayscale morphology (e.g., watersheds), but could only achieve accurate segmentation on about 60% of cell images (Figure 10.1). In 1997, we started looking at dual active contour segmentation techniques as proposed by Gunn and Nixon [72], but this method suffered from poor robustness on our images. However, Gunn [70] also suggested a fast globally optimal method based on converting the problem of finding the best circular contour into a linear trellis and then applying the Viterbi algorithm to determine the minimum energy path. This approach worked remarkably well, as reported by Bamford and Lovell [13] in 1998, and yielded 99.5% correct segmentation on a cell database of nearly 20,000 cell images.

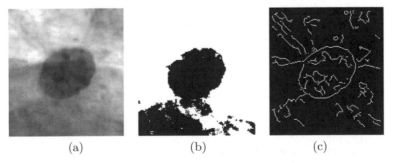

(a)         (b)         (c)

**Fig. 10.1.** Traditional bottom-up approach to cell image segmentation. (a) Original graylevel image, (b) thresholded image showing voids and artifacts, and (c) Canny edge map showing a partially complete border and other spurious edges (from [11]).

As this method was so remarkably effective on cell images, there was little incentive to improve the method for the Pap smear problem itself, but we still held a desire to develop more powerful global energy minimization techniques that could be applied to a general class of objects. In particular, the Viterbi algorithm based method would only work for objects that were convex and two-dimensional.

In 2002, Appleton and Sun [8] put the problem of minimizing the energy of closed contours unwrapped onto linear trellis onto a firm mathematical basis. Then, in 2003, Appleton and Talbot [6, 10] extended and generalized the energy minimization approach to handle the optimal segmentation of planar concave objects as well as convex images such as cells. This extension avoided dependence on a coarse discretization grid so that grid-bias could be removed. The extension to 3D was achieved in late 2003 by Appleton and Talbot [9] by converting the shortest path techniques into an equivalent continuous maximum flow/minimal surface problem.

In this chapter we briefly describe the various energy minimization segmentation techniques and show how they can be applied to solve quite difficult segmentation and reconstruction problems in diverse domains from volumetric medical imaging to multiview reconstruction.

## 10.2 Cell Image Segmentation Using Dynamic Programming

Although the use of active contours [88] is well established, it is well known that these methods tend to suffer from local minima, initialization, and stopping criteria problems [44]. Fortunately global minimum energy, or equivalently shortest-path, searching methods have been found that are particularly effective in avoiding such local minima problems due to the presence of the many artifacts often associated with medical images [51, 66].

The energy minimization method employed was based on a suggestion in Gunn's dissertation [70]. A circular search space is first defined within the image, bounded by two concentric circles centralized upon the approximate center of the nucleus found by an initial rough segmentation technique (e.g., converging squares algorithm). This search space is sampled to form a circular trellis by discretizing both the circles and a grid of evenly-spaced radial lines joining them (Figure 10.2). This circular trellis is then unwrapped in a polar to rectangular transformation yielding a conventional linear trellis.

Every possible contour that lies upon the nodes of the search space is then evaluated and an associated energy or cost function is calculated. As with the snake energy formulation of (9.3), this cost is a function of both the contour's smoothness and how closely it follows image edges. The energy [13] is defined by:

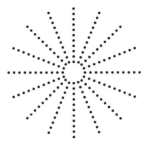

**Fig. 10.2.** Discrete search space.

$$E_{snake} = \int_0^1 E_{int}(\nu(s)) + E_{image}(\nu(s)). \qquad (10.1)$$

Using the discrete notation from Chapter 9, we have

$$E_{int} = \left( \frac{\nu_{i+1} - 2\nu_i + \nu_{i-1}}{\nu_{i+1} - \nu_{i-1}} \right) \qquad (10.2)$$

and

$$E_{image} = -|\nabla I(x, y)|^2. \qquad (10.3)$$

The internal energy consists of a thin-plate term only. The relative weighting of the cost components is controlled by a single regularization parameter, $\lambda \in [0, 1]$. By choosing a high value of $\lambda$, the thin-plate or stiffness term dominates, which may lead to smooth contours that tend to ignore important image edges. On the other hand, low values of $\lambda$ allow contours to develop sharp corners as they attempt to follow all high gradient edges, even those that may not necessarily be on the desired object's boundary. Once every contour has been evaluated, the single contour with least cost is the global solution. The Viterbi algorithm provides a very efficient method to find this global solution, as described in Section 9.5.

A data set of 19946 Pap stained cervical cell images was available for testing. The single regularization parameter $\lambda$ was empirically chosen to be 0.7 after trial runs on a small subset of the images. The effect of the choice of $\lambda$ on segmentation accuracy on this trial set is shown by the graph of Figure 10.3. This figure shows a value of $\lambda = 0.7$ as being the most suitable for these particular images. It further shows that acceptable segmentation performance can be obtained with $\lambda$ ranging from 0.1 to 0.9—an enormous range, which demonstrates the robustness and suitability of the approach. Every image in the data set was then segmented at $\lambda = 0.7$ and the results verified by eye. Of the 19946 images, 99.5% were found to be correctly segmented.

With $\lambda$ set at 0.0, the smoothness constraint from the thin-plate term is completely ignored and the point of greatest gradient is chosen along each of the search space radii. Previous studies [12] have shown that for approximately

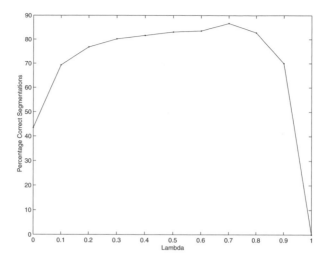

**Fig. 10.3.** Plot of percentage of correct segmentations against $\lambda$ for a set of images consisting of known "difficult" images and randomly selected images.

65% of images, all points of greatest gradient actually lie upon the nucleus-cytoplasm border, so these "easy" cell images will be correctly segmented with $\lambda = 0$. For the remaining 35% of images, a large gradient due to an artifact or darkly stained chromatin will draw the contour away from the desired border. As $\lambda$ increases, the large curvatures necessary to admit these incorrect configurations become less probable, as shown in Figure 10.4.

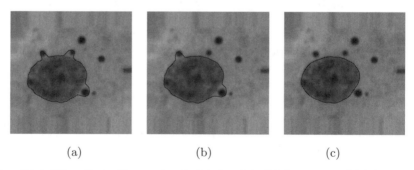

(a)                          (b)                          (c)

**Fig. 10.4.** The effect of increasing $\lambda$. (a) $\lambda = 0.1$, (b) $\lambda = 0.2$, and (c) $\lambda = 0.5$.

## Comments on the Dynamic Programming Method

We show in [110] that the above segmentation method can be viewed as the application of hidden Markov model techniques [138], where the transition matrix is determined by the curvature constraints and the observation matrix is determined by the gradient image.

A simple way to find shortest paths on the linear trellis that corresponds to the closed contours in the image domain is to replicate the $m$ nodes. Specifically, we unwrap the circular domain such that the last column of nodes in the trellis is a copy of the first column. Then if there are $m$ such nodes in a column, we would need to evaluate each of the $m$ paths, starting and finishing on the same node $i \in [0 \ldots M - 1]$. This would require $m$ evaluations of the Viterbi algorithm, as described in Section 9.5. So we use the two-pass method of Gunn and Nixon [71] based on the midpoint heuristic to find the minimum energy.

Although this heuristic works very well in practice, in theory there are clearly situations where it could fail to find the optimal solution.

**Circular Shortest Path Algorithm (CSP)**

Appleton and Sun [8] investigated this general problem of optimal circular shortest paths to address the theoretical deficiencies of the midpoint heuristic. Their circular shortest path algorithm is guaranteed to find the shortest circular path and uses a branch and bound technique [175, 99] to efficiently locate it.

The need for circular shortest paths arises when the search space is naturally periodic. Here we must satisfy the constraint that the end points of the shortest path must be connected in the periodic extension of the trellis. This constraint creates a cyclic dependency in the computation of the path cost, which prevents us from applying the standard shortest path algorithms of Section 9.5 based on dynamic programming. However, this dependency is quite simply overcome by periodically extending the trellis as follows.

We perform a rectangular to polar mapping to convert the circular search space into a linear one as before. However, in this case, the column at the cut point is replicated as the last column to provide a periodic extension. In other words, a circular search space with $N$ nodes is represented by a linear trellis of length $N + 1$ where the last column is a replica of the first. Then a contour is circular if and only if the row index of the first node $\nu_0$ is the same as the row index of the last node $\nu_N$.

The root of the branch and bound search tree consists of the entire first column of nodes. This set of nodes is recursively split in two to form the binary search tree as depicted in Figure 10.5. The Viterbi algorithm allows us to treat a set of nodes in the first column of the trellis as the source rather than using a single node as the source as described in Section 9.5. The circular shortest path algorithm progresses as follows.

The shortest path to the other end of the trellis is found from the root node (i.e., the entire first column) and this forms a lower bound on the cost of the circular shortest path. We find the destination node corresponding to the shortest path and follow the backward pointers to determine the corresponding

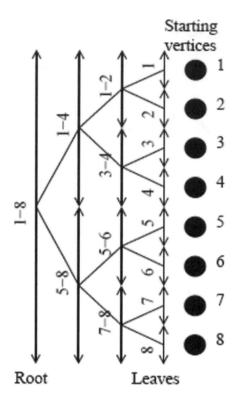

**Fig. 10.5.** The binary search tree for $m{=}8$. Only the first column of the trellis containing the potential source vertices is shown (from [7]).

source node. If the source node $\nu_0$ is the same as the destination node $\nu_N$, then we have found the circular shortest path and the algorithm terminates.

Otherwise the source node is split in two and the Viterbi algorithm is then run on the upper and lower subproblems. Since we know that a circular shortest path must start and finish on the same node, a new bound on the circular shortest path is obtained by examining the shortest path length to the corresponding upper and lower half of the destination nodes. For example, if $m = 8$, we would look for the shortest paths between source and destination nodes with row indices 0–3 and 4–7, respectively. As before, if the shortest path found is circular, the algorithm terminates.

Otherwise we recursively split the node with the lowest circular shortest path bound and continue the search. The complete algorithm is given in [7] and an example segmentation of a diatom is shown in Figure 10.6. On typical images, the CSP algortihm often identifies the optimum circular shortest path with just one run of the Viterbi algorithm, although some pathological examples may take considerably longer to compute.

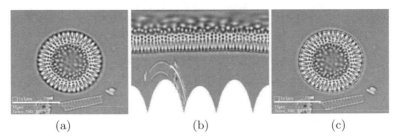

(a)                    (b)                    (c)

**Fig. 10.6.** Segmentation of *Cyclostephanos Dubius* by circular shortest path method. (a) The original microscope image of the diatom, (b) the polar unwrapping with circular shortest path overlaid, and (c) the corresponding segmentation contour (from [7]).

However, despite this improvement, a major shortcoming of all methods based on a polar to rectangular mapping is the inability to handle concave contours and higher dimensional objects, thus severely limiting their application domain.

## 10.3 Globally Optimal Geodesic Active Contours (GOGAC)

The classic active contour or snake model proposed by Kass [88] modeled a segmentation boundary by a series of point masses connected by springs. This explicit view of curves as a polygon was replaced by an implicit view of curves as the level set of some 3D surface by Osher and Sethian [129]. Level sets offer significant advantages over traditional snakes including improved stability and much better handling of topology (e.g., segmentation of multiple objects with just one contour). Another advance came in the form of geodesic active contours as proposed by Caselles *et al* [34]. They demonstrated the equivalence of their energy function to the length of a geodesic (i.e., path of least cost, path of least time) in an isotropic space. A problem with traditional geodesic active contours is that they are a gradient descent method and thus have all the usual problems of initialization, termination, and local minima associated with such methods. They simply do not have the stability and simplicity of application of globally optimal segmentation methods.

The globally optimal GOGAC method we outline here finds closed contours in the image domain itself rather than unwrapping the image through polar to rectangular transformation. Working in the image domain means that we cannot find simple shortest paths, as this would cause a bias towards small

contours that wrap tightly around the origin. Instead, we use a contour energy
of the form [7]

$$E[C] = \oint_C \frac{g}{r}\, ds \tag{10.4}$$

where g is a measure of probability of being on the boundary (e.g., image
gradient) and $r$ is the radius of the contour $C$. Thus all circles centered on
the origin would have the same contour energy.

Now we cut the image plane with an arbitrary cut line as depicted in
Figure 10.7. Let us now consider a point on the cut line, $p_{cut}$, which is mapped
to two equivalent points $p_{start}$ and $p_{end}$ in the cut plane $S'$. Now to find
the shortest circular path beginning and ending at $p_{cut}$, we just solve the
equivalent problem of finding the shortest path from $p_{start}$ to $p_{end}$ in the cut
plane $S'$ (using the Fast Marching algorithm described in the next section).

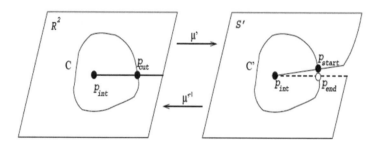

**Fig. 10.7.** A minimal closed geodesic in the image plane passing through $p_{cut}$ and
the corresponding open shortest path (*i.e.*, geodesic) in the cut plane between $p_{start}$
and $p_{end}$. (from [7]).

A problem with the above approach is that it would not allow the shortest
path to cross the cut line. This would once again restrict the algorithm to
convex shapes only. However Appleton [7] shows that if we represent the
open search space in an augmented helicoidal representation, it allows us
to represent concave contours that cross the cut line (i.e., unwrapping line)
multiple times as illustrated in Figure 10.8. Thus we can now find the shortest
closed path passing through $p_{cut}$ even if the contour wraps around the origin
several times. Thus the arbitrary choice of the cut line does not influence nor
restrict the range of image topology the GOGAC algorithm can handle.

In the above development it was assumed that $p_{cut}$, the intersection of the
shortest path and the cut line, is known in advance. This is not the case, and
an exhaustive search of all possible values of $p_{cut}$ would be quite inefficient.
Instead, we use the branch and bound approach of the CSP algorithm in
Section 10.2. Referring to Figure 10.7, we use the set of all possible points for

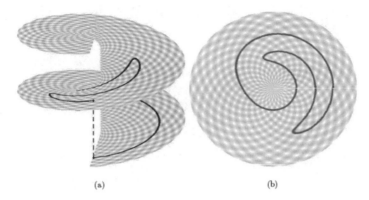

(a)                                    (b)

**Fig. 10.8.** The helicoidal representation of the cut-concave shape. (a) Open curve; (b) closed curve (from [7]).

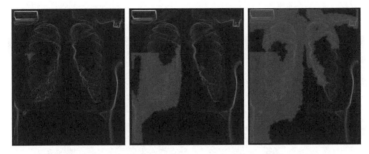

**Fig. 10.9.** Application of GOGAC to lung Xray image segmentation. Evolution of the fast marching wavefront from the cut line. (Images provided by Ben Appleton.)

$p_{cut}$ along the cut line as the source and the periodic replica of these points in the cutplane $S'$ as the destination and then proceed with the binary search in the same manner as the CSP algorithm. Figure 10.9 shows the evolution of the fast marching wavefront emanating from the cut line as it segments a lung using GOGAC. Figures 10.10 and 10.11 show other segmentation results from the GOGAC method.

### 10.3.1 Fast Marching Algorithm

We use the Fast Marching algorithm [149] to find the surfaces of minimal action whose gradient curves form shortest paths, also known as geodesics. A geodesic is a generalization of the concept of a "straight line" to "curved spaces" (i.e., Riemannian spaces) such as the surface of the earth. In the case of a sphere such as the Earth, a geodesic is a great circle. With respect to a given metric, geodesics are defined to be the shortest path between points on the space. A shortest path between two points in a curved space can be

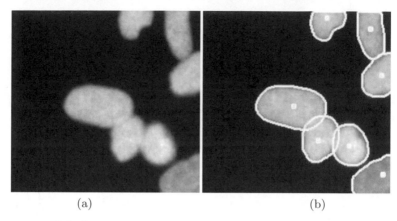

(a)                                           (b)

**Fig. 10.10.** Globally optimal geodesic active contours applied to overlapping objects. The cells (a) are separated despite the weak intensity gradient between them (b) (from [7]).

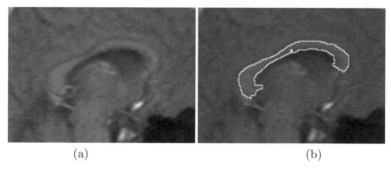

(a)                                           (b)

**Fig. 10.11.** Segmentation of MRI image of a concave contour, the corpus callosum in a human brain, from [7]. Image (a) is the original and (b) is the segmentation via GOGAC.

found by writing the equation for the length of a curve, and then minimizing the length using techniques from calculus of variations. An entirely equivalent approach is to define the energy of a curve; then minimizing the energy leads to the same equations for a geodesic. This latter formulation can better be understood when we consider how an elastic band stretched between two points will contract in length to minimize its energy—the final shape of the band is a geodesic. Thus there is an intimate relationship between the mathematical formalism of geodesics and the concepts underpinning snakes as proposed by Kass et al.

The globally minimal geodesic between two sets of points in an isotropic Riemannian space can be calculated with the fast marching method [2]. This method computes the surface of minimal action, also known as a distance

**Fast Marching Algorithm**

**Initialization:**

For all grid points $x$ in $P_0$:

- Set $U(x) = 0$
- Label $x$ as Trial and insert into $Q$

For all other grid points $x$:

- Set $U(x) = \infty$
- Label x as Far

**Main loop:**

- If Q is empty, halt
- Otherwise remove the Trial point of minimum value from the priority queue:

$$x = \operatorname*{argmin}_{x'} \{U(x')|x' \in Q\}$$

- Label x as Known
- For each neighbor $n$ of $x$ in the grid:
  - If $n$ is Known, continue to next neighbor
  - If $n$ is Far, change label to Trial and insert into $Q$
  - Update $U(n)$ by solving (10.5). Only use the values at neighboring grid points which are labeled Known.

**Fig. 10.12.** Pseudocode for the fast marching algorithm to find the surfaces of minimal action and geodesics (i.e., shortest paths)(from [7]).

function, from the starting set $P_0$ to all points in the space. It finds the surface of minimal action by considering it as the first time-of-arrival of a wavefront emanating from the starting set $P_0$ and traveling with speed $\frac{1}{g}$, where $g$ is usually the image gradient as before. This wavefront sweeps the grid beginning with the starting set $P_0$ and proceeds in order of arrival time $U$.

The algorithm is identical to Dijkstra's shortest distance algorithm [59] from Section 9.5 apart from the need to update $g$. On a rectangular two-dimensional grid in with grid step $h$, we may use the discrete gradient operator defined by

$$g^2(i,j) = \frac{1}{h^2} \max\{U[i,j] - U[i-1,j], U[i,j] - U[i+1,j], 0\}^2$$
$$+ \frac{1}{h^2} \max\{U[i,j] - U[i,j-1], U[i,j] - U[i,j+1], 0\}^2. \quad (10.5)$$

During the course of the algorithm, points that have not been considered yet are labeled *Far*. Points that have been assigned a temporary value for $U$ are labeled *Trial*. Points for which $U$ has been finalized are labeled *Known*.

The algorithm makes use of a priority queue[1] $Q$ of trial points in order to maintain efficient access to the minimum distant point. Pseudocode for the complete algorithm is provided in Figure 10.12.

Figure 10.13 shows that the fast marching algorithm calculates distance functions that behave similarly to propagating electromagnetic radiation. Indeed this example shows that the shortest path calculated via the fast marching algorithm follows Snell's Law of Refraction from the field of optics. This formula relates the angles of incidence and refraction where a ray of light crosses a boundary between different media, such as air and glass. Snell's law can be derived from Fermat's principle of least time, which states that the path taken between two points by a ray of light is the path that can be traversed in the least time–that is, a geodesic. Figure 10.14 shows a similar computation on an inverse velocity cost function.

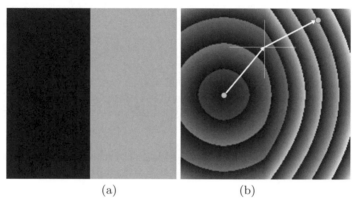

(a)                    (b)

**Fig. 10.13.** The fast marching algorithm calculates the surfaces of minimal action (b) for the two-valued cost function of (a). Note that the geodesic shown in (b) follows Snells' Law of refraction for optical and electromagnetic waves—that is, the sine of the angle of incidence divided by the sine of the angle of refraction is a constant determined by the properties of the two media at the interface (images provided courtesy of Ben Appleton).

## 10.4 Globally Minimal Surfaces (GMS)

The planar segmentation technique outlined in the last section cannot be extended to higher dimensions, so we need an entirely new approach. Minimum cuts and maximum flow techniques are naturally suited to globally optimal

---

[1] The implemention employs a heap data structure and heap sort for efficient location of the minimum.

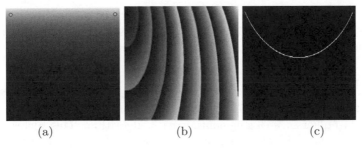

(a)              (b)              (c)

**Fig. 10.14.** The fast marching algorithm is used to compute the path of a ball rolling on an inclined plane under the influence of gravity. The path of the ball will always be a geodesic. (a) Inverse velocity metric, (b) arrival time (surfaces of minimal action), and (c) geodesic (shortest path).

segmentation in higher dimensions. Although this has been tried in the past with discrete approximations, Appleton and Talbot [9] proposed a method based on continuous maximal flows by solving a system of partial differential equations. It is shown in [7] that this method gives identical results to the previous GOGAC method in the case of planar images.

### 10.4.1 Minimum Cuts and Maximum Flows

Minimum cuts are another concept from graph theory that are related to shortest paths, although the computation is often slower and more complicated. Graph cuts may be used to determine the capacity of a communications network or to determine the minimum number of links that must fail before a network becomes disconnected—an important measure of the reliability of a network. In image analysis they have been proposed for optimally partitioning an image or volume into two regions. For example, this technique could be used to determine the most likely shape of a 3D object in an ultrasound or Magnetic Resonance Imaging (MRI) image.

Consider a finite directed graph $G$ where every edge $(u, v)$ has a capacity of $c(u, v)$, which is a non-negative real number. We identify two vertices, known as the source $s$ and the sink $t$. A cut is a partition of the nodes into two sets $S$ and $T$, such that $s \in S$ and $t \in T$. The capacity of a cut (S,T) is

$$c(S, T) = \sum_{u \in S, v \in T \mid (u,v) \text{ is an edge}} c(u, v),$$

which is just the sum of the capacity of all edges crossing the cut from region $S$ to $T$.

The *max-flow min-cut theorem* [60, 63] states that, the maximal amount of flow in a network is equal to the capacity of a minimal cut. In other words, the theorem states that the maximum flow in a network is dictated by its bottleneck—the minimum cut surface. It turns out that the maximum flow problem is convex and is consequently easier to solve than the dual problem of finding the minimum cut.

## Augmenting Path Algorithm

The best known algorithm for solving the maximum flow problem is the famous Ford-Fulkerson [63] augmenting path algorithm. This algorithm successively increases the maximum flow from source $s$ to sink $t$ by continually locating paths along which more flow may be pushed. Once all paths from source to sink are saturated, the flow is maximal. The pseudocode for the Ford-Fulkerson algorithm is given in Figure 10.15.

### Ford Fulkerson Augmenting Path Algorithm

**Initialization:**

Set $F = 0$ on each edge

**Main loop:**

- Search for an s-t path along which more flow may be pushed
- If no such path exists, halt
- Otherwise, increase the flow uniformly along this path until at least one edge
  becomes saturated

**Fig. 10.15.** Pseudocode for Ford-Fulkerson Augmenting Path algorithm (from [7]).

## Preflow Push Algorithm

An alternative to the augmenting path algorithm is the more recent preflow push algorithm of Goldberg and Tarjan [67]. One advantage of this formulation is that it is highly parallelizable compared to the Ford-Fulkerson algorithm. A preflow is like a flow, except that the total amount flowing into a vertex is allowed to exceed the total amount flowing out. The algorithm maintains a preflow in the original network and then pushes excess local flow toward the sink along what are estimated to be shortest paths.

A vertex that has greater inward flow than outward flow is called an *active* vertex—the excess being the positive difference between the two. The algorithm repeatedly pushes flow outwards from active vertices toward the sink. A height function $H$ is introduced on the vertices to guide the flow along the shortest unsaturated path toward the sink. The source and sink have fixed heights of $|V|$ and 0, respectively, and may never become active. Active vertices are stored in a queue, $Q$. The pseudocode for the Goldberg-Tarjan algorithm is given in Figure 10.16.

**Goldberg-Tarjan Preflow Push Algorithm**

**Initialization:**

- Set $F = 0$ on each edge
- Set $H$ to be the length of the shortest (unweighted) path to the sink $t$, and $H(s) = |V|$
- Set the source $s$ as active and place it in the $Q$

**Main loop:**

- If $Q$ is empty, halt
- Otherwise, retrieve an active vertex $v$ from $Q$
- For all neighboring vertices u of v:
    - If the edge $(v, u)$ is unsaturated and $H(v) = H(u) + 1$, push more flow along edge $(v, u)$ until it is saturated or $v$ has excess 0
    - If this increased the flow to $u$, set $u$ as active and place in $Q$. Note: $u$ may already be active
    - If $v$ still has positive excess, increment $H(v)$ and place $v$ in $Q$
- Otherwise, set v as inactive

**Fig. 10.16.** Pseudocode for Goldberg-Tarjan Preflow Push algorithm (from [7]).

## 10.4.2 Development of the GMS Algorithm

It is well known that maximum flow techniques work well in a discrete domain of a network, but the imposition of a coarse discretization grid on a natural image leads to quite unnatural grid-biases in the segmentation. The segmentation contours tend to follow the artificially imposed discretization grid rather than the following smooth curves in the image itself, leading to unacceptable staircase artifacts. The goal here is to develop an algorithm that works directly in the continuous image domain.

It is not at all clear how the augmenting path algorithm can be extended from the continuous to the discrete domain. On the other hand, the preflow push method is much better suited to the problem. One advantage is that the updates on vertices require only local information from the neighbors rather than global knowledge of the image. This suggests a method based on solving a system of partial differential equations—indeed in much the same way, the solution of Maxwell's equations leads to the solutions for electromagnetic fields and traveling electromagnetic waves such as light.

We relax the flow conservation constraint at each vertex by adding an additional variable at each point. This results in a scalar potential field, $P$, which will keep track of the inflow-outflow imbalance (i.e., divergence) in the (compressible) flow and provides a restoring force to drive this imbalance to zero at convergence.

One way to visualize the potential function is to think of a network of water pipes connected to an underground junction. When water initially surges down the pipes and meets at the junction, enormous pressures are generated, which

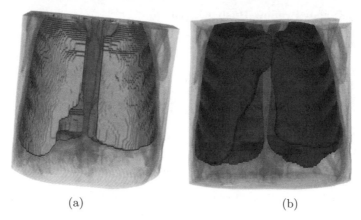

(a)                                    (b)

**Fig. 10.17.** Comparison of 3D lung MRI image segmentation using (a) discrete min-cut, and (b) continuous GMS. Note the unnatural staircase effect in the segmentation of the lower left lung due to grid bias. Computation time was 2 minutes for min-cut and 30 seconds for GMS using a 1Ghz Pentium$^{©}$ computer. (Images provided by Ben Appleton.)

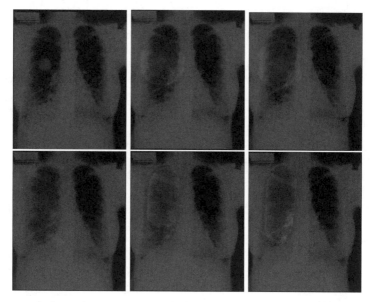

**Fig. 10.18.** Application of GMS to 2D lung Xray image segmentation. Evolution of the potential function used to find the global minimal surface. (Images provided by Ben Appleton.)

could split the pipes unless the junction box is vented. The ancient Romans knew of this problem and their solution was to relieve the pressures in their underground aquaducts with a series of vertical vents and fountains. Vents allow the excess water to rise up the vent pipe, providing a restoring force to balance the flow. Thus the water level in the vent pipe is equivalent to the potential function in the GMS algorithm.

Now consider the following system of differential equations.

$$\frac{\partial P}{\partial t} = -\mathrm{div}\vec{F}, \tag{10.6}$$

$$\frac{\partial \vec{F}}{\partial t} = -\nabla P, \tag{10.7}$$

$$\|\vec{F}\|_2 \leq g. \tag{10.8}$$

These first two equations, taken together, form a simple system of wave equations. They may be interpreted as a linear model of the dynamics of an idealized fluid with pressure $P$ and velocity $\vec{F}$. Without loss of generality and to maintain symmetry between source and sink, we fix the scalar potential field $P$ at the source $s$ and sink $t$ such that $P_s = 1$ and $P_t = -1$.

It can be shown [7] that at convergence the potential field is an isosurface of value +1 in the region connected to the source and -1 in the region connected to the sink. Thus the potential field becomes an indicator function that tells us whether we are inside or outside the minimal surface. Without loss of generality, we choose level set 0 as the minimal surface.

### 10.4.3 Applications of the GMS Algorithm

The evolution of the potential function to determine the minimal surface corresponding to a human lung is shown in Figure 10.18. Note how the potential function evolves to an indicator function separating the interior region of the lung from the exterior. Figure 10.19 shows the segmentation of volumetric MRI data to segment the hippocampus.

A less obvious application is the use of GMS to find the optimal 3D reconstruction from multiview images. Now the use of a stereo pair of images to determine ground elevation from image disparity is a well known technique from aerial photogrammetry. Unfortunately, stereo image pair photogrammetry can only provide so-called 2-1/2D rather than true 3D reconstruction—with just two frontal images, it is impossible to reconstruct the back of an object. So true 3D model reconstruction requires multiple images—hence the term multiview reconstruction.

Leung [105] developed a technique called Embedded Voxel Coloring (EVC), which employed space carving and photoconsistency contraints to the 3D reconstruction problem. He determines the 3D surface that optimally satisfied all the reconstruction constraints using the GMS algorithm. Figure 10.21

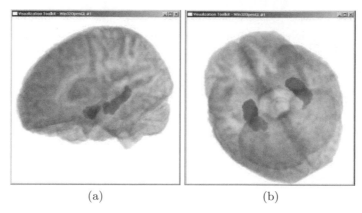

**Fig. 10.19.** Segmentation of the hippocampi from an MRI dataset using GMS. Image (a) is the view from the side and (b) is the view from below from [7].

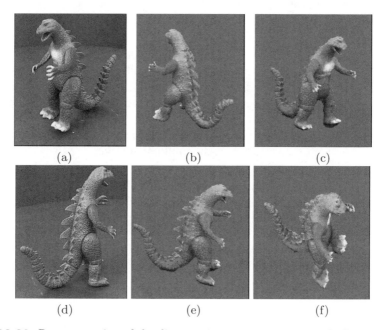

**Fig. 10.20.** Reconstruction of the dinosaur image sequence using Embedded Voxel Colouring (EVC) and adaptive thresholding via GMS. Images (a) and (d) are selected images from the dinosaur image set. Images (b), (c), (e), and (f) are new views generated from the 3D reconstruction (from [104]).

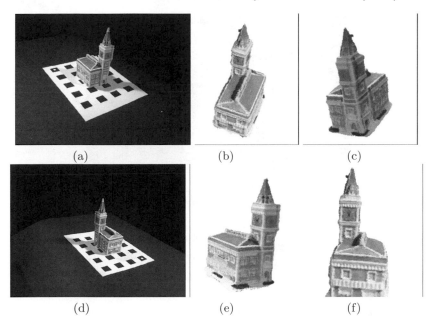

(a)          (b)          (c)

(d)          (e)          (f)

**Fig. 10.21.** Reconstruction of the Ghirardelli image sequence using Embedded Voxel Colouring (EVC) and adaptive thresholding via GMS. Images (a) and (d) are selected images from the Ghirardelli image set. Images (b), (c), (e), and (f) are new views generated from the 3D reconstruction (from [105, 104]).

shows a 3D reconstruction from multiview images using GMS as a postprocessor.

One advantage of the GMS algorithm for extraordinarily difficult segmentation tasks, such as extracting the hippocampus from MRI images, is the ability to define multiple sources and sinks to mark points that are definitely interior and exterior to the object undergoing segmentation as shown in Figure 10.22. Franklin [64] used this approach to guide the GMS algorithm so that the hippocampi of sets of human brains could be labeled fully automatically as shown in Figure 10.23. This study has now been completed on a small set of brains, yielding quite good results. It will be extended to a much larger set in the near future.

This latter work is important because there is evidence that changes in the shape of the hippocampi may be an early indicator of the onset of Alzheimer's disease (also known as dementia). The economic and social cost of Alzheimer's disease is growing rapidly due to the aging population in the western world. Indeed, Access Economics estimates that the cost of dementia to the Australian economy alone in 2004 was approximately USD 4 billion [90]. At present, the detection of Alzheimer's disease is largely performed through psychological tests that detect loss of cognitive ability once the brain is damaged. What

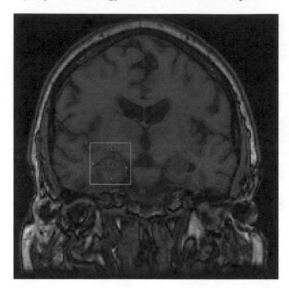

**Fig. 10.22.** The usage of multiple sources and sinks to control the evolution of the GMS algorithm for the fully automated segmentation of the hippocampus in the human brain (from [64]).

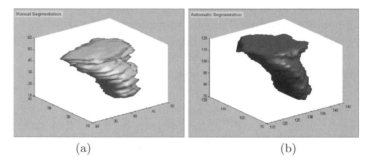

        (a)                                     (b)

**Fig. 10.23.** Comparison of manual and automatic segmentation of the hippocampus in the human brain. Image (a) is a manual segmentation by a clinician that required about 2 hours of labeling and (b) is a fully-automated segmentation via GMS using multiple sources and sinks positioned by cross-validated training on labeled images, which required just 2 minutes of computation (from [64]).

is needed is a fast, cheap, and reliable method to extract the shape of the hippocampi from brain MRI that could be used as a screening test for early Alzheimer's disease. Such a test may allow health workers to intervene before serious brain damage occurs.

## 10.5 Conclusions

These globally optimal energy minimization methods are fast, easy to apply, and tend to yield robust solutions. When using conventional active contours based on local energy minimization, a great deal of effort is expended in developing techniques for choosing the initial position of the contour, escaping local minima, and determining stopping criteria. It is certainly true that some effort must be expended on determining the search space and the energy function when using global energy minimization techniques. Yet, in our experience, these techniques are much simpler to apply in practice and yield more robust and accurate results. Note further that by carefully positioning the search space, global energy minimization techniques can always find locally minimal energy solutions. In particular, for the globally minimal surface approach, multiple sources and sinks can be used to guide the solution, providing many of the purported advantages of the original snakes of Kass et al. The converse, however, is not true—local energy minimization techniques are never guaranteed to find global solutions.

Future work is focussed on integrating these techniques with statistical shape models to develop an 3D Expectation Maximization algorithm incorporating prior shape knowledge for detection and segmentation of known shapes.

# References

1. A.S. Abutaleb. Automatic thresholding of graylevel pictures using two-dimensional entropy. *Computer Vision, Graphics and Image processing*, 47:22–32, 1989.
2. D. Adalsteinsson and J.A. Sethian. A fast level set method for propagating interfaces. *Journal of Computational Physics*, 118(2):269277, 1995.
3. A.A. Amini, T.E. Weymouth, and R.C. Jain. Using dynamic programming for solving variational problems in vision. *IEEE Trans. Pattern Anal. Machine Intell.*, 12:855–867, 1990.
4. A.C. Ansari, I. Gertner, and Y.Y. Zeevi. Combined wavelets DCT image compression. In *Proc. SPIE Int. Soc. Opt. Eng.*, volume 1699, pages 308–317, 1992.
5. A.C. Ansari, I. Gertner, and Y.Y. Zeevi. Image compression: wavelet type transform along generalized scan. In *Proc. SPIE conf. Synthetic Aperture Rader*, volume 1630, pages 99–107, 1992.
6. B. Appleton. Optimal geodesic active contours: application to heart segmentation. In B.C. Lovell and A.J. Maeder, editors, *APRS Workshop on Digital Image Computing*, volume 1, pages 27–32, Brisbane, February 2003. APRS.
7. B. Appleton. *Globally Minimal Contours and Surfaces for Image Segmentation.* The University of Queensland, 2004.
8. B. Appleton and C. Sun. Circular shortest paths by branch and bound. *Pattern Recognition*, 36(11):2513–2520, 2003.
9. B. Appleton and H. Talbot. Globally optimal surfaces by continuous maximal flows. In C. Sun, H. Talbot, S. Ourselin, and T. Adriaansen, editors, *Digital Image Computing: Techniques and Applications*, volume 2, pages 987–996, Sydney, December 2003. CSIRO Publishing.
10. B. Appleton and H. Talbot. Globally optimal geodesic active contours. *Journal of Mathematical Imaging and Vision*, July 2005.
11. P. Bamford. *Segmentation of Cell Images with Application to Cervical Cancer Screening.* PhD thesis, The University of Queensland, 1999.
12. P. Bamford and B. Lovell. Improving the robustness of cell nucleus segmentation. In P.H. Lewis and M.S. Nixon, editors, *Proc. Ninth British Machine Vision Conference, BMVC '98*, pages 518–524. University of Southampton, September 1998.

13. P. Bamford and B. Lovell. Unsupervised cell nucleus segmentation with active contours. *Signal Processing Special Issue: Deformable Models and Techniques for Image and Signal Processing*, 71(2):203–213, December 1998.

14. C.S. Barrus, R.A. Gopinath, and H. Guo. *Introduction to Wavelets and Wavelet Transforms*. Prentice-Hall, New Jersey, 1998.

15. B.A. Barsky. *The Beta Spline: Local Representation Based on Shape parameters and Fundamental Geometric Measures*. PhD thesis, The University of Utah, 1981.

16. B.A. Barsky. End conditions and boundary conditions for uniform B-spline curve and surface representations. *Comp. in Indus.*, 3:17–29, 1982.

17. B.A. Barsky. A description and evaluation of various 3-d models. In T.L. Kunii, editor, *Computer Graphics: Theory and Applications*. Springer-Verlag, New York, 1983.

18. G.A. Battle. A block spin construction of ondelettes, part-i:Lemarie functions. *Comm. Math. Phys.*, 110:601–615, 1987.

19. R.E. Bellman. *Dynamic Programming*. Princeton University Press, 1957.

20. F. Bergholm. Motion from flow along contours: a note on robustness and ambiguous case. *Int. J. Computer Vision*, 3:395–415, 1989.

21. M. Bertero, T. Poggio, and V. Torre. Ill-posed problems in early vision. In *Proc. IEEE*, volume 76, pages 869–889, 1988.

22. P.E. Bézier. Mathematical and practical possibilities of unisurf. In R.E. Barnhill and R.F. Risenfeld, editors, *Computer Aided Geometric Design*. Academic Press, New York, 1974.

23. S. Biswas. Contour coding through stretching of discrete circular arcs by affine transformation. *Pattern Recognition*, 34:63–77, 2001.

24. S. Biswas and N.R. Pal. On hierarchical segmentation for image compression. *Pattern Recog. Lett.*, 21:131–144, 2000.

25. S. Biswas, N.R. Pal, and S.K. Pal. A quantitative index for termination of iterative image smoothing algorithms. In *Proc. 3rd. Int. Conf. Automation, Robotics and Computer Vision*, pages 1107–1111, 1994.

26. S. Biswas and S.K. Pal. Approximate coding of digital contours. *IEEE Trans. Syst., Man, Cybern.*, 18:1056–1066, 1988.

27. S. Biswas, S.K. Pal, and D. DuttaMajumder. Binary contour coding using Bézier approximation. *Pattern Recog. Lett.*, 8:237–249, 1988.

28. R.E. Blahut. *Fast Algorithms for Digital Signal Processing*. Addison-Wesley, 1987.

29. J.E. Bresenham. Algorithm for computer control of a digital plotter. *IBM System Journal*, 4:25–30, 1965.

30. P. Brigger, J. Hoeg, and M. Unser. B-spline snakes: a flexible tool for parametric contour detection. *IEEE Trans. Image Processing*, 4:909–920, 2000.

31. A.D. Brink. Grey-level thresholding of images using a correlation criterion. *Pattern Recog. Lett.*, 9:335–341, 1989.

32. R. Brons. Linguistic methods for description of a straight line on a grid. *Computer Graphics and Image Processing*, 2:48–62, 1974.

33. S. Carlsson. Sketch based coding of gray level images. *Signal processing*, 15:57–83, 1988.

34. V. Caselles, R. Kimmel, and G. Sapiro. Geodesic active contours. *International Journal of Computer Vision*, 22(1):61–79, 1997.

35. B. Chanda, B.B. Choudhuri, and D. DuttaMajumder. Minimum error thresholding. *Pattern Recog. Lett.*, 3:243–251, 1985.

36. B.B. Choudhuri and N. Sarkar. Texture segmentation using fractal dimension. *IEEE Trans. Pattern Anal. Machine Intell.*, 17:72–77, 1995.

37. C.K. Chui. *An Introduction to Wavelets*. Academic Press, Inc., San Diego, CA:, 1992.

38. R. Cipolla and A. Blake. The dynamic analysis of apparent contours. In *Proc. 3rd Int. Conf. on Computer Vision*, pages 616–623, 1990.

39. R. Cipolla and A. Blake. Surface orientation and time to contact from image divergence and deformation. In *proc. 2nd European Conference on Computer Vision–ECCV'92*, volume 588 of *Lecture Notes in Computer Science*, pages 187–202, Santa Margherita Ligure, Italy, 1992. Springer.

40. A. Cohen, I. Daubechies, and J.C. Feauveau. Biorthogonal bases of compactly supported wavelets. *Commun. Pure Appl. Math.*, 45:485–560, 1992.

41. E. Cohen, T. Lyche, and R. Risenfeld. Discrete B-splines and subdivision techniques in computer-aided geometric design and computer graphics. *Computer Vision, Graphics and Image Processing*, 14:87–111, 1980.

42. E. Cohen and R.F. Risenfeld. General matrix representations for Bézier and B-spline curves. *Comp. in Indus.*, 3:9–15, 1982.

43. L. Cohen. On active contour models and balloons. *Computer Vision, Graphics and Image Processing: Image Understanding*, 53(2):211–218.

44. L.D. Cohen and I. Cohen. Finite-element methods for active contour models and balloons for 2-D and 3-D images. *IEEE Trans. Pattern Anal. Machine Intell.*, 15(11):1131–1147, 1993.

45. A.J. Cole. Compaction technique for raster scan graphics using space filling curves. *Computer Journal*, 30:87–92, 1987.

46. M.G. Cox. The numerical evaluation with B-splines. *National Physical Laboratory DNAC 4*, 1971.

47. M.G. Cox. The numerical evaluation of b-splines. *J. Inst. Math. Appl.*, 10:134–149, 1972.

48. I. Daubechies. Orthonormal bases of compactly supported wavelets. *Commun. Pure Appl. Math.*, XII:909–996, 1988.

49. I. Daubechies. *Ten Lectures on Wavelets*. SIAM, Philadelphia, PA, 1992.

50. I. Daubechies, A. Grossman, and Y. Mayer. Painless nonorthogonal expansions. *J. Math. Phys.*, 27:1271–1283, 1986.

51. C.A. Davatzikos and J.L. Prince. An active contour model for mapping the cortex. *IEEE Trans. Medical Imaging*, 14(1):65–80.

52. G. Davis. A wavelet-based analysis of fractals image compression. *IEEE Trans. Image Processing*, 7:141–154, 1998.

53. C. deBoor. On calculating with B-splines. *J. Approximation Theory*, 6:7–49, 1972.

54. C. deBoor. On calculation with B-splines. *J. Approx. Theory*, 6:50–62, 1972.

55. C. deBoor. Spline as linear combination of B-splines: a survey. In G.G. Lorenz, C.K. Chui, and L.L. Schumaker, editors, *Approximation Theory*. Academic Press, New York, 1976.

56. C. deBoor and G. Fix. Spline approximation by quasi-interpolants. *J. Approximation Theory*, 7:19–45, 1973.

57. C. deBoor and A. Pinkus. Backward error analysis for totally positive linear systems. *Numer. Math.*, 27:485–490, 1977.

58. F. Deravi and S.K. Pal. Graylevel thresholding using second-order statistics. *Pattern Recog. Lett.*, 1:417–422, 1983.

59. E. Dijkstra. A note on two problems in connexion with graphs. *Numerische Mathematik*, 1:269–271.

60. P. Elias, A. Feinstein, and C.E. Shannon. Note on maximum flow through a network. *IRE Trans. Inform. Theory*, IT-2:117–119, 1956.

61. Y. Fisher, E.W. Jacbos, and R.D. Boss. Fractal image compression using iterated transforms. In J.A. Storer, editor, *Image and Text Compression*, pages 35–61. Kluwer Academic Publishers, 1992.

62. M. Flickner, H. Sawhney, D. Pryor, and J.L. Lotspiech. Intelligent interactive image outlining using B-spline snakes. In *Proc. 28th Asilomar Conf. Signals, Systems, computers*, volume 1, pages 731–735, 1994.

63. L.R. Ford and D.R. Fulkerson. *Flows in Networks*. Princeton University Press, 1962.

64. S. Franklin. Automatic segmentation of MRI brain images. Master's thesis, The University of Queensland, 2006.

65. K.S. Fu and J.K. Mui. A survey of image segmentation. *Pattern Recognition*, 13:3–16, 1981.

66. D. Geiger, A. Gupta, A. Costa, and J. Vlontzos. Dynamical programing for detecting, tracking, and matching deformable contours. *IEEE Trans. Pattern Anal. Machine Intell.*, 17(3):294–302, 1995.

67. A.V. Goldberg and R.E. Targan. A new approach to the maximum-flow problem. *Journal of the ACM*, 35(4):921–940, 1988.

68. R.C. Gonzalez and P. Wintz. *Digital Image Processing*. Addison-Wesley, MA, 1977.

69. A. Grossman and J. Morlet. Decomposition of Hardy functions into square integrable wavelets of constant shape. *SIAM J. Math. Anal.*, 15:723–736, 1984.

70. S.R. Gunn. *Dual Active Contour Models for Image Feature Extraction*. University of Southampton, May 1996. PhD Thesis.

71. S.R. Gunn and M.R. Nixon. Snake head boundary extraction using global and local energy minimization. In *Proc. 13th Int. Conf. on Pattern Recognition*, pages 25–29. IAPR, IEEE, August 1996.

72. S.R. Gunn and M.S. Nixon. A robust snake implementation: A dual active contour. *IEEE Trans. Pattern Anal. Machine Intell.*, 19(1):63–68, January 1997.

73. E.H. Hall. *Computer Image Processing and Recognition*. Academic Press, New York, 1979.

74. R.M. Haralick and L.G. Shapiro. Image sementation techniques. *Computer Vision, Graphics and Image processing*, 29:100–132, 1985.

75. M.E. Haziti, H. Cherifi, and D. Aboutajdine. Complexity reduction in factal image compression. In *Proc. IASTED Int. Conf. Signal and Image Processing(SIP'97)*, pages 245–250, New Orleans, USA, 1997.

76. E.C. Hildreth. *The Measurement of Visual Motion*. MIT Press, Cambridge, Massachusetts, 1984.

77. B.K.P. Horn. *Robot Vision*. MIT Press, Cambridge, Massachusetts, 1986.

78. B.K.P. Horn and M.J. Brooks. The variational approach to shape from shading. *Computer Vision, Graphics and Image Processing*, 33:174–208, 1986.

79. B.K.P. Horn and M.J. Brooks (ed.). *Shape from Shading*. MIT Press, Cambridge, Massachusetts, 1989.

80. B.K.P. Horn and R.W. Sjoberg. Calculating the reflectance map. *Applied Optics*, 18:1770–1779, 1979.

81. K. Ikeuchi and B.K.P. Horn. Nimerical shape from shading and occluding boundaries. In B.K.P. Horn and M.J. Brooks, editors, *Shape from Shading*. MIT Press, Cambridge, Massachusetts, 1989.

82. L. Ji and H. Yan. Loop-free snakes for image segmentation. In *Int. Conf. on Image Processing*, volume 3, pages 193–197, October 1999.

83. S. Kamata, R.O. Eason, and E. Kawaguchi. An efficient Hilbert scanning algorithm and its application to data compression. In *Proc. Scandinavian Conf. Image Analysis*, pages 1333–1340, 1993.

84. S. Kamata, R.O. Eason, and E. Kawaguchi. An implementation of Hilbert scanning algorithm and its application to data compression. *IEICE Trans. Inform. and Syst.*, 76:420–428, 1993.

85. S. Kamata, N. Niimi, and E. Kawaguchi. Interactive analysis of multi-spectral images using a Hilbert curve. In *Proc. IAPR*, pages 93–97, 1994.

86. S. Kamata, N. Niimi, and E. Kawaguchi. A gray image compression using Hilbert scan. In *Proc. ICPR*, pages 905–909, 1996.

87. J.N. Kapur, P.K. Shaoo, and A.K.C. Wong. Gray level picture thresholding using the entropy of histogram. *Computer Vision, Graphics and Image processing*, 29:273–285, 1985.

88. M. Kass, A. Witten, and D. Terzopoulos. Snakes: Active contour models. In *Proc. Int. Conf. Computer Vision*, pages 259–268. IEEE, 1987.

89. M. Kass, A. Witten, and D. Terzopoulos. Snakes: Active contour models. *International Journal of Computer Vision*, 1(4):321–331, 1988.

90. Z. Khachaturian, H. Brodaty, T. Broe, T. Jorm, C. Masters, R. Nay, M. Haikerwal, G. Rees, and L. Low. Dementia research: A vision for australia. Technical report, Alzheimers Australia, September 2004.

91. J. Kittler and J. Illingworth. Minimum error thresholding. *Pattern Recog. Lett.*, 19:97–108, 1986.

92. J.J. Koenderink. Optic flow. *Vision Research*, 26:161–179, 1986.

93. J.J. Koenderink and A.J. Van Doorn. Invariant properties of the motion parallax field due to the movement of rigid bodies relative to an observer. *Optica Acta*, 22:773–791, 1975.

94. J.J. Koenderink and A.J. Van Doorn. Geometry of binocular vision and a model for stereopsis. *Biological Cybernetics*, 21:29–35, 1976.

95. J.J. Koenderink and A.J. Van Doorn. Depth and shape from differential perspective in the presence of bending deformations. *J. Opt. Soc. Am.*, 3:242–249, 1986.

96. Z. Kulpa. Area and perimeter measurement of blobs in discrete binary pictures. *Computer Graphics and Image Processing*, 6:434–451, 1977.

97. M. Kunt, M. Benard, and R. Leonardi. Recent results in high compression image coding. *IEEE Trans. Circuits and Systems*, 34:1306–1336, 1987.

98. M. Kunt, A. Ikonomopoulos, and M. Kocher. Second-generation image coding techniques. In *Proc. IEEE.*, volume 73, pages 549–574, 1985.

99. A. Land and A. Doig. An automatic method of solving discrete programming problems. *Econometrica*, 28:497–520, 1960.

100. J. Lane and R. Risenfeld. A theoretical development for computer generation of piecewise polynomial surfaces. *IEEE Trans. PAMI*, 2:35–46, 1980.

101. D. Lee. A provably convergent algorithm for shape from shading. In B.K.P. Horn and M.J. Brooks, editors, *Shape from Shading*. MIT Press, Cambridge, Massachusetts, 1989.

240    References

102. J.S. Lee. Digital image enhancement and noise filtering by use local statistics. *IEEE Trans. Pattern Anal. Machine Intell.*, 2:165–168, 1980.

103. P.G. Lemarie. Ondelettes a localization exponentielles. *J. Math. Pure et Appl.*, 67:227–236, 1988.

104. C. Leung. *Efficient Methods For 3D Reconstruction From Multiple Images.* PhD thesis, The University of Queensland, 2006.

105. C. Leung, B. Appleton, B.C. Lovell, and C. Sun. An energy minimisation approach to stereo-temporal dense reconstruction. In *Int. Conf. Pattern Recognition*, volume 1, pages 72–75, Cambridge, August 23-26.

106. C.W. Liao and G. Medioni. Surface approximation of a cloud of 3d points. *Graph Models Image Process.*, 57:67–74, 1995.

107. H. Lin and A.N. Venetsanopoulos. Incorporating nonlinear contractive functions into the fractal coding. In *Proc. IEEE Int. Workshop on Intelligent Signal Processing and Communication Systems*, pages 169–172, Seoul, Korea, 1994.

108. H. Lin and A.N. Venetsanopoulos. A pyramid algorithm for fast fractal image compression. In *Proc. IEEE Int. Conf. Image Processing (ICIP'95)*, pages 596–599, Washington D. C., 1995.

109. H.C. Longuet-Higgins and K. Pradzny. The interpretation of a moving retinal image. In *Proc. Royal Society, London*, volume B208, pages 385–397, 1980.

110. B.C. Lovell. Hidden Markov models for spatio-temporal pattern recognition and image segmentation. In D.P. Mukherjee and S. Pal, editors, *Int. Conf. Advances in Pattern Recognition*, volume 1, pages 60–65, Calcutta, December.

111. T. Lyche. *Discrete Polynomial Spline Approximation Methods.* PhD thesis, University of Texas at Austin, 1975.

112. T. Lyche. Discrete cubic spline interpolation. *BIT*, 16:281–290, 1976.

113. N. Macon. *Numerical Analysis.* John Wiley and Sons inc., New York, 1963.

114. S.G. Mallat. Multifrequency channel decomposition of images and wavelet models. *IEEE Trans. Accoust. Speech, Signal Processing*, 37:2091–2110, 1989.

115. S.G. Mallat. A theory of multiresolution signal decomposition: The wavelet representation. *IEEE Trans. Pattern Anal. Machine Intell.*, 11:674–693, 1989.

116. S.G. Mallat. *A Wavelet Tour of Signal Processing.* Academic Press, San-Diego, CA, 1998.

117. B.B. Mandelbrot. *Fractal Geometry of Nature.* Freeman Press, San Francisco, 1982.

118. O.L. Mangasarian and L.L. Schumaker. Discrete B-splines via mathematical programming. *Siam J. Contr.*, 9:174–183, 1971.

119. D.C. Marr and E.C. Hildreth. Theory of edge detection. In *Proc. R. Society Lond.B*, volume B-207, pages 187–217, 1980.

120. J.J. Marsden. A identity for spline functions with applications to variation-diminishing spline approximation. *J. Approximation Theory*, 3:7–49, 1970.

121. S.J. MayBank. The angular velocity associated with the optical flow field arising from motion through a rigid environment. *Proc. Royal Society, London*, A401:317–326, 1985.

122. S.J. MayBank. *A theoretical study of optical flow.* PhD thesis, Birbeck College, University of London, 1987.

123. T. McInerney and D. Terzopoulos. Topologically adaptable snakes. In *Int. Conf. on Computer Vision*, pages 840–845. IEEE, June 1995.

124. S. Menet, P. Saint-Marc, and G. Medioni. B-snakes: Implementation and application to stereo. In *Proc. Image Understanding Workshop*, pages 720–726, 1990.

125. Y. Meyer. *Ondelettes et Operateurs I.* Hermann, Paris, 1990.

126. B. Moghaddam, K.J. Hintz, and C.V. Stewart. Space filling curves for image compression. In *Proc. SPIE conf. Automatic Object Recognition*, volume 1471, pages 414–421, 1991.

127. R.C. Nelson and J. Aloimonos. Using flow field divergence for obstacle avoidance: towards qualitative vision. In *Proc. 2nd Int. conf. on Computer Vision*, pages 188–196, 1988.

128. A. Oliveira, S. Ribeiro, C. Esperanca, and G. Giraldi. Loop snakes: the generalized model. In *Int. Conf. on Information Visualisation*, pages 975–980, July 2005.

129. S. Osher and J.A. Sethian. Fronts propagating with curvature dependent speeed: Algorithms based on Hamilton-Jacobi formulations. *Journal of Computational Physics*, 79:12–49, 1988.

130. N.R. Pal and D. Bhandari. Image thresholding. *Signal Processing*, 33:139–158, 1993.

131. N.R. Pal and S.K. Pal. Entropic thresholding. *Signal Processing*, 16:97–108, 1989.

132. N.R. Pal and S.K. Pal. Object background segmentation using new definition of entropy. In *Proc. IEE.*, volume part E, pages 284–295, 1989.

133. T. Pavlidis. *Algorithms for Graphics and Image Processing*. Springer-Verlag, New York, 1982.

134. H.O. Peitjen, H. Jurjens, and D. Saupe. *Chaos and Fractals*. Springer Verlag, New York, 1992.

135. T. Pun. A new method for gray level picture thresholding using the entropy of the histogram. *Signal processing*, 2:223–237, 1980.

136. T. Pun. Entropic thresholding: a new approach. *Computer Vision, Graphics and Image Processing*, 9:210–239, 1981.

137. J. Quinqueton and M. Berthod. A locally adaptive Peano scanning algorithm. *IEEE Trans. Pattern Anal. Machine Intell.*, 3:403–412, 1981.

138. L.R. Rabiner. A tutorial on hidden markov models and selected applications in speech recognition. *Proc. IEEE*, 77(2):257–286, February 1989],.

139. B. Ramamurthi and A. Gersho. Classified vector quantization. *IEEE Trans. Communications*, 34:1105–1115, 1986.

140. J.H. Rieger and D.T. Lawton. Processing differential image motion. *J. Opt. Soc. Am.*, A2:354–360, 1985.

141. R. Rinaldo and G. Calvango. Image coding by block prediction of multiresolution subimages. *IEEE Trans. Image Processing*, 4:909–920, 1995.

142. D.F. Rogers and J.A. Adams. *Mathematical Elements for Computer Graphics*. McGraw Hill, Singapore, 1990.

143. A. Rosenfeld. Digital straight line segment. *IEEE Trans. Computers*, 23:1264–1269, 1974.

144. A. Rosenfeld and A.C. Kak. *Digital Picture Processing*. Academic Press, Florida, 1982.

145. P. Salembier. Morphological multiscale segmentation for image coding. *Signal Processing*, 38:359–386, 1994.

146. I.J. Schoenberg. Contributions to the problem of approximation of equidistant data by analytic functions. *Q. Appl. Math.*, 4:45–99, 1946.

147. I.J. Schoenberg. Cardinal spline interpolation. *J. Soc. Indust. Appl. Math*, 12:1–119, 1973.

148. L.L. Schumaker. Constructive aspects of discrete polynomial spline functions. In C.C. Lorenz, editor, *Approximation Theory*. Academic Press, New York, 1973.

149. J.A. Sethian. A fast marching level set method for monotonically advancing fronts. *Proc. National Academy of Sciences*, 93(4):1591–1595, 1996.

150. J.A. Sethian. *Level Set Methods and Fast Marching Methods—Evolving Interfaces in Computational Geometry, Fluid Mechanics, Computer Vision, and Materials Science*. Cambridge University Press, 1999.

151. C.E. Shannon and W. Weaver. *The Mathematical Theory of Communication*. University Illinois Press, Urbana, 1949.

152. L. Shen and R.M. Rangayyan. A segmentation based lossless image coding method for high resolution medical image compression. *IEEE Trans. Medical Imaging*, 16:301–307, 1997.

153. W. Skarbek, T. Agui, and M. Nikajima. Compression of dithered binary images using Hilbert scan. *Trans. IEICE*, 72:1235–1242, 1989.

154. N. Sorek and Y.Y. Zeevi. On-line visual data compression along a one dimensional scan. In *Proc. SPIE conf. Visual Communication and Image Processing*, volume 1001, pages 764–770, 1988.

155. R.J. Stevens, A.F. Lehar, and F.H. Preston. Manipulation and presentation of multidimensional image data using peano scan. *IEEE Trans. Pattern Anal. Machine Intell.*, 5:520–526, 1983.

156. G. Strang. Wavelets and dilation equations:A brief introduction. *SIAM Rev.*, 31:614–627, 1989.

157. M. Subbarao. Bounds on time-to-collision and rotational component from first-order derivatives ofimage flow. *Computer Vision, Graphics and Image Processing*, 50:329–341, 1990.

158. Y.Y. Tang, L.H. Yang, J. Liu, and H. Ma. *Wavelet Theory and Its Applications to Pattern Recognition*. World Scientific, Singapore, 2000.

159. N.T. Thao. A hybrid fractal-DCT coding scheme for image compression. In *Proc. IEEE Int. Conf. Image Processing (ICIP'96)*, pages 169–172, Lausanne, Switzerland, 1996.

160. L. Thomas and F. Deravi. Region-based fractal image compression using heuristic search. *IEEE Trans. Image Processing*, 4:832–838, 1995.

161. D.W. Thompson and J.L. Mundy. Three-dimensional model matching from an unconstrained viewpoint. In *Proceedings of IEEE Conference on Robotics and Automation*, 1987.

162. A.N. Tikhonov and V.Y. Arsenin. *Solutions of Ill-posed Problems*. V.H. Winston and Sons, Washington, D. C., 1977.

163. S. Ullman. *The Interpretation of Visual Motion*. MIT Press, Cambridge, Massachusetts, 1979.

164. P.P. Vaidyanathan and P.Q. Hoang. Lattice structures for optimal design and robust implementation of two channel perfect reconstruction QMF banks. *IEEE Trans. Acoust. Speech and signal Processing*, 36:81–93, 1988.

165. M. Vetterli and C. Herley. Wavelets and filter banks: theory and design. *IEEE Trans. Signal Processing*, 40:2207–2232, 1992.

166. M. Vetterli and J. Kovacevic. *Wavelets and Subband Coding*. Prentice-Hall, Englewood-Cliffs, 1995.

167. A.J. Viterbi. Error bounds for convolutional codes and an asymptotically optimum decoding algorithm. *IEEE Trans. Inform. Theory*, 13(2):260–269, April 1967.

168. D. Walford. Rock wall segmentation using spatial and image information fusion. Technical report, The University of Queensland, 2006.

169. G.K. Wallace. The JPEG still picture compression standard. *Communications of The ACM*, 34(4):30–44, 1991.

170. M. Wang, J. Evans, L. Hassebrook, and C. Knapp. A multistage optimal active contour model. *IEEE Trans. Image Processing*, 5:1586–1591, 1996.

171. A.M. Waxman and S. Ullman. Surface structure and three-dimensional motion from image flow kinematics. *Int. Journal of Robotics Research*, 4:72–94, 1985.

172. A.M. Waxman and K. Whon. Contour evaluation, neighborhood deformation and global image flow: planar surfaces in motion. *Int. J. Robotics Research*, 4:95–108, 1985.

173. J.S. Weszka. A survey of threshold selection techniques. *Computer Graphics and Image Processing*, 7:259–265, 1978.

174. J.S. Weszka and A. Rosenfeld. Threshold evaluation techniques. *IEEE Trans. Syst., Man, Cybern.*, 8:622–629, 1978.

175. P.H. Winston. *Artificial Intelliegence*. Addison-Wesley Publishing Company Inc, 1984.

176. L.D. Wu. On the chain code of a line. *IEEE Trans. Pattern Analy. Machine Intell.*, 3:347–353, 1982.

# Index

Printed in the United States of America